KU-744-170

Finance for the non-accountant

FINANCE
FOR THE NON-ACCOUNTANT

L. E. Rockley, B COM (LOND), AIMTA, AMBIM

Principal Lecturer, Lanchester Polytechnic, Coventry

Business Books Limited

London

First published 1970
Second impression 1970

ISBN 220 79891 0 5

This book has been set in 10 on 12 point Times New Roman and printed in England at the Pitman Press, Bath, for the publishers, Business Books Limited (Registered office: 180 Fleet Street, London EC4) Publishing offices: Mercury House, Waterloo Road, London SE1

MADE AND PRINTED IN GREAT BRITAIN

By the same author

Capital Investment Decisions, 1968

TO ANNE AND RICHARD

Contents

Preface

Too many people are bemused by the ways in which an accountant talks about profit and loss, debit and credit, or costs and incomes. Furthermore the content of balance sheets and profitability statements is rarely explained or presented in terms understandable by the layman. Yet most business managers and directors, having little or no training in finance, need to have financial data given to them in unequivocal clear form. They need to know where the figures in financial statements come from, what they mean and what the limitations are of the figures in those statements.

For several years therefore I have been testing methods of educating students and managers in the subjects of financial analysis and financial management. This book is, in part, the result of those years of trial and evolution. Here, the gradual development of a company from its first balance sheet up to the stage where it possesses a wide variety of assets and liabilities, is shown clearly. The reader is taken through a study of revenue cost analysis and an evaluation of capital expenditure proposals. The emergence of profit and loss accounts, of balance sheet statements of company worth is explained so as to show the relationships existing between different kinds of financial data. The utility of ratios for measuring business performance is presented in a way which will ensure a thorough understanding of their value.

I trust that the veil of obscurity will be lifted from the financial reports of companies and other organizations, for those who read this book.

Kenilworth, 1970 L. E. ROCKLEY

CHAPTER 1 The Balance Sheet

Introduction

Accountancy is a service; it is the service that gathers together all the data and facts about the operation of a concern or other venture and presents this information in financial terms to the managers of the concern. The skill with which the information is presented, and the facts that can be obtained from it may be referred to broadly as 'financial analysis', whilst the use to which the data is put in making business decisions is called 'financial management'. To have any success in the beneficial use of this data does not, however, necessitate a detailed knowledge of the techniques of book-keeping and accounting which recorded all the information and distributed it around the various accounts of the concern. Of prime importance is a knowledge of what financial statements can contain and how they materialize from the accountant's records. To achieve such a confident facility in accounts' analyses our study must commence with a clear understanding of a balance sheet, a profit and loss account, and the relationship of these two to the cash account.

Looking at any balance sheet the reader will see, at the top, the name of the concern and the fact that it is a balance sheet as at a particular date. The object of this statement is to give a picture of the firm at a specified point in time, thus the balance sheet is styled 'as at 31 December 1969' or other date. It is not a description of what has happened to the concern or the venture over any period of months or weeks, it does not describe a continuing process; it is simply a still picture of the firm at the close of business on the day stated in the balance sheet heading. As an immediate comparison the profit and loss account is given as a recording of the events, i.e. the making of a profit or loss, for the period ended on such and such a date, and this period is always given in the caption or title above the account itself. Here we have the vital difference between two particular statements. The profit and loss account is very similar to a ciné camera's picture of something occurring over a period of time whilst the balance sheet may be one of the 'stills' taken at any stage during the run of that particular ciné film. Of course, it is customary that we have a profit and loss account for a period of, say, 12 months, depicting the result of the activities of the firm during the 12 months, and the balance sheet is drawn up on the very last day of that 12 months. So, taking up the analogy of the previous sentence, the profit and loss account represents the run of the ciné film over the whole of the 12 months, giving a monetary expression to the physical business of buying, making and selling the firm's products during that period. The balance sheet is the enlarged final frame of the whole ciné film. In this instance, however, the enlarged final frame states the whole of the ownings and the whole of the owings of the firm when that last stage is reached.

Capital and revenue

Earlier on it was stated that the balance sheet gave the picture of the firm at the close of business on the day the document was prepared. The very precise intent of this remark must be appreciated for the balance sheet statement does refer to the circumstances existing at *one* very precise point in time only. Business is dynamic. Firms are trading throughout each and every day and thus, whilst a balance sheet may show that a firm possesses so much cash and has so many debts owing to it, on the day next following the publication of the balance sheet if someone enters the offices of the business, and pays some money in the settlement of a debt, then the picture of that firm's existence in terms of assets has immediately changed. Cash has been increased and debtors have been decreased and for this reason only, if nothing else happened, the previous day's balance sheet would not now show the true *current* position of this firm's possessions. Such a process of change is going on continuously with a firm in business; stocks are being bought on credit, they are placed in the production line, become work in progress, subsequently being styled finished goods which are sold, in many instances on credit, thus becoming debtors. The process then continues until the debtor comes along and pays his cash, and perhaps some of this cash may be used to settle debts owed by the firm. All this interaction of the dynamic business can be reflected in the drawing up of many balance sheets —one each day, for example—but it is customary, and more sensible, that the day to day working operations of a concern are recorded in the statement called the profit and loss account. Frequently termed a revenue account or an income and expenditure account, the profit and loss account will give the total of the firm's expenditure and the total of its income during a time of trading activity of buying and selling, or manufacture and selling. Where this activity is undertaken at a profit, then that profit will be shown in the accounts also, for it will stem from the total income being greater than total expenditure. At the end of the period the worth of the firm in terms of things it possesses such as finished goods or debtors, will have increased simply because the value of these assets will be greater than the value of the physical things consumed in the productive process. This increased value is reflected in the accounts of the business from which the balance sheet is drawn up. The balance sheet preparation and layout after such a period of activity reflects this growth and demonstrates, as we shall see shortly, the amount of profit made.

Before going on to some simple examples of balance sheet changes resulting from an interaction of the company's amalgam of assets and liabilities in earning of profits, we should give some consideration to the reasons why the profit and loss account deals with certain kinds of expense but not all, and why the balance sheet always deals with other types of spending. The content of either of these two statements, balance sheet and profit and loss account, depends upon the nature of the expenditure involved. For identification of the nature of an expense it is necessary to understand the accounting terminology which puts the various types of spendings into two major initial categories. These two categories are termed 'capital expenditure' and 'revenue expenditure'.[1] The first of these two terms relates to expenditure on objects of a more or less permanent nature; this

[1] The distinction between capital and revenue expenditure is extremely important, because the former *results in, or is due to,* the acquisition of assets which must appear in the balance sheet, while the latter represents the expenses incurred in the business and is charged against profit.

When expenditure *results in* the acquisition of a *permanent asset,* or in the permanent improvement of, or the addition to, or the extension of an existing asset, which is capable of, and *intended for repeated or continuous use* in the earning of profits or revenue, it is capital expenditure. An example is the purchase price of machinery with which a manufacturer converts raw material into a saleable product.

All expenditure which cannot properly be debited to an asset account is revenue expenditure.

VICKERY, B. G., *Principles and Practice of Book-keeping and Accounts,* page 235, Cassells, Seventeenth edition 1963.

would include, for example, land and buildings, plant and machinery, equipment, vans, and to some extent, loose tools. On the other hand the profit and loss account is concerned with items of revenue expenditure. In this context, revenue expenditure means the cost of day to day management or running of a concern. We may define capital expenditure in an easier fashion, by saying that this represents the substitution of cash by an asset of a more or less permanent nature, i.e. having a value in use beyond the end of the accounting period in which it was purchased. This acquisition of an asset of a more or less permanent nature will include extensions to existing assets, or major modifications to existing assets which add to their permanent worth. Revenue expenditure, which as has been stated, covers the day to day operating costs of an organization includes a multitude of items such as rent, rates, insurance, salaries, wages, repairs and maintenance, licences, petrol and oil. The essential part of this particular category is that the money spent or the expenditure incurred results in the acquisition of commodities and services in the furtherance of the trade of the organization, whereas these things and services bought *are entirely consumed in the productive processes* of the current period, leaving nothing whatever available for future consumption. When the productive process is continued and the need for more of the day to day operating materials and services are required, then further expenditure must be incurred to obtain these additional productive factors. On the other hand as the business needs premises in which to work, and machinery to utilize inside these premises, one cannot similarly say that these kinds of assets can be used up entirely in a short period of industrial activity; at the end of a normal period of trading operations there will be left standing—the buildings, still operating—the machines, the lorries and the vans, which are needed for all of the concern's business activities, and no-one could say that expenditure on these items had been wholly and completely absorbed in the output of the company's product in a short period of account. Some of the expenditure has been consumed however and this is accounted for by the depreciation charges for fixed assets. These items will be discussed more fully in Chapter 2.

The accounting period and business planning

The repeated reference to the short period has in mind the normal accounting period of 12 months and thus where the balance sheet shows fixed assets of land and buildings, this is an acknowledgment of the fact that these possessions, having a more or less permanent existence, belong to the business and are being used by the business in its productive activities but, and what is more important, have not been *used up*. Thus we can go forward with the knowledge that a capital good lasts, whilst a revenue good will be used up during the current period in the trading venture for which that revenue good was acquired. This will not entirely satisfy the perceptive reader however, who may note that amongst the assets of any balance sheet we may find, under a heading entitled current assets, some stock, some work in progress, and perhaps some finished goods. Confusion may arise here by thinking that stock once purchased for the purpose of productive operations is intended to be used up, and therefore, should not be shown in a balance sheet, but rather should be listed amongst the expenses of a profit and loss account. This misapprehension can be quickly dispelled when the reader considers that the business manager must look ahead and must plan, at least in some small measure, for his future activities. Planning results in the acquisition of stock and a labour force based upon an anticipation of future need. Therefore, we have a storehouse in which stocks of materials and components, to be used in the manufacturing process are stored. Once an item leaves the storehouse and is embodied in a product being made, then that expenditure has been incurred, that current asset (stock) has been used, and its appropriate financial value shown in the profit and loss account represents the cost of materials consumed in the manufacturing of the firm's output.

The goods which are left in the storehouse and are waiting for future activity, are short-term assets possessed by the firm and will appear in the balance sheet drawn up at that time. They are recorded in the balance sheet under the heading 'current assets' because at that time they are assets of the *current* period only and not possessions that will last into the future or into other periods. In so far as goods remain in the storehouse, or products are in course of manufacture (work in progress) at the date of the balance sheet, in so far as finished goods are in the warehouse and not yet sold to clients, these possessions are assets of the current period. In a few days, weeks or months, they may no longer be the assets of the firm for they will have passed into the hands of customers and will be replaced in the balance sheet by the term 'debtors'. In this form the output of the business remains until such times as the debtors pay the amounts due and finally the worth of the commodities made is represented by cash. The cash itself, a current asset, will be the cash of the day upon which the balance sheet was drawn up and, as we have seen previously, a few hours after the date of the balance sheet money can be received, can move out as payments to creditors, changing in a vital fashion the appearance of the balance sheet and its story of the worth of the firm as to possessions and liabilities. Sometimes the group of assets called current assets are referred to as 'circulating assets'. The reason for this name is explained by the fact that they do not (in a dynamic concern) remain in this condition for any length of time: they are assets that are constantly on the move, changing into something else, reverting into cash, cash settling creditors bills, more stock being received, and so on.

The impact of trading

The following series of hypothetical balance sheets will show the interaction of the assets and liabilities as they would appear in a balance sheet drawn up immediately after each separate transaction.

EXHIBIT 1

R.E.A. Limited

BALANCE SHEET AS AT ....

	£		£
Subscribed Capital		*Current Assets*	
10,000 Ordinary shares of £1 each	10,000	Cash	10,000
	£10,000		£10,000

In Exhibit 1 a business, R.E.A. Limited, has just opened its doors after having issued 10,000 Ordinary shares of £1 each, and having received all the money for each of the shares from the members of the public who subscribed for them. The balance sheet thus shows the liabilities as shares of £10,000 and amongst the current assets cash of £10,000. The reader may wonder why shares of £10,000 are shown amongst the liabilities of the balance sheet. This is because the balance sheet shows, in respect of the name of the firm at the top, the assets of that firm and the liabilities of that firm. In the instance provided, R.E.A. Limited have received from the shareholders £10,000 in response to the issue of 10,000 shares: the liability exists therefore for the company to account for the £10,000 to those shareholders who have purchased these shares and therefore subscribed the money for the company's initial operations.

At this stage an important concept can be injected to the exposition of balance sheet terminology. This is that the left-hand side of a balance sheet shows where the firm obtained its money or credit, thereby showing how it has been financed in the circumstances existing at the date of the statement. The right-hand side of a balance sheet shows how that financing was used, what it was spent on in terms of goods not yet used up in the productive process. The reader should apply the above narration to the series of balance sheets we shall now study.

EXHIBIT 2

R.E.A. Limited

BALANCE SHEET AS AT ....

	£		£
Subscribed Capital		*Fixed Assets*	
10,000 Ordinary shares		Buildings	4,000
of £1 each	10,000	Plant and machinery	3,000
		Current Assets	
		Cash	3,000
	£10,000		£10,000

Exhibit 2 demonstrates the next stage in the life of our company. Using the cash which they received from the shareholders, buildings costing £4,000 and plant and machinery costing £3,000 have now been purchased. This is to enable the company to get to work, and it can be seen that cash has decreased in the balance sheet to the extent of the payments made for the buildings and plant and machinery purchased. The reader may now see that the firm possesses fixed assets worth £7,000: this sort of spending we have referred to previously as capital expenditure, being payments made in respect of items that are not going to be wasted away or used up in a short period: these assets should remain for the use of the firm over several years. Continuing to give a precise statement of the firm's possessions the balance sheet now recognizes that the amount of cash which was previously held, £10,000, does not now apply to the new state of the firm because it possesses £3,000 only.

EXHIBIT 3

R.E.A. Limited

BALANCE SHEET AS AT ....

	£		£
Subscribed Capital		*Fixed Assets*	
10,000 Ordinary shares		Buildings	4,000
of £1 each	10,000	Plant and machinery	3,000
Current Liabilities		*Current Assets*	
Creditors	3,000	Stock	3,000
		Cash	3,000
	£13,000		£13,000

Exhibit 3 shows the firm now ready to go into production. It has bought stocks of raw materials worth £3,000 but has not paid for them, obtaining the goods on credit. Thus amongst its current assets is listed the stock and its purchase price, whilst on the liabilities side of the balance sheet is recorded the liability of the business to meet this particular debt. The new liability, a debt of the current period, is shown under current liabilities and is the £3,000 owing for stock purchased.

Let us now assume that our businessmen engage in production using some of the stock and paying cash for the labour involved in manufacture; they produce goods which are sold on credit for £5,000. These goods, we shall assume were produced at the expense of the consumption of £2,000 worth of stock, and the payment of £2,000 to the labour force. This is a simple example ignoring all other complications of rent, rates, light heat etc. The balance sheet would now appear as shown in Exhibit 4. We can now see that the

EXHIBIT 4

R.E.A. Limited

BALANCE SHEET AS AT ....

	£		£
Subscribed Capital and Reserves		*Fixed Assets*	
10,000 Ordinary shares		Buildings	4,000
of £1 each	10,000	Plant and machinery	3,000
Profit	1,000		
Current Liabilities		*Current Assets*	
Creditors	3,000	Stock	1,000
		Debtors	5,000
		Cash	1,000
	£14,000		£14,000

sale of goods for £5,000 is shown amongst the current assets where debtors for £5,000 now appear. The consumption of £2,000 worth of stock has reduced the previous stock value figure to £1,000, whilst the payment of £2,000 in cash to the labour force has reduced the balance of cash to £1,000. Now here is the important point: the difference between the cost of manufacturing these goods and actually selling them is £1,000 and this is the profit made on this particular series of operations. The £1,000 profit is now shown in the balance sheet close to the shareholders' subscribed capital of £10,000. It is shown there, connected with the shareholders because the profit has been made by the business, a business which they theoretically own, and the profit of which belongs to the shareholders.[1] In the previous balance sheet the section entitled 'subscribed capital' was being shown at £10,000. The title is now changed and refers to subscribed capital and reserves. This title will include any balance

[1] The statements in this sentence which describe the business and its profits as belonging to the shareholders contain the substance of much argument. The library on this topic is extensive and the serious student should refer to:
The Corporation in Modern Society, edited by Edward S. Mason, Harvard University Press, 1959.
SWOPE, G., 'Some aspects of corporate management', *The Harvard Business Review*, pages 314–22, 1945.
MANNE, H. G., 'The higher criticism of the modern corporation', *The Columbia Law Review*, pages 399–432, March 1962.

left on the profit and loss account because profit made and left in the business, referred to as 'ploughed back', is in fact a reserve retained for the operation of the business out of its gainful working.

R.E.A. Limited now carry on their trade and we obtain a balance sheet as shown in Exhibit 5. In this balance sheet we are able to see

EXHIBIT 5

R.E.A. Limited

BALANCE SHEET AS AT ....

	£		£
Subscribed Capital and Reserves		*Fixed Assets*	
10,000 Ordinary shares of £1 each	10,000	Buildings	4,000
		Plant and machinery	3,000
Profits	1,000		
Current Liabilities		*Current Assets*	
Creditors	3,000	Stock	1,000
		Debtors	2,500
		Cash	3,500
	£14,000		£14,000

that some of the debtors, £2,500 worth, settled their debts. In the balance sheet therefore, the debtors figure is reduced by that amount and the cash figure is increased. If the reader examines these last two balance sheets closely, he will see that this sort of transaction is not affecting the worth of the business to the shareholders, for this worth still stays at £11,000 and the total assets owned still stands at £14,000: all that has varied is the composition of those assets.

Total shareholders' interest

Now our next statement of this company's possessions, Exhibit 6, will show that creditors have been settled to the tune of £2,500. The balance sheet shows that cash has been dispersed to the extent of £2,500, by payments to creditors and as a result of this the amount of creditors still awaiting payment, therefore still a liability of the firm, is shown in the balance sheet at £500. Our company at this stage possesses assets, fixed and current, totalling £11,500. At the same time it owes to persons trading with the company £500, leaving £11,000 to be expressed as the worth of the proprietors' interest in

EXHIBIT 6

R.E.A. Limited

BALANCE SHEET AS AT ....

	£		£
Subscribed Capital and Reserves		*Fixed Assets*	
10,000 Ordinary shares		Buildings	4,000
of £1 each	10,000	Plant and machinery	3,000
Profit	1,000	TOTAL FIXED ASSETS	7,000
TOTAL SHAREHOLDERS' INTEREST	11,000	*Current Assets*	
Current Liabilities		Stock	1,000
Creditors	500	Debtors	2,500
		Cash	1,000
	£11,500		£11,500

the business. It should be noted particularly that in this balance sheet the total of £11,000 has for the first time been given a name, 'total shareholders' interest', being the expression of the worth of the business to those who hold shares in it. Beyond saying that this monetary expression of worth is based upon the book values of the assets—not market values necessarily—nothing more will be said at this stage. One other addition to the information in the balance sheet is the totalling of the values attributed to fixed assets: thus we have a section of the statement called 'total fixed assets'. The analyst can conclude that 64 per cent of the total shareholders' interest is invested in long-term, lasting assets—a matter to be discussed in later chapters.

The company now prepares to commence another cycle of production and to enlarge its activities; these have their effect on the balance sheet as shown in Exhibit 7. At this stage the firm has purchased a vehicle for £1,000 and bought £2,500 worth of stock; all of these purchases were made on credit. On the left-hand side therefore, the balance sheet shows an increase in the statement of amounts due by the firm to those who trade with it, from £500 to £4,000. Thus the reader may see that, in the section 'current liabilities', creditors may refer not only to current assets but to fixed assets also. The important point about these current liabilities is the fact

EXHIBIT 7

R.E.A. Limited

BALANCE SHEET AS AT ....

	£			£
Subscribed Capital and Reserves		*Fixed Assets*		
		Buildings		4,000
10,000 Ordinary shares		Plant and machinery		3,000
of £1 each	10,000	Vehicles		1,000
Profit	1,000			
		TOTAL FIXED ASSETS		8,000
TOTAL SHAREHOLDERS' INTEREST	11,000			
Current Liabilities		*Current Assets*		
Creditors	4,000	Stock	3,500	
		Debtors	2,500	
		Cash	1,000	
				7,000
	£15,000			£15,000

that they must be regarded as liabilities for the *current period* only, and very likely must be regarded as being due for payment early in the next accounting period. The reader should not conclude that current liabilities are always going to be eliminated in the succeeding operating period. The continuous nature of business brings forward other credit transactions; thus whilst the particular creditors shown in Exhibit 7 will be discharged, they will be replaced by other current liabilities arising from R.E.A.'s transactions in this next operating period.

This concept of the quantity of current liabilities and its comparison with the current assets leads on to the expression 'working capital'. Now current assets are considered to be the assets most readily convertible into cash; this transference is the object and result of the productive process and thus the availability of such relatively liquid assets is a measure of the extent to which creditors can expect to be paid reasonably promptly. In the case of our most recent balance sheet we can see the immediate debts are £4,000 whilst the assets of the current period are £7,000. These current assets are now totalled in order to facilitate comparison with current liabilities so that the reader of the balance sheet can see that R.E.A. Limited had a working capital of £3,000 (£7,000 – £4,000) on the date referred to in the heading. A satisfactory state of solvency is thereby revealed.

For the purposes of the next statement we will assume that production was engaged, and that stocks were transferred into the productive process, a balance sheet being drawn up before the productive

EXHIBIT 8

R.E.A. Limited

BALANCE SHEET AS AT ....

	£			£
Subscribed Capital and Reserves		*Fixed Assets*		
		Buildings		4,000
10,000 Ordinary shares		Plant and machinery		3,000
of £1 each	10,000	Vehicles		1,000
Profit	1,000			
		TOTAL FIXED ASSETS		8,000
TOTAL SHAREHOLDERS' INTEREST	11,000			
Current Liabilities		*Current Assets*		
Creditors	4,000	Stock	2,000	
		Work in progress	1,500	
		Debtors	2,500	
		Cash	1,000	
				7,000
	£15,000			£15,000

process was finished, before labour was paid, and before any goods could be sold. The result is shown in Exhibit 8. The only change in this balance sheet demonstrates the transfer from stock of materials worth £1,500, which are in the factory, being worked upon but not yet converted into saleable finished products.

Our company is proceeding with its business and on this occasion it has sold goods on credit for £5,000. To produce these goods, the work in progress of £1,500 was completed, further stocks costing £500 were utilized, and the labour force was paid £2,000. The cost of achieving the sales was, therefore, £4,000 making a profit for the firm of £1,000. This £1,000 is the difference between the sales value £5,000 of goods sold to debtors and the cost of production, £4,000.

EXHIBIT 9

R.E.A. Limited

BALANCE SHEET AS AT ....

		£			£
Subscribed Capital and Reserves			*Fixed Assets*		
10,000 Ordinary shares			Buildings		4,000
of £1 each		10,000	Plant and machinery		3,000
Profit		2,000	Vehicles		1,000
			TOTAL FIXED ASSETS		8,000
TOTAL SHAREHOLDERS' INTEREST		12,000			
Current Liabilities			*Current Assets*		
Creditors	4,000		Stock	1,500	
Bank overdraft	1,000		Debtors	7,500	
		5,000			9,000
		£17,000			£17,000

There is an interesting development during this period of trade however, for the reader will notice that in Exhibit 8 the firm possessed cash resources of £1,000. During the recent trading cycle, when goods worth £5,000 were manufactured, it was necessary to pay to the labour force £2,000, thus using up the entire cash resources of the firm, and with the assistance of the bank, to negotiate an overdraft for the remaining £1,000. We now have a balance sheet (see Exhibit 9) showing assets possessed by the firm totalling £17,000 whilst the liabilities to persons with whom the firm does business are £5,000 (creditors £4,000 plus an overdraft from the bank of £1,000). The £1,000 profit made as a result of this transaction has been added to the previous figure of profit of £1,000 now making the new total profit, retained in the business, of £2,000. During this productive cycle, work in progress has been completely manufactured and a further £500 worth of stock has been used. The consequences of the factory's actions was the sale of products worth £5,000: this being a credit sale has raised the debtors to a sum of £7,500. The reader may now find it interesting to note that the increase of profit ploughed back from £1,000 to £2,000, cannot be identified with any particular asset or liability anywhere in the balance sheet. The increase in profit, or to use another term, increase in reserve has resulted from the fixed assets, buildings and plant and machinery, being used in the shaping and manufacture of the stock and work in progress into a finished commodity, but nowhere in the balance sheet can there be any identification of this increase in worth of the company which is now measured at a net value of the total proprietors' interest of £12,000.

EXHIBIT 10

R.E.A. Limited

BALANCE SHEET AS AT ....

		£			£
Subscribed Capital and Reserves			*Fixed Assets*		
			Buildings		4,000
10,000 Ordinary shares			Plant and machinery		3,000
of £1 each		10,000	Vehicles		1,000
Profit		1,000			
			TOTAL FIXED ASSETS		8,000
TOTAL SHAREHOLDERS' INTEREST		11,000			
Current Liabilities			*Current Assets*		
Creditors	4,000				
Bank overdraft	1,000		Stock	1,500	
Dividend payable	1,000		Debtors	7,500	
		6,000			9,000
		£17,000			£17,000

We will now assume that the directors of the company decide to pay the shareholders a dividend in view of the results of the period's trading activities. We will assume this dividend to be a 10% dividend upon the subscribed value of the shares; thus with a subscribed Share Issue of £10,000, a 10% dividend will result in a payment to shareholders of £1,000. For the next balance sheet in the life of the company (Exhibit 10) it will be accepted that the dividend has been declared at 10% but not yet paid. Here the balance sheet displays amongst the current liabilities a sum of £1,000 which is described 'dividends payable'. As dividends are payable out of profit[1], then the amount which has been set aside for payment to shareholders has been deducted from the profit figure of £2,000. The profit now remains at £1,000 and the total shareholders' interest is reduced from £12,000 to £11,000. The reader should find this quite reasonable to accept for the company has publicly stated its intention to return to the shareholders a sum of £1,000 from the totality of their interest in the company.

End of a trading cycle

Our final balance sheet (Exhibit 11) will demonstrate several transactions. Here we shall assume that debtors have paid to the firm's

EXHIBIT 11

R.E.A. Limited

BALANCE SHEET AS AT ....

	£			£
Subscribed Capital and Reserves		*Fixed Assets*		
10,000 Ordinary shares		Buildings		4,000
of £1 each	10,000	Plant and machinery		3,000
Profit	1,000	Vehicles		1,000
		TOTAL FIXED ASSETS		8,000
TOTAL SHAREHOLDERS' INTEREST	11,000	*Current Assets*		
		Stock	1,500	
		Debtors	1,500	
				3,000
	£11,000			£11,000

[1] The reference to dividends being payable out of profits begs several questions. There is no desire on my part to complicate the trend of thought at this stage but a good reference on this subject is *The Principles of Auditing* by de Paula (Pitman), Chapter X, 'Profits Available for Dividend'.

cashier £6,000 of the money owing by them. We shall further assume that £6,000 has been used to pay the whole of the creditors, to pay the dividends due to the shareholders leaving £1,000 to eliminate the overdraft at the bank. Our final balance sheet thus shows after a period of considerable business and movement of the firm's assets that the company owns assets of £11,000 and owes liabilities of £11,000. In this instance the liabilities represent the liability of the firm to account to the shareholders for their total interest in this business which over its period of life has grown in value from £10,000 to its present worth of £11,000, even after shareholders have had a return of £1,000 in the form of dividend.

Questions for discussion

1. How does the balance sheet come into existence? Where does the information it gives originate?
2. What values are the balance sheet figures based upon?
3. How is the net worth of a firm shown in a balance sheet?
4. What is profit? How does it arise?
5. Does the balance sheet figure of profit relate to any specific assets?
6. Why is profit shown in the balance sheet as a liability?
7. What do current assets and current liabilities represent?
8. What is working capital?
9. How do you define and distinguish between capital expenditure and revenue expenditure?

Recommended reading

CHAMBERS, R. J., *Financial Management*, Sweet & Maxwell, 1967.

HOWARD, B. B., and UPTON, M., *Introduction to Business Finance*, McGraw-Hill, 1953.

BOND, G. D., *Financial Aspects of Industrial Management*, Butterworths, 1955 (new edition in preparation).

TOVEY, P., and DE PAULA, F. C., *Balance Sheets: How to Read and Understand Them*, Pitman (out of print).

MAGEE, B., *Accounting*, Gee, Seventh edition, 1968. (at this stage read Section IV only).

CHAPTER 2 Depreciation

Introduction

In Chapter 1 we were able to see how the company progressed through a trading cycle, how the changing nature of the company was reflected in the various balance sheets and how a simple statement of profit has its impact upon the amalgam of assets and liabilities appearing in that balance sheet. The perceptive reader will have had certain reservations concerning the profits shown in the previous paragraph. These reservations would undoubtedly have referred to the lack of charge, against the profit earned, for the use of the capital equipment. Now with our knowledge of the balance sheet and of the company's various expenses we can begin to think further about the nature of these capital assets in land, buildings, plant and machinery, equipment, vans, etc.

In any business environment fixed assets such as these are held, not for resale, but with the object of enabling the firm to carry on its business and earn its profits. Having accepted this, and in the knowledge that physical assets in general do not last for ever, the reader must have appreciated that any surplus of income over expenditure which is earned by a business must be regarded as having been made with the aid, or with the use, of its fixed assets. Consequently, in a true determination of profit, some estimate of the cost of usage of fixed assets or of their deterioration in worth to the company must be assessed. Whatever is regarded as the cost of using an asset in the earning of profit, must be set against that profit, thus reducing its size. This expense which we calculate as being the cost of use of the plant and machinery in producing turnover and obtaining profit is called depreciation. The term depreciation has many connotations and there are many different opinions with regard to its object. Basically it is that part of the initial cost of an asset which is not recovered by the owner when that asset is sold by him. The reader knows that the assets in the balance sheet are there for the purpose of the company's aims and that the business manager must set out to recover from his profit, the cost to him of the fixed assets available for use during the period in which the profit was made. Assessing the cost of fixed assets used in a productive process is a topic of considerable argument but for the moment we will say that such fixed asset cost to the proprietor or manager is comprised of:

1 The original payment he made for the plant, etc.

less

2 What he sells it for when it is finally disposed.

The difference between these two sums, the net cost of the asset to the businessman, is the total sum which should be set against the profits of the various periods during which that asset was held by the company or firm.

Let not the reader concern himself at this stage with the problems of replacing plant and equipment and other fixed assets where it is felt that the cost of replacement will, more often than not, be considerably higher than the price paid for the asset being discharged from service. The relationship of depreciation to replacement of fixed assets will be considered later on in this chapter, but just let us consider that this charging of fixed asset cost against profits made is merely a means of *allocating net cost over life:* this is the function of depreciation to which we shall give attention now.

Opinion in the final accounts

There are several ways of determining the amount to be charged against profit in each year; each method involves an amount of estimation and of personal opinion. It is here that our balance sheet first begins to reflect the views of the person drawing up that statement. Let it not be thought that limited companies are permitted to publish their final accounts in any way, with any content which they think fit. The law of the land demands that certain things are shown in published balance sheets, that certain information is given either as notes to that statement or in an accompanying published profit and loss account. In Appendix A will be found an extract of the requirements of the Companies Act 1967, in so far as the figures included in published balance sheets, published profit and loss accounts, and statements accompanying those documents are concerned.

However, there is still room for judgement or opinion or in assessing the expected life of a capital asset—for this is capable of determination only within fairly wide boundaries. Whether maintenance can improve the performance of an asset or increase its life; whether continual use will reduce its efficiency from the point of view of producing a quality article or from the point of view of speed of output, each of these and other factors will have some impact upon the assessment of useful life for the firm of any of its assets. Such assessments are made upon acquisition of long life assets for the purpose of cost allocation; on occasions one finds that re-assessments of expected life are made during active use of, for example, plant and equipments. Such prognostications are not easily made and past records or information of similar plants or other equipment can always be of use in making this estimation, but estimation it is, and estimation it will remain. Moreover, once asset life is determined the businessman must make an evaluation of yet another future occurrence—the expected receipts to be obtained from selling the plant! It is this sum which is deducted from the original cost to give the net cost of the asset to the businessman, which net sum is spread over the operating life of the asset. Now bearing in mind the need to recover the capital cost, and putting aside for the moment the fact of the impact of personal opinion upon this allocation of cost, let us consider some of the methods fairly widely used in industry today for calculating the annual cost of use of capital assets in earning profits, this sum being called provision for depreciation. Notice that the terminology has changed in an attempt to identify the accounting transaction in that, in allocating cost, we are making a provision to cover the cost of asset use. The previous term depreciation really referred to the *physical* reduction in value or fall in worth only.

Of the several methods of apportioning the cost of an asset over its useful life the ones most generally used (and incidentally the easiest to calculate) are the straight-line method and the reducing-balance method. The first, dealt with below, is the straight-line method.

STRAIGHT-LINE METHOD OF DEPRECIATION

Using the initial cost less an estimated amount to be received on retirement of the asset, this method gives the total sum to be divided by the expected number of years of useful life of the plant. In this way an equal annual charge to the profit and loss account, in respect of the use of the asset in earning the profit, can be calculated. The point to notice is that the charge against profit will be the same each year. This means that a fixed proportion of the cost of the asset to the business is recovered from each year's profits during the asset's operating life. Here we have the rudimentary assessment of the cost of providing the services of plant in producing turnover and earning profit. This particular method is widespread in use in this country and in the United States and Canada, though in the latter two countries there are other methods and other taxation provisions with regard to the determination of depreciation. (Such taxation provisions have affected those foreign companies' determination of the provision for depreciation, very widely.) Having decided to use the straight line method of depreciation there are two principal ways in which this calculation may be shown in the books of account. The reader should understand that the charge thus calculated is placed in the profit and loss account to be levied against the income received, thus enabling a more truthful statement of profit to be achieved. Truthful in this context refers to the inclusion not only of costs of running the business from day to day, but also an estimate of the costs of having plant and capacity available to do the work. Now these two methods of recording depreciation both have, as an essential point, charging the profit and loss account with the sum determined as the cost of use of the physical assets. The divergence then occurs in how the asset itself is to be affected by this charge which is really an assessment of the reduction in value or the depreciation in worth of the asset as a result of its use or wear and tear. This measure of depreciation which we have just calculated can be credited direct to the asset account, thus reducing the asset's money value in the books: alternatively it can be credited to a separate account called 'provision for depreciation'. This latter account which grows with each year's depreciation sum transferred is then offset against the asset cost in the balance sheet. The resultant figure is the unrecovered part of the original cost of the asset and it is shown in the final cash column of the balance sheet. Now a limited company is required to show in its balance sheet the cost, or the valuation of its assets less the total amount of depreciation charged to date, thus producing a net figure of unrecovered cost in respect of all its fixed assets. In the following examples it will be seen that the information required by law for the balance sheet can be more easily obtained when the asset account is maintained at cost together with a separate 'provision for depreciation' account showing each year's depreciation amount, which has been charged to that year's profit and loss account. The depreciation sum for each period is then carried forward into an aggregated total of the whole depreciation up to a particular date. The following examples will show the operation of the charge for depreciation and its impact on profits if we look at the assets in the balance sheet on page 9 (Exhibit 4) of the previous chapter. In the example chosen goods have been sold for £5,000 'at the expense of the consumption of £2,000 worth of stock and the payment of £2,000 to the labour force'. Clearly these transactions had been completed by the use of the firm's machinery which is situated in the firm's buildings. Therefore let us assume that this financial result is the effect of one year's trading; we will further assume operating lives of 60 years for the building and ten years for the machinery. Estimating a residual value of £400 for the buildings and a nil value for the machinery at the end of the assumed operating lives, the yearly charges for depreciation will be as shown in Exhibits 12 and 13.

EXHIBIT 12

$$\text{Buildings} = \frac{\text{Cost less residual value}}{\text{Number of years of life}}$$
$$= \frac{£4{,}000 - 400}{60} = \frac{£3{,}600}{60}$$
$$= £60 \text{ per annum}$$

EXHIBIT 13

$$\text{Plant and machinery} = \frac{£3{,}000}{10}$$
$$= £300 \text{ per annum}$$

The effect of these costs upon one year's profit, and upon the asset values shown in the balance sheet, is now demonstrated in the balance sheet as amended (see Exhibit 14).

EXHIBIT 14

R.E.A. Limited

BALANCE SHEET AS AT ....

	£	£		£	£
Subscribed Capital and Reserves			*Fixed Assets*		
10,000 Ordinary shares of £1 each		10,000	Building at cost	4,000	
Profit	1,000		*Less* depreciation to date	60	
Less depreciation	360				3,940
		640	Plant at cost	3,000	
			Less depreciation to date	300	
TOTAL SHAREHOLDERS' INTEREST		10,640			2,700
			TOTAL FIXED ASSETS		6,640
Current Liabilities			*Current Assets*		
Creditors		3,000	Stocks	1,000	
			Debtors	5,000	
			Cash	1,000	
					7,000
		£13,640			£13,640

REDUCING-BALANCE METHOD OF DEPRECIATION

In using this method the previous information is still required, i.e. original costs, less estimated residual value and expected useful life of the asset. The reducing-balance method does not attempt to place against each successive year's profit a constant proportion of original price less residual sales value. Each year a percentage of the balance on the asset account is determined as the depreciation sum. The percentage figure is the same used each year, and is applied to the original cost which has been reduced by depreciation sums calculated in previous years. This method too is pretty widely used in this country, but the reader should understand that it involves relatively heavier charges in the earlier years of life of an asset and the fact should be noted that the percentage required, under the reducing balance method, to write down the asset at the end of its expected useful life to its residual value needs to be two or three times greater than that percentage used in the straight-line method. (Though the straight-line method of depreciation is not calculated by means of a percentage, the actual sum evolved from dividing net costs by expected years of useful life can be expressed as a percentage of original cost.) There is one thing to emphasize about the reducing-balance method—no matter how long the asset is possessed, calculating depreciation and thus writing it down by this method will never delete the asset entirely from the books of the firm. On the other hand the straight-line method eliminates the asset from the books of account at the end of its useful life to the firm. The success of these calculations depends upon accurately forecasting useful lives and potential sales values of discharged assets at the ends of those lives.

EXHIBIT 15

		£
Year 1	Cost of plant at beginning of year	3,000
,,	Depreciation: 25 per cent of cost for 12 months	750
,,	Written down value at end of year	2,250
Year 2	Depreciation: 25 per cent of written down value	562
,,	Written down value at end of year	1,688
Year 3	Depreciation: 25 per cent	422
,,	Written down value	1,266
Year 4	Depreciation: 25 per cent	317
,,	Written down value	949
Year 5	Depreciation: 25 per cent	237
,,	Written down value	712
Year 6	Depreciation: 25 per cent	178
,,	Written down value	534

Exhibit 15 shows the effect of assessing the depreciation charge, by the reducing-balance method, for the plant and machinery in the balance sheet of Exhibit 14.

By carrying this calculation to the end of life of the assets, the wide variations in annual depreciation charges under these two methods can be seen. The impact upon asset values shown in the balance sheet, and upon profit, is shown in the revised balance sheet of Exhibit 16. (In this instance depreciation in respect of buildings has been left at £60, the straight-line charge.)

EXHIBIT 16

R.E.A. Limited

BALANCE SHEET AS AT ....

	£	£		£	£
Subscribed Capital and Reserves			*Fixed Assets*		
			Buildings at cost	4,000	
10,000 Ordinary shares of £1 each		10,000	*Less* depreciation to date	60	
Profit	1,000				3,940
Less depreciation	810		Plant at cost	3,000	
		190	*Less* depreciation to date	750	
					2,250
TOTAL SHAREHOLDERS' INTEREST		10,190			
			TOTAL FIXED ASSETS		6,190
Current Liabilities			*Current Assets*		
Creditors		3,000	Stock	1,000	
			Debtors	5,000	
			Cash	1,000	
					7,000
		£13,190			£13,190

The reader will see that, had the first year's depreciation for the fixed assets been increased by a small amount, the profit would have entirely evaporated.

Text books and other theoretical appraisals of accounting practices point out that plant and machinery, in the earlier years of its life, suffers less from the need for repair and maintenance. Thus profit in those earlier years of life has to bear a lower charge for keeping the assets in an operating condition than in the later years of its life. Therefore, it is argued that the calculation of depreciation by the reducing balance-method when the charge in the earlier years of life is at its highest, should result in a more even total charge against profits for the use and operation of this machinery, when one also considers rising costs of maintenance. There are some deficiencies in this argument and in particular the reader must consider settling in costs, initial trial and testing costs, which with some complicated machinery can be quite expensive. Such problems may result in the first year of life of new plant and equipment being the most expensive period of its operating life, contributing little to the over-all productive efficiency of the concern. Furthermore one cannot foresee with certainty the future trend of repairs and maintenance expenditure with regard to all types of plant; these costs may increase at a gradually growing rate in subsequent periods; they may not present any particular pattern at all especially in the years when a major overhaul is necessary. Such comments all point to the fact that it is not possible to forecast, with any certainty, future repairs and maintenance costs. It is possible, however, in a number of instances to indicate in the first year or years of life of expensive complicated machinery that installation and running costs may be inordinately high in comparison with succeeding years. In view of these comments it does not seem a sound hypothesis to opt for the reducing-balance method simply because it may have the function of spreading more evenly over the life of an asset the costs of use and operation of that asset in each of those years of life.

Review of basic data

Whichever method is adopted for the calculation of depreciation, the bases upon which that calculation was made, i.e. expected useful life, expected residual value, should be reviewed periodically. As an example, some years ago one of this country's most famous companies reviewed its depreciation charges which were calculated on the straight-line basis. Attention was paid to asset initial cost, expected life, expected residual value, and in this instance to the replacement cost also. During their examination the company's accountants discovered that depreciation charges which had been levied in past years had resulted in an overcharge of depreciation to those past years, simply because it now became evident that the plant and equipment was going to last longer than was originally estimated. Here then is a problem; should the accountant re-open the past years' accounts, charge to those accounts the revised computations of depreciation for those years? Or should they re-calculate the depreciation provision for the future years bearing in mind the now extended expected future life of the assets involved? What actually happened was the latter; the balance remaining on the books representing the unrecovered costs of the assets was now to be spread over a longer period in the future than was originally thought.

In the succeeding years the charges for depreciation calculated on the straight-line method in respect of these assets was therefore reduced.

Replacement or historical cost

So far we have been concerning ourselves with depreciation as a means of recovering the original cost of the asset, less its expected sale value on discharge. In his *Principles of Economics*, Pigou says 'the manufacturer knows that his machinery wears out, and if his capital is to remain unimpaired he must set aside something annually to replace it. If he is to secure a permanent profit he must reckon these amounts as part of his expenses'. If as may be implied here depreciation must be regarded also as a means of providing for the replacement of assets when they wear out, then some consideration must be given to the potential cost of replacing the asset, especially in times of inflation. Having studied the impact of depreciation upon building and plant values shown in the balance sheet of Exhibit 15, the reader has been able to see also the effect upon profit left after charging depreciation. The appreciation of this effect upon profit is important for the net profit remaining after all operating costs and taxation charges have been met, is the source of dividend appropriations and ploughing back for the growth and development of the business. Thus it is clear that erroneous calculations of depreciation, or varying calculations of depreciation, will have a decisive impact upon the amount available for the payment of dividends. Now we may assess depreciation by basing our calculations on the historical cost, having the view that the function of depreciation is to provide a means of allocating historical cost over active life. Alternatively we may assess depreciation based upon some future estimated replacement price with the object of retaining in the business sufficient sums to replace the capital equipment when it is worn out. Whichever method is used there must be no doubt that some estimate of the cost of the usage of assets must be placed against the income of a firm in a particular year. However there is some divergence of view as to what the function of depreciation is: we also must think of the effect upon the accounts and upon profits by regarding the charge for depreciation as having some element in it of providing a savings bank to meet the cost of replacing those assets which will become obsolete or wear out and need replacing.

Now the first object of the accounts of a firm is to show to the owners how their funds have been used. Here the reader will remember that the balance sheet states on the left-hand side how the business has been financed, and, on the right-hand side, how the money was spent. The other major final account statement, the profit and loss account, is intended to show the cost of obtaining output or turnover, or sales of the firm in the specified period. In the past both of these records have been in the form of an historical record, in as much as the costs entered in them or the values of items entered in them have referred to those prices and those costs which arose at the time of purchase of the asset or the time of use of the service. There is one very great benefit of this historical cost accounting and that is it records, as closely as possible, *fact*: it is concerned with a cost which existed and which can be proved from bills and invoices and documents within the firm. As soon as the preparer of the accounts departs from this principle it enlarges the area in the accounts where fact is no longer the major determinant of value. It is realized in any system of accounting for depreciation that some element of opinion must creep in, if only from the point of view of how long the asset is likely to last; that estimate will affect the charge for depreciation. However, as soon as other matters are introduced, such as what will be the cost of this plant when we have to replace it in several years' time, then further expressions of opinion have their effect upon the accounts.

It is not intended in this book to go into the question of replacement accounting to any great length, or to discuss the pros and cons of the subject. It is considered, however, that the reader should have some knowledge of the methods available for levying against profits a depreciation cost which will have as its object not just the allocation of original capital outlay, but also the provision of amounts needed to meet the cost of asset replacement. Considerable doubt surrounds the estimation of replacement cost, and therefore must attach to the consequent calculations involved in the replacement cost method of assessing the depreciation charge. Except in the very short period replacement cost cannot be calculated with extreme accuracy; neither can one be sure that a piece of plant and equipment will be replaced by exactly the same item. These qualifications and doubts must restrict one's possible approval of replacement cost theories. But I do not think that the improbability of a replacement of one item of plant by another piece of precisely similar equipment is a vital issue. What is vital is the 'guesstimation' of any replacement cost. However, in striving for a better statement of profit and a more accurate statement of company worth in the balance sheet one can secure a more realistic depreciation charge by various methods, though the accounting for these methods in the ledgers need not concern the reader. The first example to which one would give consideration is the replacement cost of dealing with fixed assets: this bases the charge or charges for depreciation upon an assessed expense of replacing assets at some time in the future. A second method takes the step of writing up fixed assets to a new current level of worth. Such a process has the effect of treating the business as though it has just started again with current values attributed to its capital assets in the balance sheet. Where this method is used depreciation is charged on the higher values and here again we are making a greater charge against current profits in respect of the use of physical assets which we bought some time ago. A third method concerns the current value method of dealing with depreciation, and the object of this assessment is to charge for the consumption of the capital assets at current values and not upon an historical cost analysis. Again depreciation would not be regarded as spreading the original cost over the life of the asset but as a measure of consumption of the physical values embodied in this asset. The broad effect of charging depreciation on current values would be as if new assets had been purchased in that particular year at that particular year's prices with depreciation then levied in the profit and loss account at those up-to-date prices.

Finally, a more refined method of judging the change in value of an asset; here the change in cost of replacement is effected by the use of an index method. This index is understood to be an index to reflect the changes in the purchasing power of money. Much has been written on this topic and widely varying views exist as to whether it is possible to produce an index of the purchasing power of money. This method recognizes most clearly that the problem of replacement accounting and determination of profit revolves around the fact that the profit obtained from the sale of commodities is expressed in turnover in terms of the currency of today, i.e. in today's prices and today's values. On the other hand the capital assets utilized in producing the turnover, earning the income and gaining the profit, are very frequently expressed in the currency of the period when those assets were purchased. Now, in a period of inflation, these two monetary values are by no means equal. The object of this index value method for determining depreciation would therefore be to reduce the element of difference between the monetary value determining the sales income and the monetary value determining the cost of use of assets. In practice this method would be applied to increase the value of the assets by the amount of the index increase and thus increase the amount of depreciation charged.

The reader should always remember, however, in discussing replacement accounting that much of the emphasis has been laid, quite naturally, during the last 20 years on rising prices. This has concentrated attention on the provision for replacing assets at increased costs, but if such a system is used for the purpose of replacement costing then it should be used consistently. This must give thought to what needs to be done in the event of a falling price level. In these instances the replacement of plant and equipment would cost less than in the past. Here a depreciation provision which was based upon a replacement cost which is expected to be lower than the original cost may not eliminate the original price of the asset from the books, when that asset is thrown out of use at the end of its life. Therefore, the problem of saying what is profit is a difficult one, and when we say that profit is the excess of income over the cost of getting that income we must remember that 'cost' includes capital costs as well as revenue costs and that these capital costs should not just pay for the original purchase price of fixed assets but should provide for replacement. If this is profit, then the definition must apply in periods of falling prices also. The reader should begin to think of the effect of replacement cost accounting upon the firm's profits in a deflationary age. These final comments are not intended to place undue emphasis upon any particular price trend but to ensure a thorough understanding of the general implications.

Questions for discussion

1. What causes depreciation? What are the objects of the charge for depreciation in a profit and loss account?
2. What factors affect the calculation of the charge for depreciation?
3. How does personal opinion affect these calculations?
4. What is the straight-line method of depreciation? How is it calculated?
5. What is the reducing-balance method of depreciation? How it is calculated?
6. Why does the charge for depreciation reduce the net worth of the business?
7. What do you understand by historical cost? What is the object of valuing assets at replacement cost?
8. What does *replacement* cost *mean*, and how can it be measured?

Recommended reading

THRASHER, J. P. and LEACH, R., 'Countering the hidden effects of inflation', *Financial Times*, page 11, 5 January 1967.

JONES, F., *Guide to Company Balance Sheets and Profit and Loss Accounts*, Heffer, 1964.

BAXTER, W. T. and DAVIDSON, S., *Studies in Accounting Theory*, Sweet & Maxwell, 1962.

HELFERT, E., *Valuation: Concepts and Practice*, Wadsworth, 1966.

CHAPTER 3 Determination of Income

Introduction

The object of the income (profit and loss) account is to show how the profit was made, or loss incurred, during a specified period. This statement therefore is vitally concerned with the company's trading during that period. For this reason it is important to note that the heading of the account will always state that it is the Profit and Loss Account *for the Year Ended* 31 December 1969, or any other relevant date. Thereupon the reader knows that each of the items of expenditure and of income relate to the costs and gains of that period only, the period given at the head of the account itself. Now when the accountant talks of expenditure and income, he has a mental picture of the value of goods and services[1] consumed in obtaining a quantity of sales. The fact that some of this resource consumption, or sales output, may not have been paid for is not a main criterion for judging the money values to be entered in the profit and loss account. Naturally the businessman must pay for the resources he uses, and will expect to be paid for the sales he achieves but such *money* transactions will be found in the cash book—the other name for which is the receipts and payments book.

Income and expenditure

This essential difference between expenditure and payments, between income and receipts must be thoroughly appreciated before any further understanding of finance can be pursued. Broadly, expenditure relates to the total cost of the resources *used* during the period stated at the head of the account, to obtain the quantity of sales shown in that account. Payments on the other hand refer to *money*

[1] For example, materials, labour, light, heat, insurance, etc.

paid during the same operating period, for such goods and services as the business has used or will use *at any time*: payments although made during an operating period do not necessarily relate to resource consumption in that particular operating period only. Some amounts may be paid in advance of next year's planned output; some amounts may be paid in arrear, being outstanding debts from last year's trading. Again, income represents the value of sales achieved by the firm during the period given at the head of the account: this should match with the value of goods despatched to customers from the factory or shop, during that same period.

These remarks have analysed the content of the profit and loss account from the accounting concepts of income and expenditure, in comparison with the more widely understood notions of receipts and payments. These two definitions of two groups of business transactions, the consuming and the paying functions, are but further analyses of the main categories of commercial spendings—capital expenditure and revenue expenditure. The reader should be acquainted (see pp. 3–4) with the impact of capital costs upon the balance sheet picture of the firm, and the impact of revenue costs upon the profit picture of the firm. At this stage it can be said that the profit and loss account contains in it, items of revenue expenditure and revenue income, whilst capital transactions go to the balance sheet to add to the value picture of the whole firm. Without this statement one would imagine that the profit shown in the profit and loss account represents the ultimate change in the cash possessions of the firm, because sales must bring money to the company from the customers who bought the firm's goods. At the same time the expenditure on resources used to manufacture goods and procure sales must also result in cash flowing away from the firm to pay for those goods and services consumed. But the change in a company's cash position is not brought about just by the revenue operations of its trading: some money will flow from the company in respect of the purchase of capital assets and these would not appear in the profit and loss account[1], at least not all at once. Now this phrase should cause reflections upon the subject of depreciation: in Chapter 2 a cost called depreciation was charged against profit and was shown to arise from the use of capital assets in the productive process. The financial sum indicating the extent of this charge was calculated by reference to the original cost (amongst other things)

[1] Neither would *payments* made in advance, of course.

of the relevant capital assets. In this way a portion of the original capital expenditure, listed amongst the fixed assets in the balance sheet, is transferred to the profit and loss account as an expense item. Quite certainly this is a very proper and prudent way of ensuring that the year's profit is declared only after *all* costs have been taken into consideration.[1]

Cash flow and the profit and loss account

Leading on from this, the reader will be able to accept the statement that a simple profit and loss account will give a measurement of the movement of cash to and from the firm resulting from trading operations, *provided that* the figure of net profit made is increased by such *non-cash* charges as depreciation.

Before proceeding to a study of the detailed construction of the profit and loss account and the determination of cash flow, three further illustrations of balance sheet variations will be examined.

Using Exhibit 11 (page 16) as the starting point of a new trading period, the reader is invited to complete the following balance sheet outline, after considering the undermentioned transactions[2]:

1 New machinery costing £500 is purchased on credit.
2 Additional stock at £1,500 is purchased on credit.
3 £500 is received by the Company's cashier, from a debtor.

Now let the further development of the firm be presented by incorporating the next group of changes in yet another balance sheet:

4 Land and buildings are purchased on credit for £2,000.
5 New plant and machinery costing £500 is purchased for cash.
6 An old vehicle is sold for £500 for cash.
7 Additional stock at £4,000 is purchased on credit.
8 The cashier pays £2,000 to creditors: he receives £1,000 from debtors.
9 Using stock valued at £3,000 and paying £3,000 for manufacturing expenses, the company sells goods priced at £10,000. The goods are sold on credit.

[1] As explained in Chapter 2 the point of argument will always centre around the correctness of the amount charged for depreciation, in view of the various factors affecting its calculation.

[2] The answers to the problems posed in Exhibits 17 and 18 are given in the appendix at the end of this chapter.

EXHIBIT 17

R.E.A. Limited

BALANCE SHEET AS AT ....

	£	£		£	£
Subscribed Capital and Reserves			*Fixed Assets*		
10,000 Ordinary shares of £1 each			Buildings		
Profit			Plant and machinery		
			Vehicles		
			TOTAL FIXED ASSETS		
TOTAL SHAREHOLDERS' INTEREST					
Current Liabilities			*Current Assets*		
Creditors			Stock		
			Debtors		
			Cash		
		£			£

EXHIBIT 18

R.E.A. Limited

BALANCE SHEET AS AT ....

	£	£		£	£
Subscribed Capital and Reserves			*Fixed Assets*		
10,000 Ordinary shares of £1 each			Land and buildings		
Profit			Plant and machinery		
			Vehicles		
			TOTAL FIXED ASSETS		
TOTAL SHAREHOLDERS' INTEREST					
Current Liabilities			*Current Assets*		
Creditors			Stock		
Bank overdraft			Debtors		
			Cash		
		£			£

For the purposes of the balance sheet (Exhibit 18) the reader is requested to treat the vehicle (item 6) as being sold for the amount at which it is shown in the books: no study of capital profits or losses are intended at this stage. Nevertheless the information given in adjustment 9 to Exhibit 18 does give sufficient information for determination of a simple profit and loss account to show the operating results of this period. In its most rudimentary form such a statement would be presented as shown in Exhibit 19.

This profit of £4,000 is shown in the new balance sheet (Exhibit 18) to have been added to the profit shown in the previous balance sheet (Exhibit 17). Clearly in the simplest form of profit statement (Exhibit 19), the profit figure of £4,000 must be the assessment of cash *currently flowing* to the firm as a result of its manufacturing and trading operations. This positive statement can be made because all of the items in the account are cash receipt or payment transactions; there is no non-cash expense such as depreciation.

EXHIBIT 19

R.E.A. Limited

PROFIT AND LOSS ACCOUNT FOR THE YEAR ENDED ....

	£		£
Stock	3,000	Sales	10,000
Manufacturing expenses	3,000		
Profit	4,000		
	£10,000		£10,000

Turning to the balance sheet which includes this profit, the total value of the assets is shown to be £24,500: the firm has grown from an asset strength of £13,000 in Exhibit 17, an improvement of £11,500. Whilst this growth in asset size has been happening, the firm has made a profit of £4,000 which has been referred to as an 'assessment of the cash currently flowing to the firm'. It may therefore seem strange that the cash balance in Exhibit 17 has vanished, when Exhibit 18 is completed to show an overdraft of £3,500! Such a variation is not entirely unusual and by the preparation of a statement which details the source of company funds and their disposal, the reasons for the changing cash balance can be seen. Such a statement which compared the company state in Exhibit 17 with that demonstrated in Exhibit 18 is now presented (see Exhibit 20).

EXHIBIT 20*

R.E.A. Limited

SOURCE AND APPLICATION OF FUNDS STATEMENT FOR THE PERIOD ENDED . . . ., (i.e. EXHIBIT 18)

Source of funds	£
Increased profit	4,000
Increase in creditors	4,000
	£8,000
Application of funds	
Increased expenditure on fixed assets	2,000
Increased expenditure on stocks	1,000
Increase in debtors	9,000
	£12,000
Total net cash movement	—£4,000
(Therefore £500 cash in hand becomes £3,500 overdrawn.)	

* The source and application of funds may also be set out as follows:

Application of Funds			£
Increased expenditure on fixed assets			2,000
Increase in working capital:			
	Exhibit 17	Exhibit 18	
	£	£	
Current assets	4,500	14,000	
Current liabilities	2,000	9,500	
Working capital	£2,500	£4,500	
Therefore increase in working capital in the period			2,000
			£4,000
Source of funds required to meet above expenditure			
Profit			£4,000

Appropriation of profit

The profit shown in Exhibit 19 is an important figure: it is from this sum that amounts due for taxation on profits are deducted: similarly it represents the fund from which transfers to reserves may be made, and dividends paid. Furthermore it is one half of a vital business efficiency ratio—return on sales. In this instance the £4,000 profit would be expressed as 40 per cent of sales. In commercial parlance our profit and loss account shows a return before tax, before depreciation, of 40 per cent on sales. Before moving on to further studies of corporate development, the reader should realize that profit and loss accounts are never so simple as that shown in Exhibit 19. With even the limited number of transactions brought into that statement, the professional accountant would produce a more informative profit and loss such as that given below.

EXHIBIT 21

R.E.A. Limited

PROFIT AND LOSS ACCOUNT FOR THE PERIOD ENDED ....

		£	£		£
Materials consumed:*				*Sales*	
Opening stock	(Exhibit 17)	3,000			10,000
Purchases	(Exhibit 18)	4,000			
		7,000			
Closing stock	(Exhibit 18)	4,000			
			3,000		
Manufacturing expenses			3,000		
Profit			4,000		
			£10,000		£10,000

It now remains to demonstrate the process of sharing out the profit between taxation, reserves and dividends, as well as to bring to account the impact of the charge for depreciation. In the next example the amount given as the company's corporation tax assessment is not a precisely calculated sum, but a figure used for the purpose of demonstration only. This amount and other transactions to be incorporated into our next balance sheet are:

1 Debtors paid £5,000 to the company.
2 Inland Revenue agreed Corporation Tax assessment of tax payable—£2,000.

* See pages 35 and 42.

3 Stock in Exhibit 18 to be divided into the following groups:

a Raw materials £2,500.
b Work in progress £1,000.
c Finished goods £500.

4 For entry in the balance sheet, work in progress is to be valued at £1,250: the increase of £250 represents cash spent on manufacturing operations.
5 For entry in the balance sheet, finished goods are to be valued at £1,000: the increase of £500 represents the cost of manufacturing operations; of this sum £250 has been paid in cash and £250 is still owing.
6 Transfer £2,000 from profit and place in a general reserve.
7 Pay creditors £1,500.

The balance sheet of R.E.A. Limited, after taking note of the above adjustments is as shown in Exhibit 22. This balance sheet shows that with a total profit of £3,000 the directors decided to transfer £2,000

EXHIBIT 22

R.E.A. Limited

BALANCE SHEET AS AT ....

	£	£		£	£
Subscribed Capital and Reserves			*Fixed Assets*		
			Land and buildings		6,000
10,000 Ordinary shares			Plant and Machinery		4,000
of £1 each		10,000	Vehicles		500
General reserve	2,000				
Profit	1,000		TOTAL FIXED ASSETS		10,500
		3,000			
TOTAL SHAREHOLDERS' INTEREST		13,000			
Current Liabilities			*Current Assets*		
Creditors	4,500		Raw materials	2,500	
Expenses due	250		Work in progress	1,250	
Taxation	2,000		Finished goods	1,000	
Bank overdraft	500		Debtors	5,000	
		7,250			9,750
		£20,250			£20,250

to a new general reserve, thus giving some indication of their present desire to retain at least that amount of profit in the business. If we assume that Exhibit 22 reflected the position of R.E.A. Limited at the end of a year's working, then with a final profit balance of £1,000 after tax, after transfers to reserves, it would appear that a dividend could be paid to the shareholders. As the company has a subscribed share capital of £10,000 of Ordinary shares, a 10% dividend could be paid.[1] However, as has been emphasized previously, profits result from the consumption of goods and services in the efficient production of goods for sale. The price at which the firm's output is sold must in the long run cover not only the material and labour charges, but also the costs of use of capital assets such as plant and machinery. Therefore in order to find out the true cost of turning raw materials into products ready for sale, further adjustments have to be made to the balance sheet in Exhibit 22 to take account of the capital assets used in the productive process. In making the conventional 'rule of thumb' calculations for depreciation, certain assumptions must be made about the assets' expected economic lives. In Exhibit 23 an expected sixty-year life has been attributed to the buildings, a ten-year life for plant and machinery and a four-year life to the vehicles. With the final assumption that these assets will have a nil salvage value at the end of the expected life, annual charges for depreciation[2] are shown to be:

1 Land and buildings—one sixtieth of cost, i.e. £100.
2 Plant and machinery—one tenth of cost, i.e. £400.
3 Vehicles—one quarter of cost, i.e. £125.

As a result of the above decisions being applied to the assets and profits shown in Exhibit 22, the picture of the firm now emerges as shown in Exhibit 23.

The full effect of the concept of 'charging for use' of the fixed assets is now seen to reduce:

1 The book value of each asset.
2 The book value of the total fixed assets.
3 The balance of the profit and loss account.
4 The value of the total shareholders' interest.

[1] A company rate of ordinary dividend is given as a percentage of the amount paid up on the Ordinary shares—*not* as a percentage of the face value of those shares.
[2] According to the straight-line depreciation method—see pages 21–22.

EXHIBIT 23

R.E.A. Limited

BALANCE SHEET AS AT ....

	£	£	£		£	£
Subscribed Capital and Reserves				*Fixed Assets*		
10,000 Ordinary shares				Land and buildings at cost	6,000	
of £1 each			10,000	*Less* depreciation	100	
						5,900
Reserves				Plant and machinery		
General reserve		2,000		at cost	4,000	
Profit and loss				*Less* depreciation	400	
Account	1,000					3,600
Less depreciation				Vehicles at cost	500	
charges	625			*Less* depreciation	125	
		375				375
			2,375			
				TOTAL FIXED ASSETS		9,875
TOTAL SHARE-HOLDERS' INTEREST			12,375			
Current Liabilities				*Current Assets*		
Creditors		4,500		Raw materials	2,500	
Expenses due		250		Work in progress	1,250	
Taxation		2,000		Finished goods	1,000	
Bank overdraft		500		Debtors	5,000	
			7,250			9,750
			£19,625			£19,625

and thus:

5 The value of the whole firm as it is represented in the totals of the balance sheet.

It should be noted further that the profit and loss account, which is the source of dividend payments, is reduced to £375. In these circumstances a dividend of £3·75% is all that can be recommended if one is to ignore the general reserve; expressed in another way, the charges for depreciation have reduced the sum of money which the firm might distribute in the form of dividend from £1,000 to £375. So one can say that charging for depreciation has not only produced a more realistic profit statement, but it has resulted in the company being persuaded to conserve some of its cash resources by *not* paying out *un*realistic dividends.

Appendix—Answers

ANSWER TO EXHIBIT 17

R.E.A. Limited

BALANCE SHEET AS AT . . . .

		£			£
Subscribed Capital and Reserves			*Fixed Assets*		
10,000 Ordinary shares			Buildings		4,000
of £1 each		10,000	Plant and machinery		3,500
Profit		1,000	Vehicles		1,000
		———	TOTAL FIXED ASSETS		8,500
TOTAL SHAREHOLDERS' INTEREST		11,000			
Current Liabilities			*Current Assets*		
Creditors		2,000	Stock	3,000	
			Debtors	1,000	
			Cash	500	
				———	4,500
		£13,000			£13,000

ANSWER TO EXHIBIT 18

R.E.A. Limited

BALANCE SHEET AS AT . . . .

		£			£
Subscribed Capital and Reserves			*Fixed Assets*		
			Land and buildings		6,000
10,000 Ordinary shares			Plant and machinery		4,000
of £1 each		10,000	Vehicles		500
Profit		5,000			
		———	TOTAL FIXED ASSETS		10,500
TOTAL SHAREHOLDERS' INTEREST		15,000			
Current Liabilities			*Current Assets*		
Creditors	6,000		Stock	4,000	
Bank overdraft	3,500		Debtors	10,000	
	———	9,500		———	14,000
		£24,500			£24,500

Questions for discussion

1. Why does the profit and loss account include income and expenditure rather than receipts and payments?
2. If the profit and loss account is not concerned with receipts and payments, how can it portray cash flow?
3. What is the effect of charging depreciation upon the ultimate profit shown in the final accounts? If you consider that the relevant fixed assets were paid for years ago, why charge depreciation *now*?
4. What is the value of a source and application of funds statement?
5. Do you consider that a company should distribute all of its profits as dividends?
6. If a company consistently paid no dividends to its shareholders, what would happen to the market price for its shares?

Recommended reading

JAEDICKE, R. K. and SPROUSE, R. T., *Accounting Flows: Income, Funds and Cash*, Prentice Hall, 1965.

EDEY, H. C., *Introduction to Accounting*, Hutchinson, 1963.

SIDEBOTHAM, R., *Introduction to the Theory and Context of Accounting*, Pergamon Press, 1969.

CHAPTER 4 Return on Capital Employed

Functions of depreciation

The inclusion of a charge for depreciation in the profit and loss account has been presented in the previous chapters as a step towards the assessment of a realistic profit. Some reference has also been made to the effect of depreciation upon profit available for dividend and thus upon the ultimate cash assets retained by the company. It is possible therefore to argue several functions for the depreciation provision—an aid to asset valuation, a determinant of income (as a result of the charges to the profit and loss account) and a conserver of cash resources. Nothing more will be said here about the depreciation controversy beyond emphasizing that charging the profit and loss account for asset use[1] is a wise action: it is the action of a prudent businessman. There is no requirement at law, either in statute or case law, for a company to charge for the depreciation of its *fixed* assets against its profit. In fact, excess depreciation provision can be written back to the income account if the managers of the firm so desire.

The effects of the depreciation charge

It is now our intention to demonstrate how the various accepted methods of assessing depreciation will seriously affect

Asset valuation in the balance sheet.
Profit in the profit and loss account.
The total sum available for dividends.

[1] Again the reader is reminded of the problems attaching to the determination of the charge. Should depreciation be based upon (historical) cost, current cost or replacement cost? The answer to this question lies in the objective of business endeavour. Is it aimed at reimbursing the past cost of its present existence? Should it be concerned with recovering the current cost of using its present physical resources or should it be concerned with showing the cost of ultimate replacement of those resources? Whichever decision is made will determine the basic figure upon which depreciation is to be calculated.

For the purpose of a graduated analysis of the growth of R.E.A. Limited, we will assume that the directors, upon studying the balance sheet in Exhibit 23, decided to recommend a 3% dividend. Being concerned about the firm's lack of liquid resources and the need to finance further expansions, they also issued £5,000 worth of 7% debentures which were secured by a mortgage on the fixed assets of the company. The ensuing Exhibit 24 shows the state of the company after these transactions have been entered in the accounts.

EXHIBIT 24

R.E.A. Limited

BALANCE SHEET AS AT ....

	£	£	£		£	£
Subscribed Capital and Reserves				*Fixed Assets*		
10,000 Ordinary shares of £1 each			10,000	Land and building at cost	6,000	
Reserves				*Less depreciation*	100	5,900
General reserve		2,000		Plant and machinery at cost	4,000	
Profit and loss account	375			*Less* depreciation	400	
Less dividend	300					3,600
		75		Vehicles at cost	500	
			2,075	*Less* depreciation	125	
						375
TOTAL SHAREHOLDERS' INTEREST			12,075	TOTAL FIXED ASSETS		9,875
Loan Capital						
7% Debentures (secured on the fixed assets)			5,000	*Current Assets*		
Current Liabilities				Raw materials	2,500	
Creditors		4,500		Work in progress	1,250	
Expenses due		250		Finished goods	1,000	
Taxation		2,000		Debtors	5,000	
Dividends payable		300		Cash	4,500	
			7,050			14,250
			£24,125			£24,125

Now Exhibit 24 has much more to reveal. The reader will observe that profit has been reduced by the 3% dividend which now becomes a current liability, assuming that the dividend is voted by the shareholders at their annual general meeting. The proposed amount has been transferred from the profit and loss account balance to current liabilities because it will be payable by the company in the very near future: it cannot therefore, by definition be a part of retained profits!

Additionally a new form of liability grouping called 'loan capital' has been introduced. This kind of company financing does not form part either of the corporate share capital or of the total shareholders' interest. It is quite simply a long term loan which will have to be paid back some day.

Finally the firm's liquid position has considerably improved from having an overdraft of £500 to where a healthy bank balance of £4,500 is displayed. Taking into account the dividend declaration and the issue of debentures, the working capital of the business has risen from £2,500 to £7,200[1] giving a sound credit worthy picture of R.E.A. Limited. Exhibit 24 now presents information about the company which with certain other data will be sufficient to meet the requirements of the various Companies Acts. These other details which must accompany the published balance sheet are given at Appendix A. Briefly they refer to:

1 Amounts set aside to be used to prevent undue fluctuation in charges for taxation.
2 Aggregate of loans to the company where the loans are not wholly repayable in five years, showing terms of repayment and rate of interest payable on each loan.
3 Notes of liabilities due by the company, whether secured or not, by law, on any assets of the company.
4 Capital expenditure approved by the directors but not yet embodied in formal contracts.
5 Method of valuation of fixed assets and the total amount of such assets bought and disposed of in the year.
6 The detailed nature of the companies interest in land.
7 Manner of computation of raw material and work in progress valuations.
8 More information upon investments and certain special provisions concerning holding and subsidiary companies.

The narrative balance sheet

So far the balance sheets of R.E.A. Limited have been set out in the orthodox two-sided form. We can however present this same

[1] Working capital calculations:

Exhibit 23: Current assets £9,750 –
current liabilities £7,250 = £2,500.

Exhibit 24: Current assets £14,250 –
current liabilities £7,050 = £7,200.

EXHIBIT 25

R.E.A. Limited

BALANCE SHEET AS AT ....

Fixed Assets	£	£	£
Land and buildings at cost		6,000	
Less depreciation		100	
			5,900
Plant and machinery at cost		4,000	
Less depreciation		400	
			3,600
Vehicles at cost		500	
Less depreciation		125	
			375
TOTAL FIXED ASSETS			9,875
Current Assets			
Raw materials		2,500	
Work in progress		1,250	
Finished goods		1,000	
Debtors		5,000	
Cash		4,500	
TOTAL CURRENT ASSETS		14,250	
Less: Current Liabilities			
Creditors	4,500		
Expenses due	250		
Taxation	2,000		
Dividends payable	300		
TOTAL CURRENT LIABILITIES		7,050	
NET WORKING CAPITAL			7,200
NET CAPITAL EMPLOYED			17,075
Less Loan Capital			
7% Debentures (secured on the fixed assets)			5,000
NET WORTH OF THE COMPANY			£12,075

The above net worth of the company has been financed as follows:

Subscribed Capital		
10,000 Ordinary shares of £1 each		10,000
Reserves		
General reserve	2,000	
Profit and loss account	75	2,075
TOTAL SHAREHOLDERS' INTEREST		£12,075

information in an entirely different way. This other method of presentation, which meets all the legal requirements for publishing corporate financial data, is shown in Exhibit 25.

The above balance sheet is written in what is called the 'narrative form' and it is the form of display which will be adopted throughout the remainder of this book. Here, it is the order of presenting the relevant facts of the company's possessions which is important. The values of the fixed assets are still the same but they are shown first because they are the (more or less) permanent expression of the firm's power to do business, to produce and deliver its goods. Next in order of priority, the reader should note the sequential positioning of current assets and current liabilities which enables the amount of working capital to be revealed as an essential logical step in the assessment of the company's viability. The balance sheet, as now drawn up, reflects the business man's approach to planning when he thinks of the costs of setting up and running a commercial enterprise. Most managers would express this total investment in terms of the cost of the necessary fixed assets plus the amount of working capital needed to run the concern. Exhibit 25 gives that total sum and specifies it as 'net capital employed £17,075': more will be said of this definition in due course. The value of the debentures, because they are (normally) secured against some or all of the fixed assets of the company, are then deducted from the total net capital employed to give a book value of 'net worth of the company'. Net worth of a firm is meant to convey the net value of the company to the shareholders, after all corporate debts to outside parties have been accounted for. It is the total value (not the face value) of the proprietors' holdings of shares in the company, and is frequently called 'total shareholders' interest'. In the narrative balance sheet this proprietors' interest subscribed shares, reserves and profit retentions is defined as the means of financing the existence and growth of the firm up to the date of the balance sheet. Thus we have an explanatory statement showing

1 The total net capital employed and how it is made up.
2 How working capital is comprised and how much it is in money terms.
3 The net worth of the company.
4 How the business in its present state has been financed.

Capital employed

It must be stressed at this stage that the figures in the balance sheet, which enable the above four items of information to be calculated, result from the transactions in the books of account. They are book figures only and they arise from dealings in the past: they do not presume to be the current market values of the assets listed.[1] The reader will surely have noted that if no depreciation has been charged for the use of fixed assets, the capital employed would have been £625 greater! The expression 'capital employed' does have several possible interpretations. The total of £17,075 used in Exhibit 25 looks at the net long-term assets available to the company: also it takes in these possessions after deductions for depreciation. Current liabilities have been the source of a further reduction because they are short-term items which fluctuate in size from month to month throughout the year, especially in a seasonal trade. Such short-term liabilities are matched to a great extent by short-term assets such as stocks of materials on the other side of the balance sheet. Again debentures have not been eliminated from the capital employed total because they refer to the borrowing of money for periods of say 20 years, frequently for long-term expansion and the provision of additional fixed assets and *permanent* working capital. Here then net capital employed is the financial book value of the extent to which corporate assets are held throughout the year, available for the earning of profit.

Capital employed is also frequently referred to as the total assets possessed by the firm and shown in its balance sheet—no deductions being made for any liabilities. This measures the total book value of all assets at the disposal of the company to enable it to pursue its trading. But such is not all of the possible combinations leading to an assessment of the capital employed by any company. Commonly used practices include also:

[1] Some reservations need to be made here with regard to the valuation of the current assets. The monetary values of these assets will, indeed must, be approximating more closely to their actual values. Current assets change much more frequently than fixed assets and therefore their values are more 'up to date'. Furthermore any losses through, for example, obsolescence, changes in demand or bad debts, must be written off to the profit and loss account *before* their resultant values are entered in the balance sheet. Even so, the current asset valuations are assessed for the firm *in business as a going concern*. The value of work in progress within this concept can only be a value to the company intending to convert the work in progress to a finished good for sale to its customers.

1 Calculating fixed assets at gross cost, i.e. no depreciation.
2 Calculating fixed assets at current cost or at replacement cost —either with or without deductions for depreciation.
3 Regarding capital employed as those assets available throughout the year and therefore taking the average of capital employed at the beginning and at the end of the year.

These other expressions of capital employed are given to show the potential variety of the basic expression of corporate earning power.[1] It is very important that the sundry values which may be given to our index of earning power should be realized, for the return on capital employed is our major ratio of comparison of industrial performance. Care must always be taken therefore to ensure the comparison of like with like.

Whilst there are good reasons for differing computations of this concept, it is intended that we should restrict our study of return on capital employed by utilizing the book value of fixed assets plus working capital as our definition of the capital invested in the firm's operations. The reader should understand that this is done because:

1 It is the most common interpretation for comparison of corporate and industrial performance.
2 It is not proposed to develop this book beyond the preliminary stages of accounts analysis.
3 It does represent a view of earning power available to the firm, in the longer term without too much influence of opinion on the valuation of assets.

However it must be acknowledged that, for internal business comparisons of the profit earning efficiency of different divisions of a large organization, other considerations will prevail. For example, it is not uncommon in these instances for capital employed to be calculated by reference to the total gross cost of the assets available for use, excluding cash. Cash is eliminated from the evaluation because it represents an amount which is not always within the power of the divisional manager or factory manager to affect. It should not therefore be regarded as a part of the capital employed upon which he must earn a specific return.

[1] For the impact of the different values, of capital employed, upon the evaluation of company performance, see 'Uses of comparison' by Anthony Harris in the *Financial Times*, 22 May 1968. Also on 23 June 1967 in the same paper 'How to impress your board with lower profits', by John Murray.

Profit and the appropriation account

Pursuing the notion of return on capital employed it is high time that the profit and loss account was re-examined. The simple expositions of this account given in Exhibits 19 and 21 are now to be extended to show the transactions which have transformed Exhibit 18 into Exhibit 25. The reader will recall that in this change of R.E.A. Limited's wealth, certain dealings have affected the asset and financing structure *only* of the company. Other dealings have affected the income only and it is these matters with which we shall be concerned in preparing the formal profit and loss account. Our account will show the results of trading over a period of time and will include the undermentioned consequences of operations and decisions:

1 The earning of £4,000 profit by selling goods, costing £6,000 for £10,000—see Exhibit 18.
2 The appropriation or setting aside of £2,000 by transfer of this sum to a general reserve—see Exhibit 22.
3 The liability of the company to pay corporation tax of £2,000, assessed on its profits—Exhibit 22.
4 A charge for depreciation of fixed assets used in the production process—Exhibit 23.
5 The declaration of a dividend of £300 payable from the profits referred to in 1 above—Exhibit 24.

The resultant profit and loss account is given in Exhibit 26.

Section of the profit and loss account

The outline of business trading as given in Exhibit 26 is too limited for it to represent a picture of the company's whole performance. The reader has progressed step by step to the stage where a professional appreciation, of the logic of appropriately grouped numerical statements, can be developed. Therefore the accounts must now show the whole process of R.E.A. Limited's conversion of raw materials into saleable products. Here we shall consider the various costs involved in the successive stages of making and marketing goods for sale and finally the disposal of the ultimate profit together

EXHIBIT 26

R.E.A. Limited

PROFIT AND LOSS ACCOUNT FOR THE PERIOD ENDED ....

		£	£		£
(Exhibit 17)	Opening stock	3,000			
(Exhibit 18)	Purchases	4,000		Sales	10,000
		7,000			
(Exhibit 18)	*Less* closing stock	4,000			
	Materials consumed		3,000		
(Exhibit 18)	Wages		3,000		
(Exhibit 23)	Depreciation		625		
	Profit before taxation		3,375		
			£10,000		£10,000
	Corporation tax		2,000	Profit before tax	3,375
	Profit after taxation		1,375		
			£3,375		£3,375
(Exhibit 22)	Transfer to General Reserve		2,000	Profit for the period after tax	1,375
(Exhibit 24)	Dividends payable		300		
(Exhibit 25)	Balance of profit remaining to carry forward to next period		75	Balance of profit from the previous period (Exhibit 17)	1,000
			£2,375		£2,375

with the firm's liability for tax upon that profit. In truth the profit and loss account is four or five accounts rolled into one, each of which has its vital information giving service to perform.

First of all comes the manufacturing function and the relevant 'Manufacturing Account' should show the cost of raw materials used up in producing the factory output during the period stated at the head of the account. Together with labour costs of production, the wages of those workmen actually operating the machines and fashioning the raw materials or components, the account must show the 'Prime Cost' of production. Prime cost refers to the material and labour expenses indissolubly linked with the firm's products and which can be *seen* to be incorporated in the product *as it is being made*. If a commodity is being made then prime costs are automatically incurred: if there is no production then there can be no expense on the factors included in prime cost.[1] This statement cannot be made about overhead expenses which will be considered next in the study of the complete income account.

New production lines are operated within factory buildings and therefore the costs of the firm's output must include the expenses of servicing and maintaining this manufactory shell—the buildings. Furthermore the costs of using plant and equipment within this building, the supervisory salaries, drawing office wages and other essentials for the proper running and organization of the production function, are other expenses to bring to account. This list of ancillary expenses, termed overheads, should be segregated in an appropriate grouping of the financial accounts.[2] Exhibit 27 sets out the form of a complete profit and loss account dividend into its various sections and showing the manufacturing account to be the first part of this financial story. Prime cost and the total of factory overhead costs are both given: a series of several years' manufacturing accounts can therefore show the proportion that such expenses bear to the total sales value of the works output.

Exhibit 27 goes on to show the results of trading and the gross profit achieved from the sales. Gross profit is an important control ratio for not only does it show the accomplished mark up on sales,

[1] Prime cost is more frequently referred to as 'direct cost' or 'marginal cost' although the latter definition presents the concept of changes in total cost brought about by the changes in level of production.

[2] This book is predominantly concerned with financial accounts and their analysis: cost accounts may be prepared in conjunction with financial accounts and would be aimed at an appraisal *in detail* of the whole costs of operation and management.

but it represents the sum from which all other corporate expenses of administration, selling, distribution and financing are met. It is the amount which should make possible the ultimate declaration of a dividend and the ploughing back of retained profits to company reserves so that further expansion can be undertaken. The sequence of the account's details are of interest here, in that before the

EXHIBIT 27

R.E.A. Limited

MANUFACTURING, TRADING AND PROFIT AND LOSS ACCOUNT
FOR THE PERIOD ENDED ....

Manufacturing account	*Materials Consumed*	£	£		£
	Opening stock	xxx		Cost of goods manufactured transferred to trading account	xxxx
	Purchases	xxx			
		xxx			
	Less closing stock	xxx	xxx		
	Production Wages		xxx		
	PRIME COST		xxxx		
	Factory Overhead Expenses				
	Supervisory wages	xxx			
	Light, heat power	xxx			
	Rent and rates	xxx			
	Repairs and maintenance	xxx			
	Depreciation—plant	xxx	xxxx		
			xxxx		
	Work in Progress				
	At commencement of period	xxx			
	Less: at end of period	xxx	xx		
			£ xxxx		£ xxxx
Trading account	Opening stock of finished goods		xxx	Sales	xxxxx
	Cost of goods manufactured		xxxx		
			xxxx		
	Less closing stock of finished goods		xxx		
	COST OF SALES		xxxx		
	Gross profit transferred to profit and loss account		xxxx		
			£xxxxx		£xxxxx

Profit and loss account	*Administration Expenses*				
	Directors' fees	xx		Gross profit brought from trading account	xxxx
	Salaries	xx			
	Printing and stationery	xx			
	Rent and rates, etc.	xx	xxx		
	Selling Expenses				
	Sales salaries	xx			
	Advertising	xx			
	Delivery expenses, etc.	xx	xxx		
	Financing Expenses				
	Discounts allowed	xx			
	Bad debts	xx			
	Debenture interest	xx	xxx		
	Depreciation				
	Land and buildings	x			
	Vehicles	xx			
	Equipment	xx	xxx		
	Profit before tax		xxx		
			£ xxxx		£ xxxx
	Corporation tax		xx	Profit before tax	xxx
	Profit after tax		xx		
			£		£
Appropriation account	Transfer to reserve		xx	Profit after tax	xx
	Dividends paid		xx	Balance of profit brought from previous year	xx
	Dividends payable		xx		
	Tax on dividends		xx		
	Balance to balance sheet		xx		
			£ xxx		£ xxx

question of dividend can be considered the profit and loss account proper is prepared. In the continuing statement the reader will observe that *general* organizational overheads of administration and selling are listed together with a total of certain depreciation charges. It must be understood that the particular depreciation expenses given may well be found more appropriately placed in other parts of the whole income statement. For example, if the vehicles are used solely for distribution of the firm's goods then the relevant depreciation sum should be sited amongst the selling and distribution costs.[1]

The final part of Exhibit 27 denotes the disposal of the profit remaining after all the costs of production, management and selling,

[1] Similarly buildings depreciation may be allocated to the manufacturing, administration or selling functions, according to the proportionate usage of the buildings by those functions.

plus the liability for corporation tax on profits, have been accounted for. The disposal of profit is effected in what is termed the 'Appropriation Account' and here the unapportioned balance from the previous year is brought forward to take part in the current year's disposals. As the appropriation account contains the gross amounts of dividends paid and proposed, it is frequently called by another name—the 'Dividend Fund'. This proforma layout of the manufacturing, trading and profit and loss account will be used in a later chapter where forecasting and budgeting will be studied. The reader should not therefore be too disturbed at the sudden appearance of such an extensive example.

Depreciation, profit and return on capital

Exhibit 23 introduced the effect, upon asset and upon profit, of accounting for the cost of using fixed assets. That particular example was based upon a calculation of depreciation by the straight-line method. A total sum of £625 was deducted from the cost of fixed assets and from the balance of the profit and loss account as shown in the balance sheet. In order to show more clearly the effect of such changes, we shall see the impact on profit and on the balance sheet figures of using the reducing balance method of calculating depreciation. Now the *annual rate of* asset diminution must be larger when using the reducing balance method than when the straight-line method of depreciation calculation is used.[1]

In these circumstances the three types of asset will be reduced by the following percentages per annum, remembering that this annual rate of asset diminution is *not* based upon cost but *upon the reducing book value* at the commencement of each year:

Land and buildings	3 per cent
Plant and machinery	25 per cent
Vehicles	60 per cent

Previously with the complete elimination of asset book value as practised by the straight-line method, the proportion of initial cost charged in each year's accounts had been:

[1] Accepting that in both instances the asset cost is to be spread fully over its economic working life.

Land and buildings	1/60th (1·7 per cent)
Plant and machinery	1/10th (10 per cent)
Vehicles	1/4 (25 per cent)

Exhibit 28 shows the comparative annual reductions in asset value and profit, for the first four years of the firm's operations, resulting from the application of the two methods of calculating depreciation which we have discussed. The table demonstrates the variations in individual and total amounts which could be used as appropriate depreciation charges, i.e. the assessment of the cost of fixed asset use or the means of asset valuation (see page 44). The first column which deals with the straight-line method of calculation is shown once only for there would be no change, in subsequent years, in

1 The total depreciation sum for each of the first four years.
2 The amount of buildings' depreciation for sixty years.
3 The amount of plant depreciation for ten years.
4 The amount of vehicles' depreciation for four years.[1]

EXHIBIT 28

R.E.A. Limited

DEPRECIATION CHARGES: STRAIGHT-LINE AND REDUCING-BALANCE METHODS

Details	Straight-line method	Reducing-balance method			
		Year 1	Year 2	Year 3	Year 4
	£	£	£	£	£
Land and buildings	100	180	175	169	164
Plant and machinery	400	1,000	750	562	422
Vehicles	125	300	120	48	19
ANNUAL TOTALS	£625	£1,480	£1,045	£779	£605

The figures in Exhibit 28 speak for themselves. With a similar asset structure the charge for depreciation can vary from £605 to £1,480, depending upon the business manager's opinion of expected

[1] This assumes, of course, no further additions to or disposals of these assets within the periods stated, and accepts that the forecasted economic lives of the assets will remain unchanged.

EXHIBIT 29

R.E.A. Limited

COMPARATIVE PROFIT AND LOSS ACCOUNT:
SHOWING THE EFFECTS OF THE VARIOUS DEPRECIATION METHODS

Details	From Exhibit 26		Reducing-balance method			
			Year 1		Year 2	
	£	£	£	£	£	£
Sales		10,000		10,000		10,000
Less						
Materials	3,000		3,000		3,000	
Wages	3,000		3,000		3,000	
Depreciation	625		1,480		1,045	
		6,625		7,480		7,045
Profit before tax		3,375		2,520		2,955
Less Corporation Tax		2,000		2,000		2,000
Profit after tax		1,375		520		955
Profit from previous year		1,000		1,000		1,000
Available for appropriation		£2,375		£1,520		£1,955
To general reserve		2,000		1,220		1,655
Dividends payable		300		300		300
Balance to next year		75		—		—
		£2,375		£1,520		£1,955

asset lives and upon his preference for one or other method of calculating the cost of fixed asset usage. The variations become more meaningful if the profit and loss account in Exhibit 26 is reconstructed in narrative form to take account of the differences in total depreciation charge.

Assuming a dividend policy costing £300 each year, then the amount of book profit available for retention and transfer to reserves is:

Year 1 (straight line) = £2,000 + £75 = £2,075
Year 1 (reducing balance) = £1,220
Year 2 (reducing balance) = £1,655

But the depreciation expense shown in the profit and loss account is not itself a cash payment: it is the annual apportionment of some past cash payment which occurred when the fixed assets were first bought. When this is recognized, and when depreciation is regarded as a special kind of 'ploughback', then the total of these retentions is seen to be:

Year 1 (straight line) = £2,075 + £625 = £2,700
Year 1 (reducing balance) = £1,220 + £1,480 = £2,700
Year 2 (reducing balance) = £1,655 + £1,045 = £2,700

After elimination of the £1,000 balance of profit brought forward from the previous year we are left with a total retentions figure, attributable to the current year's operations, of £1,700. This is the company's cash flow for this year.

However it is the return on capital employed by which a company's performance is so frequently judged. The table now presented shows the financial expression of the same company's worth, using alternative depreciation charges taken from Exhibits 28 and 29.

Stock valuation

Economic business management involves the planning of consumption of material resources for the production and sale of finished commodities. Production lines must be adequately serviced and

EXHIBIT 30

COMPARATIVE BALANCE SHEETS OF R.E.A. LIMITED SHOWING THE EFFECTS OF THE VARIOUS DEPRECIATION METHODS

		From Exhibit 25		Reducing-balance method	
	£	£	£	£	£
Fixed Assets					
Land and buildings at cost		6,000		6,000	
Less depreciation		100		180	
			5,900		5,820
Plant and machinery at cost		4,000		4,000	
Less depreciation		400		1,000	
			3,600		3,000
Vehicles at cost		500		500	
Less depreciation		125		300	
			375		200
TOTAL FIXED ASSETS			9,875		9,020
Current Assets					
Raw materials		2,500			
Work in progress		1,250			
Finished goods		1,000			
Debtors		5,000			
Cash		4,500			
TOTAL CURRENT ASSETS		14,250		14,250	
Less: Current Liabilities					
Creditors	4,500				
Expenses due	250				
Taxation	2,000				
Dividends payable	300				
		7,050		7,050	
			7,200		7,200
NET CAPITAL EMPLOYED			17,075		16,220
Less Loan Capital			5,000		5,000
NET WORTH OF THE COMPANY			£12,075		£11,220

The above net worth of the company has been financed as follows:

	From Exhibit 25		Reducing-balance method	
	£	£	£	£
Subscribed Capital				
10,000 Ordinary shares of £1 each		10,000		10,000
Reserves				
General reserve	2,000		1,220	
Profit and loss account	75	2,075	—	1,220
TOTAL SHAREHOLDERS' INTEREST		£12,075		£11,220

N.B.

(1) Profit before tax as a percentage of capital employed	19·7	15·5.

. . . and the whole of the above figures related to the same company!

supplied with labour and materials in order to avoid the potentially heavy losses which stem from a cessation or breakdown in the manufacturing (or selling) operations. For these reasons firms carry stocks of raw materials and finished goods: industrial concerns inevitably have some unfinished production—work in progress—which is working its way through the complete process. Valuation of these assets:

Raw materials
Work in progress
Finished goods

can also be the subject of opinion and can have their effects upon profit and upon return on capital. Such influences are no less important and no less startling, in their ultimate impact upon book rate of return, than the results we have seen from using only two alternative methods of calculating the depreciation charge. In a period of unstable prices it is possible for raw materials to be charged to production at varying prices depending upon when the goods were bought. The problem is—which price shall be used in costing materials to production and hence against profit? The price of the goods bought two months ago, or the price of goods bought yesterday? Again the value of work in progress must consist, in some measure, of the labour and materials embodied in the unfinished article as it exists on the date of valuation. But this is not all: whilst the commodity is in course of manufacture, it has 'used' the corporate services of machines, factory buildings and management, light and heat, etc. Should not the direct labour and materials cost of work in progress have some amount or percentage added to them to bring to account these other costs also?

Similar questions can be asked about the valuation of finished goods. Most of the expenses of keeping the firm in existence, except selling and distribution costs, have resulted from these very manufacturing and administrative services which have finally brought the finished goods into the warehouse, ready for sale to a customer. How should these expenses be apportioned in the valuation of finished goods shown in any balance sheet? However it is not the intention of this book to study costing practices or theory, or to study asset valuation solely. Nevertheless it is most necessary that concepts of asset valuation and their effects should be put before the reader in sharp outline.[1] To enable those interested to pursue the matter further, the reading list at the end of this chapter has been carefully chosen to give adequate additional sources of information on stock valuation. All that is required of the reader of this publication is that he should appreciate that asset valuation must be affected by opinions such as those views of:

1 The engineer re asset life.
2 The accountant re depreciation method to be used for fixed assets.
3 The cost accountant and business manager re the methods of stock valuation to be used.

If this is accepted, if the impact on profit and on return on capital employed is understood, then one of the objectives of the study of R.E.A. Limited's progress has been achieved.

Questions for discussion

1. Why do accountants adhere to cost in their valuation of fixed assets?
2. Why is the cost of a fixed asset not charged to profit and loss account in the year of its purchase?
3. Compare the effects of using LIFO and FIFO methods of stock valuation on profits, and on return on capital employed.
4. Is the published balance sheet of a company a sound basis for an analysis of that firm's financial condition?
5. To what extent are (*a*) reserves, (*b*) depreciation, represented by cash balances in the balance sheet?
6. What do you understand by cash flow? In what way is this important in company planning?
7. Why is it advisable to have several sections of the profit and loss account?
8. What is the dividend fund?

[1] For an appreciation of impact of stock valuation upon profit, Exhibit 26 should be studied. If the same closing stock of materials had been valued at £5,000 instead of £4,000 then the ultimate profit would have been increased by £1,000 and the return on capital (Exhibit 30) using straight-line depreciation for fixed assets, increased from 19·7 to 24·2 per cent! Again all the figures relate to the same company in the same physical state.

Recommended reading

ROBINSON, R. I., *Financing the Dynamic Small Firm*, Prentice Hall, 1966.

HELFERT, E., *Valuation*, Prentice Hall, 1966.

THE INSTITUTE OF CHARTERED ACCOUNTANTS OF SCOTLAND, *The Companies Act 1967—some requirements and implications.*

BIGG, W. W., *Cost Accounts*, MacDonald & Evans, 1959 (a simple book with easily readable sections on stock accounts and stock valuation).

SYDENHAM, H. W., 'Some considerations in relation to the accounting treatment of stock-in-trade and work-in-progress,' *Accountancy*, pages 547–57, September 1960.

CHAPTER 5 Planning and Forecasting

Introduction

The management accountant is an interpreter to the business planners: he is able to represent the forecasts of production, administration and sales activities into statements of profit and company worth. The forecast profit and loss account and balance sheet are compiled from the data in a plan of proposed business development. These statements enable managers to see what the return on capital will be if the plan is put into action. Similarly, they can see whether this return will bc adequate or whether other proposals should be examined to improve the forecast. Frequently areas of high cost can be studied, before the event, in the search for economies and greater efficiencies which could bring the budgeted return more into line with business requirements. Profit figures and return on capital targets are thus established and, week by week, the firm's actual progress can be checked against the approved plan.

The progress of R.E.A. Limited is now to be followed in such an exercise. Certain plans for the company's future have been made and are presented in the case study below. Before proceeding with the preparation of a forecast profit and loss account and balance sheet, however, some recapitulation of the relationships between these statements and the cash account must be undertaken. The reader should be aware of the essential nature of the profit and loss account —it is a statement of income and expenditure. The figures of income describe the monetary values of the firm's products which have finally *left the works on their way to customers, as sales*, during the whole of the period stated at the head of the account. It is not necessary that the goods should have been paid for, before the relevant value can appear amongst the sales in the profit and loss account. *Money* receipts are entered in the cash book. Any difference between (*a*) the credit sales value, and (*b*) the cash received, at the balance sheet date, in respect of those sales, will be shown in the balance sheet amongst sundry debtors.[1] In the same way the profit and loss account shows expenditure, *not* payments. Expenditure is the monetary cost of the physical goods and services used, during the period of account, to make the sales shown in that account. Where such goods and services are received on credit, then those tems not paid for by the balancing date, will be shown amongst the various creditors under the title 'current liabilities' in the balance sheet.

The following demonstration of the preparation of budgeted, i.e. forecast, final accounts will commence with a cash budget. This is an important document because it shows the expected cash flow during the forthcoming period. The corporate liquidity path can be traced, and a watch kept on the ability of the company to meet its debts. It is not sufficient to be profitable only: too frequently the growth of sales has been achieved at the expense of prompt payment of creditors' accounts. This kind of situation indicates a company which is overtrading: operating at a level of business beyond that which can be sustained by its own long-term financial resources. Where these circumstances are foreseen, then arrangements can be made to obviate financial embarrassment and the consequent loss of the company's creditworthy reputation. The use of short-term creditors to finance company long-term growth is a dangerous practice which can lead to bankruptcy. Preserving the firm's liquidity or debt-paying ability may be secured by obtaining a bank loan or an overdraft, issue of shares or debentures or by the sale of investments. In each of these cases greater chances for the success of any financing operations will ensue, when the firm is able to support its requests for money with forecast cash and profit figures. Where investments are to be sold, this can be done gradually without disturbing the market. Sales can be effected at prices to suit the company—not as a result of panic measures to meet unforeseen events. This is the benefit of planning.

Exhibit 31 sets out a flow diagram of the interrelationships involved in preparing the company's activity plans. The reader will see how *all* roads lead ultimately to the cash book which contains not only day to day (running cost) payments but also payments for capital items.

[1] This postulates that settlements are received in arrear (goods sold on credit) and that no *over*payments are received.

EXHIBIT 31

DEVELOPMENT OF PROFIT AND LOSS BUDGET

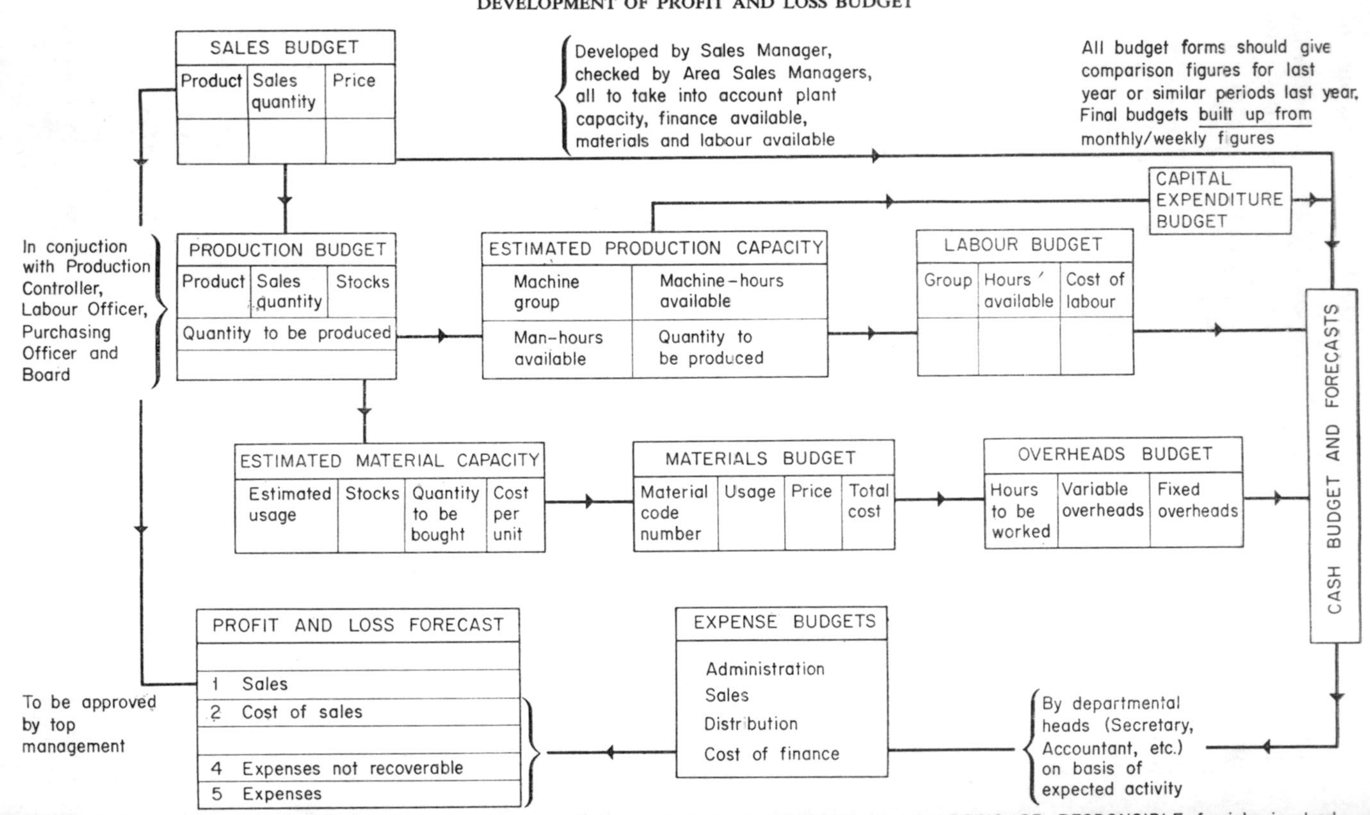

THE CASE STUDY

R.E.A. Limited

CASH BUDGET, PROJECTED PROFIT AND LOSS AND BALANCE SHEET FOR NEXT THREE MONTHS

1 THE PLAN R.E.A. Limited decided to develop some of their promising lines and to enter new fields of production. A market study by a firm of consultants indicated that, with carefully planned production and distribution arrangements, sales should reach the following targets in the next three months:

	£
1st month	6,000
2nd month	7,200
3rd month	7,800

Exhibit 30 (straight-line version) shows the existing state of the company and it soon became apparent, when production facilities were being compared with the sales forecast, that additional expenditure on fixed assets would be necessary. Therefore with a re-arrangement of the layout of the shops, additional machinery was installed. This expenditure on machinery was phased as follows:

	£
1st month	3,000
2nd month	2,000

whilst in the 3rd month, £1,000 was spent on new vehicles.

2 BUDGET The proposed extensions of company activity meant that fresh detailed budgets for the various departments of R.E.A. Limited had to be worked out. With the assistance of the Finance Director, heads of departments came forward with the undermentioned estimates of expenditure for the ensuing quarter. The final agreed income and expenditure budgets are tabulated in Exhibit 32.

The Finance Director was then requested to produce a profit and loss account for the next three months showing the anticipated profit for that forthcoming period. He was also expected to show the anticipated balance sheet at the end of the period.

EXHIBIT 32

R.E.A. Limited

OPERATING BUDGETS FOR THREE MONTHS ENDED ....

Details	Month 1	Month 2	Month 3	Totals to profit and loss account
(1)	(2)	(3)	(4)	(5)
	£	£	£	£
Wages	600	720	760	2,080
Factory overheads	500	500	600	1,600
Administration overheads	250	250	300	800
Selling overheads	500	500	630	1,630
Research and development	200	200	400	800
Welfare and Medical	50	50	70	170
TOTALS	£2,100	£2,220	£2,760	£7,080

Past practices showed that actual cash disbursements in respect of the above budgeted expenditures would occur as follows:

Wages: $\frac{3}{4}$ being paid in the month of the statement;
$\frac{1}{4}$ paid in the following month.

Factory, administration and selling overheads: Paid in full in the month following that shown in the statement.

Research and development / *Welfare and medical*: $\frac{1}{2}$ paid in the month of the statement; $\frac{1}{2}$ paid in the following month.

3 STOCKS It was decided that enough raw materials should be purchased in each month to support the sales of that month. As the raw material cost is expected to be $\frac{3}{4}$ of anticipated sales value these purchases would be £4,500 in the 1st month. In order to build up stocks, purchases of raw materials in each month should be supplemented by additional purchases of

£1,000 per month. Stocks at the end of the three-month period would be planned to achieve

	£
Raw materials	5,500
Work in progress	2,750
Finished goods	2,500

The company takes two months' credit before paying its suppliers so that purchases in month 1 are paid for in month 3. Furthermore the creditors shown in Exhibit 30 represent two months' accounts, due from the previous trading period.

4 GENERAL Other details pertinent to the planning period are given below:

a Debtors are given two months credit.

b Taxation of £2,000 shown in Exhibit 30 as being due, is paid in month 3.

c Dividends of £300 also shown in Exhibit 30 are paid in month 1.

d Expenses of £250 shown in Exhibit 30 as being outstanding represent amounts due as follows:

(i) Wages £100.
(ii) Factory overheads £50.
(iii) Administration overheads £50.
(iv) Selling overheads £50.

These sums are to be paid in Month 1.

e Capital expenditure acquisitions are paid in the month of the planned installation.

f Assume depreciation to be charged for the quarter as follows:
(i) Land and buildings £25.
(ii) Plant and machinery £100.
(iii) Vehicles £25.

Cash budget[1]

The above information shows what the managers of R.E.A. Limited think that they will be able to achieve in the next three months. Budget periods are not limited to three months—indeed many firms

[1] To aid the explanation of the cash budget it should be assumed that the balance sheet in Exhibit 30 was compiled to show the position as at December 31st. In this case the debtors and creditors in that balance sheet would refer to November and December of the period leading up to December 31st. Months 1, 2 and 3 of the budget plan would then relate to January, February and March of the next year.

prepare such a statement to cover a period of 12 months. Longer term plans are generally supported by re-examinations and revisions of the proposed activities every quarter. In those instances of quarterly (or monthly) revision, it is quite common for the planners to look forward over the *next period of 12 months from the date* of

EXHIBIT 33

R.E.A. Limited

CASH BUDGET FOR THREE MONTHS ENDED ....

Line number	*Details*	*Month 1*	*Month 2*	*Month 3*	*Totals*	*To balance sheet*
	RECEIPTS	£	£	£	£	£
1	Balances b/fwd	4,500	625	o/d 3,315	1,810	Debtors
2	From debtors	2,500	2,500	6,000	11,000	7,200 + 7,800
3	Totals	7,000	3,125	2,685	12,810	
	PAYMENTS					Creditors
4	Materials	2,250	2,250	5,500	10,000	6,400 + 6,850
5	Wages	550	690	750	1,990	190
6	Factory overheads	50	500	500	1,050	600
7	Administration overheads	50	250	250	550	300 } 1,955* (lines 5–10)
8	Selling overheads	50	500	500	1,050	630
9	Research	100	200	300	600	200
10	Welfare	25	50	60	135	30
11	Taxation	—	—	2,000	2,000	Capital expenditure
12	Capital	3,000	2,000	1,000	6,000	6,000
13	Dividends	300	—	—	300	
14	Interest	—	—	—	—	
15	Totals	6,375	6,440	10,860	23,675	
16	Balances c/fwd	625	o/d 3,315	o/d 8,175	o/d 10,865	
17	Total receipts (above)	7,000	3,125	2,685	12,810	

* The figure of £1,955 represents the total due but unpaid, at the end of the budget period, in respect of the running expenses listed on lines 5 to 10. This amount is a liability of the firm at that date. It is therefore shown in the balance sheet, under the heading current liabilities on page 79.

revision. Thus business forecasts may be 'rolling over'—consisting of successive month by month projections, each projection covering a forthcoming period of 12 months.

The cash budget for the next three months, based upon the data in the case study, is given in Exhibit 33.

The layout of the budget gives details and totals of expected receipts in each month (lines 1 to 3). Here are shown balances brought forward plus the estimated cash flow from debtors. The receipts' total for each month therefore gives the assessment of monies expected to be available to meet the expenses of the firm in that month. Forecasted payments are listed for each separate group of costs and the totals of those payments are also given for each month of the plan (line 15). The difference between receipts and payments (line 16) represents the expected balance of cash at the month's end.

A note of warning must be sounded at this point. The flow of cash expressed by the cash budget does not necessarily imply that payments are made each month *after* the receipts of that month have arrived at the firm's bank account. Thus if there is an uneven or delayed stream of cash receipts to match with an earlier pattern of outgoings, then the figure of cash in hand (month 1, line 16) could be misleading. It may conceal the fact that, for most of the month, there was an overdraft *not* a balance in hand! Now, to trace the completion of the budget shown in Exhibit 33, the reader must turn to Exhibit 30. Amongst the current assets, at that balance sheet date, cash is shown to be £4,500. Our forecast period is taken to be a continuation of the firm's business from the situation given in Exhibit 30. Therefore, the commencing cash balance for the forecast period must be £4,500 and this amount begins the cash budget at line 1 for month 1.

In this simple example, an assumption will be made in order to make our calculations the easier. The assumption relates to debtors and creditors which are shown as £5,000 and £4,500 respectively (see Exhibit 30). As the case study, at paragraphs 3 and 4a, indicate that the periods of credit taken and given is two months, then the totals of debtors and creditors are taken to refer in equal proportions to the final two months leading up to the balance sheet date.[1] This

[1] Obviously in a practical situation we should *know* the periods to which debtors and creditors relate. They would rarely arise from a series of month's sales—in ***equal proportions for each month.***

means that the total debtors of £5,000 include:

£2,500 due from November sales and
£2,500 due from December sales.

Similarly the total creditors of £4,500 relate to

£2,250 owing for November's purchases and
£2,250 owing for December's purchases.

In view of the two months' credit periods which apply equally to debtors and creditors it is expected that cash will be received from debtors as follows:

November's £2,500 in month 1, and
December's £2,500 in month 2.

Payments are similarly planned to be made to creditors so that the outward cash flow for these items will show that

November's £2,250 will be paid in month 1, and
December's £2,250 will be paid in month 2.

The above transactions are shown in the cash budget on lines 2 and 4 respectively.

Now paragraph 1 of the case study quoted the forecast sales during the planning period as

	£
Month 1	6,000
Month 2	7,200
Month 3	7,800

In view of the continuing credit periods of two months, these three amounts should be received in that given order, in months 3, 4 and 5. Thus the reader will find that the receipts from debtors (line 3) in month 3 are entered as £6,000. The two months still outstanding at the end of the planning period will be shown in the balance sheet as 'sundry debtors' £15,000. This is recorded as a note in the final column of Exhibit 33.

The same process is repeated in respect of the cost of material purchases, but here some calculation has to be completed first. Paragraph 3 of the case study states:

'It was decided that enough raw materials should be purchased in each month to support the sales of that month. As the raw material cost if expected to be $\frac{3}{4}$ of anticipated sales value, these purchases would be £4,500 in the 1st month. In order to build up stocks, purchases of raw materials in each month should be supplemented by additional purchases of £1,000 per month.'

These instructions relating to the purchases of, and payments for, materials are tabulated in Exhibit 34. Here one can trace the monthly

EXHIBIT 34

RAW MATERIALS: COMPUTATION OF EXPENDITURE AND PAYMENTS DURING THE PLANNING PERIOD

Details (1)	Sales (2)	Purchases of raw materials ($\frac{3}{4}$ of column 2) (3)	Additional materials purchases (4)	Total purchases of materials (columns 3 + 4) (5)	Entries (6)
	£	£	£	£	
Month 1	6,000	4,500	1,000	5,500	Month 3 of cash budget
Month 2	7,200	5,400	1,000	6,400	} Balance sheet
Month 3	7,800	5,850	1,000	6,850	
TOTALS	21,000	15,750	3,000	18,750	Profit and loss account

incidence of expenditure and of payments and see how they affect the cash budget demonstrated at Exhibit 33. Entries to be made in the final accounts—profit and loss account and balance sheet—will be demonstrated in subsequent pages. By this system of methodical calculation, and it is only elementary arithmetic, all of the remaining entries in the budget lay out can be verified. The relevant data for verification of these other payments are found in paragraphs 2, 3 and 4 of the case study.

Paragraph 4d is of prime importance here for it explains how the item 'Expenses £250', amongst the current liabilities of Exhibit 30, is compiled. Furthermore, paragraph 2 of the plan gives details of how payments are made for the other main groups of expense. By using these instructions, the pattern of disbursements for wages can be seen (Exhibit 35). The amount unpaid of third month's wages,

EXHIBIT 35

WAGES: COMPUTATION OF MONTHLY PAYMENTS

Details (1)	Amount due per Exhibit 32 (2)	Amount paid ($\frac{3}{4}$ × Column 2) (3)	Amount due from previous month (4)	Total payments (Columns 3 + 4) (5)	Entries (6)
	£	£	£	£	
Month 1	600	450	100*	550	Cash budget, line 5
Month 2	720	540	150	690	
Month 3	760	570	180	750	
TOTALS	2,080	1,560	430	1,990	

which is £190 ($\frac{1}{4}$ of £760) ill be found in the final column of the cash book layout.

The profit and loss account

Exhibit 36 is the completed projection of the manufacturing, trading and profit and loss accounts for the coming three months.

The sequence of items in this account follows the natural progress of materials, through the production process until the results of sales are revealed in the ultimate profit or loss. The first item therefore sets out the expected consumption of raw materials in attaining the output of the budget period. Commencing stocks are brought forward from the previous account (Exhibit 30—where they were the stocks at the *end* of that period). This amount, together with the raw materials to be purchased (Exhibit 34, column 5), gives the total

* This sum relates to the previous year: it forms a part of the £250 'expenses' due which are listed amongst the current liabilities of Exhibit 30.

EXHIBIT 36

R.E.A. Limited

PROJECTED MANUFACTURING, TRADING AND PROFIT AND LOSS ACCOUNT FOR THREE MONTHS ENDED ....

Materials Consumed	£	£		£
Opening stock	2,500		Cost of goods manufactured transferred to trading account	18,030
Purchases	18,750			
	21,250			
Less closing stock	5,500	15,750		
Wages		2,080		
PRIME COST		17,830		
Factory overheads	1,600			
Depreciation	100			
		1,700		
		19,530		
Add work in progress at commencement	1,250			
Less work in progress at end	2,750			
		1,500 (CR)		
COST OF PRODUCTION		£18,030		£18,030
Opening stock of finished goods		1,000	Sales	21,000
Cost of goods manufactured		18,030		
		19,030		
Less closing stock of finished goods		2,500		
COST OF SALES		16,530		
Gross profit		4,470		
		£21,000		£21,000
Administration overheads		800	Gross profit	4,470
Selling overheads		1,630		
Research and development		800		
Welfare and medical		170		
Debenture interest*		88		
Depreciation	£			
Land and buildings	25			
Vehicles	25			
		50		
		3,538		
Profit before taxation		932		
		£4,470		£4,470

* Interest on debentures has not been introduced before this exhibit as the author wished to present the gradual development of the company, without raising too many

value of materials available for use by the production department during the three months of the plan. As we are trying to find the accounting cost[1] of the goods manufactured during a specified period, then we must deduct any raw materials which remain unused at the end of that period. In this instance the value of the closing stocks of raw materials is given in the case study, at paragraph 3, as £5,500. Deducting this amount will reveal the cost of materials used to be £15,750.

The various headings in the manufacturing trading and profit and loss accounts have been discussed in Chapter 4. Consequently this study of the compilation of the whole profit and loss account will be concerned with the determination of the amounts entered therein only. The reader must be reminded again that here we are ascertaining income and expenditure: *cash* is not a part of the profit and loss statement.[2] In this case, Exhibit 32, column 5 gives the planned expenditures which are expected to be incurred in obtaining the forecast income. Each item of the table can be traced to its appropriate place in the final income account shown in Exhibit 36. Only the totals appear in the account because its object is to show the aggregate income—expenditure relationships—over the period given. The division of the total expenditure into monthly amounts is an essential part of the planning process. Such greater detail of the *monthly* incidence of, for example, purchases, is necessary for the following:

1 Cash planning—cash budget.
2 Scheduling, purchasing and storing materials so that sufficient materials shall always be available to the production function to enable it to meet the requirements of the sales programme.

Similar comments explaining the month by month analyses of the likely expenditure on overheads, research and medical facilities can be specified.

issues at one time. Clearly all profit and loss accounts which have been presented since the issue of debentures (Exhibit 24) should have borne an appropriate interest charge. As the profit and loss account above covers 3 months, the costs should include $\frac{3}{12} \times \frac{7}{100} \times £5{,}000$: this being the relevant proportion of the total annual interest charge for £5,000 worth of debentures, issued at 7 per cent per annum.

[1] The various concepts of cost will be discussed in a later chapter.

[2] In so far as an entry in the final accounts reflects the ultimate *movement* of cash, this statement is not strictly true of course. The amounts of cash which flow to and from the firm are shown in the cash account: the statement says therefore that entries in the profit and loss account, whilst reflecting the *movement* of cash, do not *mirror exactly* cash payments. The account is concerned with income and expenditure and nothing else.

To return to the manufacturing account: one item remains to be charged to the costs of manufacture, i.e. depreciation. The proposed depreciation provisions are given at paragraph 4f of the case study and it will be noted that a charge for plant and machinery depreciation has been shown in the manufacturing account. That entry is necessary because the goods produced could not have been completed without the aid of the company's machines. On the basis of assessing the total costs of manufacture, some recognition must be given to fixed asset use: this recognition is achieved in some measure by the fixed assets' depreciation charges. But depreciation of buildings and vehicles has been shown in the profit and loss account and one may wonder why some proportion of, for example, the buildings cost is not apportioned to the costs of manufacture. This is a very proper observation and in practice some allocation, of the appropriate buildings' depreciation charge, to manufacturing process, to the administration and selling departments, would be determined. The allocation could be based upon actual areas of buildings space used by the various departments. The function of the vehicles, whether for interfactory movement of goods, transfers around the shop floor, or for delivery of finished goods would determine the allocation of the depreciation charge for these assets also.

Before proceeding to examine the forecast balance sheet, a word on the transfer of balances in the profit and loss is necessary. The summation of charges in the manufacturing account is described as 'cost of goods manufactured, transferred to the trading account—£18,030': this represents the total manufacturing cost of goods produced during the period stated at the head of the account. These are the goods passed to the sales and distribution departments for delivery to customers. Manufacturing costs are a part of the cost of sales of finished goods: the whole cost is shown in the trading account to be £16,530, but this figure takes into account the opening and closing stocks of finished goods. Now at this point the reader must observe one of the most important items of information which the profit and loss accounts give—gross profit. If this amount is expressed as a percentage of sales, we ascertain the mark up which has been achieved on total sales. This mark up or gross profit, however it is termed, is a vital absolute sum also. It is the total amount which is available from trading to meet the overhead expenses shown in the profit and loss account proper. Therefore the gross profit sum, determined in the trading account, is passed to the profit and loss account in order to be set against the expenditures of administration and selling, etc. Finally when the taxation liability is taken into account we may see how much is left for dividends or for transfer to reserves. Thus the size of the gross profit, the achievement of mark up on sales, must ultimately influence both the shareholders' dividends and the growth of the company through retentions.

The balance sheet

The compilation of totals for the balance sheet should now be relatively easy. As this statement presents a static picture of the firm at the end of a series of trading transactions, it will include the results of that trading. Thus the new balance sheet will incorporate the period's profit or loss, together with any variation in the quantity of fixed assets. The other factors affected by trading, e.g. debtors, creditors and stock, will be listed at the values attributed to them on the balancing date.

Whilst the case study did not plan any effect on the firm's possessions of land and buildings, it did state that £5,000 was to be spent on machinery and £1,000 on new vehicles. Exhibit 38 shows the expected balance sheet at the end of the three months planning period.

The reader will note that the cost of land and buildings remains at £6,000, but machinery now stands at £9,000 (£4,000 + £5,000 additional expenditure). Similarly the cost of vehicles owned by the firm is shown as £1,500, after adding the expenditure of £1,000 on new vehicles. The depreciation charges which have been deducted from the fixed assets are given in the case study (paragraph 4f): these amounts have already been charged to the profit and loss account. If the whole of the proposed plan is implemented therefore, the total value of fixed assets possessed by R.E.A. Limited, will reach the sum of £15,725. Each of the remaining items in the balance sheet can now be traced either from the case study or from the various statements which have been completed in this chapter, e.g.:

Stocks	Case study paragraph 3 (note also that these amounts have been deducted from the costs in the profit and loss account, as they represent the *unused part* of available materials, etc.)

EXHIBIT 38

R.E.A. Limited

PROJECTED BALANCE SHEET AS AT ....

Fixed Assets		£	£
Land and buildings at cost		6,000	
Less depreciation to date		125	
			5,875
Plant and machinery at cost		9,000	
Less depreciation to date		500	
			8,500
Vehicles at cost		1,500	
Less depreciation to date		150	
			1,350
TOTAL FIXED ASSETS			15,725
Current Assets			
Stock		5,500	
Work in progress		2,750	
Finished goods		2,500	
Debtors		15,000	
TOTAL CURRENT ASSETS		25,750	
Less Current Liabilities	£		
Creditors	13,250		
Expenses	1,955		
Debenture interest	88		
Cash overdrawn	8,175		
TOTAL CURRENT LIABILITIES		23,468	
NET WORKING CAPITAL			2,282
NET CAPITAL EMPLOYED			18,007
Less 7% debentures			5,000
NET WORTH OF THE COMPANY			£13,007

The above net worth of the company was financed as follows:

Subscribed Capital			
10,000 Ordinary shares of £1 each			10,000
Reserves			
General reserve		2,000	
Profit and loss account	£		
Brought forward	75		
Forecast	932		
		1,007	
			3,007
TOTAL SHAREHOLDERS' INTEREST			£13,007

(continued)

Exhibit 38 (continued)

The performance of the company as a result of the proposed activities can be expressed as

$$\frac{\text{Profit}}{\text{Capital employed}} = \frac{\text{Profit}}{\text{Sales}} \times \frac{\text{Sales}}{\text{Capital employed}}$$

and inserting the figures from the above accounting statements we have

$$\frac{932}{18{,}007} = \frac{932}{21{,}000} \times \frac{21{,}000}{18{,}007}$$

which to the nearest second decimal place is

$$5{\cdot}2 = 4{\cdot}4 \times 1{\cdot}2 \text{ for 3 months}$$

and for 12 months the ratios would be, at this level of trading performance

$$20{\cdot}8 = 4{\cdot}4 \times 4{\cdot}7$$

Debtors, creditors and expenses	Exhibit 33, final column
Cash overdrawn	Exhibit 33, line 16, month 3

Lastly, the forecast profit of £932 shown in the profit and loss account is the only change in the shareholders' capital invested.

Whereas the balance of the profit and loss account was given in Exhibit 30 as £75, the addition of the expected £932 will bring the undistributed profit figures to £1,007 and the total shareholders' interest to £13,007.

The ratios of business performance which are shown at the end of Exhibit 38 presage the studies to be encountered in the next chapter. For the moment it will be sufficient if the reader verifies these calculations by looking at the forecast profit and loss account and balance sheet. Clearly the ratios would show to the directors whether the performance of R.E.A. Limited would be satisfactory, consequent upon accepting the proposed plan of action set out in the case study. If the forecast returns are inadequate, steps can be taken to amend the plan, to revise costs and generally improve the potential performance, *before the event*.

Questions for discussion

1. What advantages accrue to the business manager from the preparation of a cash budget?
2. Would you consider it just as necessary for the smaller business to prepare forecast accounts, as for the large limited company?
3. 'A budget though desirable is not essential to the production of accounting information for control purposes.' What other information is regularly available in the accounting period for use as a control factor?
4. What are accruals and prepayments?
5. When referring to the 'allocation of expenditure' in accounting, what does the word 'allocation' mean?
6. If two companies have the same total shareholders' interest in the balance sheet, but one company has a larger investment in fixed assets than the other, will it experience greater difficulty in earning a profit than the second company?

Recommended reading

CHAMBERS, R. J., *Accounting, Evaluation and Economic Behaviour*, Prentice Hall, 1966.

WHEELER, L. V., *Management Accounting*, Gee (out of print).

HELFERT, E. A., *Techniques of Financial Analysis*, Irwin, 1967.

CHAPTER 6 Analysis of Accounts and Company Worth

Introduction

At the close of the previous chapter, three measures of business performance were given. These measures, or ratios, facilitate an easy appraisal of the results of specific aspects of the firm's activities. The appraisal is made easier because the results of business activity are reduced to simple percentages, or simple unit comparisons, of otherwise complicated aggregations of financial data. The ratios which were used in Exhibit 38 are explained below.

1 RETURN ON CAPITAL EMPLOYED This is a common enough expression for evaluating an investment in any venture. A decision, to put one's money in a Building Society rather than the Post Office Savings Bank, is made as a result of, for example, comparing the rates of interest offered for deposits with either institution. A business man does much the same thing if, when reviewing his business performance, he is concerned with the rate of return (cf. interest) which he makes upon his investment. Return on capital employed is an over-all measure of a firm's efficiency-of-use of its total assets.

2 MARK-UP ON SALES Here we have a term which expresses the net profit mark-up as a percentage of the value of sales obtained in the period of account. The mark-up on individual sales indicates the level of gross profit planned by a business, whilst the total net mark-ups actually achieved are revealed by the net profit in the profit and loss account. In connection with this ratio, all other items and groups of items in the manufacturing, trading and profit and loss accounts can be shown similarly as a percentage of sales. These subsidiary ratios will enable clarification of

a The cost importance of each item or group of items in relation to total cost.

b The impact of changes in cost structure from one period to another, i.e. whether any single expense or group of expenses is getting out of line.

Sales mark-up is a measure of the cost efficiency of the firm throughout the whole process of manufacturing and distributing its products.

3 TURNOVER OF CAPITAL EMPLOYED The extent to which the firm's physical assets are used to earn profit is represented in this ratio. Clearly if full-time working is achieved, more goods will be produced than if short-time working is in force. Similarly a business which has an efficient production flow at the shop floor will produce more, in the same period, than a firm with disorganized workshops. Both of these instances (full time working, efficient production flow) lead to a greater out turn of goods from identical operating assets. This is what turnover of capital employed is, and it expresses the extent to which the company's physical assets are used to create new wealth; it is a measure of the efficiency of use of the available assets in producing output.

A relationship

The above three ratios are the 'front line' appraisals of a firm's activity: they evaluate the use of resources. They are not independent measures however. The reader should note carefully that, if the mark-up on sales is raised whilst the turnover of capital remains the same, the return on capital employed *must* increase. These interrelationships are displayed by the equation

$$\text{Return on capital employed} = \text{Mark-up on sales} \times \text{Turnover of capital employed}$$

which is the same as saying

$$\frac{\text{Profit}}{\text{Capital employed}} = \frac{\text{Profit}}{\text{Sales}} \times \frac{\text{Sales}}{\text{Capital employed}}$$

Whilst return on capital employed is used in comparisons of different firms and industries, the reader should remember that profit and capital employed can be seriously affected by different methods of valuing assets. The impact of the various ways of calculating depreciation provisions has already been shown.[1] Again profit has several connotations: it may refer to

Profit before tax.
Profit after tax.
Profit before tax and interest.
Profit before tax and depreciation.
Profit after tax and depreciation.

The list of alternatives is not complete: consistency of approach is the important criterion however, and it is suggested here that 'profit' should mean

Profit before tax and debenture interest but after depreciation[2].

Solvency

The writer has stated earlier in this book that profitability and efficiency are not the only considerations for ensuring successful business continuance. In a complete appraisal of company performance, the question of whether the firm can pay its way must be answered. Here the size of the net working capital is a vital factor in a satisfactory answer to the problem of liquidity. Now previous exhibits have demonstrated that

Working capital = Current assets − Current liabilities

At the end of the planning period envisaged in the case study (pages 67–69) working capital was expected to be £2,282 as shown in Exhibit 38. Therefore, if during the ensuing trading period current assets each realized the values attributed to them, then short term creditors would be able to be settled from current income. Where prompt settlement of creditors' accounts is not effected, due to lack of sufficient cash and income earning current assets, the firm will

[1] Different expressions of capital employed are used also. Such other computations will have regard to the objectives of the person making the analysis. For example a prospective investor in the company's shares will be concerned with the rate of return on the shareholder's interest. For a fuller treatment of capital employed concepts see *Practical Financial Statement Analysis* by R. A. Foulke, Chapter 2.

[2] Later on in this chapter when examining the concept of earnings per share, an after tax profit computation will be recommended.

lose its good name, its creditworthy status will diminish and petitioning creditors can force liquidation. A ready appraisal of working capital, so that comparisons can be made with other periods is essential therefore. The form of a working capital ratio is calculated, and expressed, in the equation below:

$$\frac{\text{Current assets}}{\text{Current liabilities}} = \frac{25{,}750}{23{,}468} = 1{\cdot}09 \text{ to } 1$$

The desired level of the working capital ratio will vary from industry to industry, and at different periods of the year. A company engaged in a seasonal trade will require a larger working capital in the close season period, because at this time it will be manufacturing largely for stock. However it is generally recognized that a ratio greater than unity, i.e. current assets money value being greater than the money value of current liabilities, is desirable. A relationship of 2 to 1 is advisable for a sound financial basis for current business operations.

Even so the net working capital sum, or the equivalent ratio, is not a *wholly* adequate indicator of a company's liquidity. Stocks of raw materials, work-in-progress and finished goods, which are included in current assets, are vital elements in the calculation of working capital. Such goods are valued in anticipation of their being converted into sales and thus into cash flowing to the firm's bank account. Should the change from stock to sales and cash be fairly speedily completed, any risk of loss through depreciation of stock values is thereby reduced. In order to emphasize the importance of truly liquid current assets, the *liquidity ratio* is used. It is considered to be a better indicator of a firm's ability to meet the demands of its creditors and is calculated by

$$\frac{\text{Current assets—stocks}}{\text{Current liabilities}} = \frac{15{,}000}{23{,}468} = 0{\cdot}64 \text{ to } 1$$

Again the desired level of the liquidity ratio should be at least unity. In the example above, the liquid ratio does show the potential dependence of R.E.A. Limited upon its stocks for its solvency status.

The importance of observing the impact of inventories upon a working capital assessment can be brought out by showing stocks as a percentage of working capital. R.E.A's total stocks in Exhibit 38 are valued at £10,750. Working capital is given as £2,282 and therefore if the value of the various stocks were to fall by only 20 per cent, current assets would be reduced to £23,600! In this event working capital would be cut to £132. A fall in the value of raw material stocks, of work in progress and of finished goods can arise relatively easily and with very little warning. Changes in consumer taste, the appearance of new products, currency valuation changes and loss of markets can each have their influence upon the worth of a firm's stocks on hand. The existence of a situation which could lead to an 'overnight' loss of working capital, in the way suggested above, can be revealed by expressing the total stocks' value as a percentage of working capital. Here stocks of £10,750 are 471 per cent of the working capital of £2,282![1] Though this ratio should give a warning of the true liquidity of our company, there is yet one more consideration to examine.

Stock turnover ratios

The continuing analysis of company liquidity[2] demands a study of inventory movement, and this means finding out how long the average item of stock remains on the company's books. The speed of transference of stock into sales is referred to as the *turnover of stock*. The greater the rate of turnover, the smaller the risk of loss of value whilst the goods are in the charge of the manufacturer. Now the turnover rate of raw material stocks is demonstrated by

$$\frac{\text{Cost of materials used}}{\text{Average stock of raw materials}}$$

$$= \frac{15{,}750^{3}}{4{,}000}$$

$$= 3{\cdot}9 \text{ times in the period of account}$$

One must not be too rigid in the approach to this problem. It may well be advisable for stocks to be bought in a certain time in the year, because that is the best (or only) time of the year to buy them. This can apply to the supply of natural resources such as animal hides, sheep's wools etc. Again a seasonal trade may justifiably carry heavy stocks in readiness for the normal surges of trade at some other time in the year.

[2] The figures used in the next series of ratios are taken from Exhibits 36 and 38, respectively.

[3] Where published accounts are used to find out the stock turnover rate, only two inventory valuations are normally available. These are the valuations at the beginning and at the end of the year and it is from these two totals that an *average* stock would be calculated. This is what has been done in the determination of materials turnover rate in this example. A more accurate turnover rate will result from calculating an average stock by using the *monthly* valuations in, say, a twelve-month period.

As the period of account is three months, the actual time during which the material would be in stock is shown by

$$\frac{3}{3{\cdot}9} = 0{\cdot}77 \text{ months} = 23 \text{ days approximately}$$

Whether this period is a reasonable one is a matter of fact and can be determined by such criteria as

1 The time taken to obtain new supplies.
2 The optimum order size to apply when obtaining new stocks.
3 The level of activity of the works.

Work in progress and finished goods

The rate of turnover for these sections of the total inventory should be calculated also. The rate for work in progress will be arrived at by

$$\frac{\text{Cost of goods manufactured}}{\text{Average stock of work in progress}}$$

$$= \frac{18{,}030}{2{,}000}$$

$$= 9{\cdot}01 \text{ times in the period of account}$$

Again, as the period of account is three months, the actual time during which work in progress would be passing through the works is shown by

$$\frac{3}{9{\cdot}01} = 0{\cdot}33 \text{ months} = 9{\cdot}9 \text{ days approximately}$$

An efficient production control system, aided by a good shop floor layout, will operate to keep this ratio down to acceptable levels. Furthermore the quantity of work in progress must also be influenced by the sales programme and the need for finished goods. Thus the turnover rate for finished goods, the next ratio to be studied, will give an indication of

1 The pressure of demand for the company's goods.
2 The efficiency with which they are inspected, packaged and despatched to customers.

The speed of transfer of finished goods to satisfy orders, the finished goods turnover rate, is expressed as

$$\frac{\text{Cost of sales}}{\text{Average cost of finished goods}}$$

$$= \frac{16{,}530}{1{,}750}$$

$$= 9{\cdot}44 \text{ times in the period of account}$$

Once again the reader will appreciate that a more meaningful index is created if this ratio is converted into months or days. As the plan in the case study covered a period of three months, then the time during which the average stock of finished goods would be in the company warehouse is calculated as

$$\frac{3}{9{\cdot}44} = 0{\cdot}32 \text{ months} = 9{\cdot}6 \text{ days approximately.}$$

Credit manipulation

From a study of the management teams of different organizations, one can see that some companies are marketing oriented whilst others place great stress upon the financial or production aspects of the firms' activities. On the other hand it appears that the really successful businesses base their operations upon an appreciation of the need for a complete integration of the planning and functioning of all departments. Only in this way can the progress and expansion of the business be controlled and carried out profitably and safely. In other words, it is of little use to aim for ambitious targets in one section of the firm whilst leaving the other departments to adapt themselves to the requirements of targets which have been fixed without *full interdepartmental* discussion. A rapidly expanding sales programme calls for more and more production and/or supplies of materials and finished goods. These requirements cannot be met without additional finance to

1 Pay for the increased production and additional supplies of materials which must be held in stock.
2 Furnish the greater absolute quantity of credit which follows upon an increasing number of customers at the higher level of sales.

It should be emphasized that it is the *continuous rapid* expansion of sales which gives rise to these problems of lack of adequate company finance. The first indications of corporate overtrading are revealed in the debtor–creditor relationships shown in the balance sheet. When the firm's bank balance is under pressure, the first reaction of the management may well be to seek earlier settlements of debtors' bills. At the same time creditors of the firm could find themselves waiting longer and longer for payment of sums due to them, from the company. Such a situation has the tendency to grow worse and worse until certain creditors will wait no longer.[1] If this crisis arises, and the company cannot obtain sufficient extra funds, then the impatient creditors might commence legal proceedings to recover their money. Liquidation may not be far away.

Now in all businesses there are some standard relationships which have emerged during the normal trading operations. One of these is the *average collection period* for debts. The ratio is calculated from

$$\frac{\text{Debtors}}{\text{Average daily sales}} = \text{Number of days which accounts remain unpaid}$$

and a study of the trend in this ratio is very material to the analysis of corporate liquidity. Conclusions drawn from this study must have regard to the terms of sale in force, because a firm operating net settlement conditions of 30 days will have a different ratio from one where a 60-day credit period is in operation. However, after allowing for particular specialities, the accounts analyst can see whether the average collection period is lengthening or shortening. To consider this concept in relation to the volume of creditors, it is necessary to compare the cash sum of outstanding creditors with the current level of material purchases.

$$\frac{\text{Current level of material purchases per annum}}{\text{Creditors}}$$

$$= \text{Average number of months which creditor accounts remain unpaid}$$

[1] Variations in the relationships between outstanding debtors and creditors may well arise from other causes. The income section could be operating more efficiently, thus bringing money in more quickly and reducing balances unpaid. If at the same time a corresponding efficiency in the payments section does not materialize, then debtor balances will fall in relation to creditor balances. The point is that the reason for a change in a ratio must be sought: the ratio itself is but an indication of a need for investigation.

A comparison of the two ratios above will indicate how the firm is managing its short term financing; it may be revealed that the creditors listed amongst current liabilities are forming a larger and larger proportion of the total funding of the company's operations. (A word of warning must be repeated here. Ratios are but demonstrations of matters needing further scrutiny. They rarely give final answers to any problem by themselves alone; it is the ensuing scrutiny of underlying reasons for change which should present management with a plan of action to correct any undesirable developments.)

By using the figures in Exhibits 36 and 38, the two ratios can now be calculated as shown below:

$$\frac{\text{Debtors}}{\text{Average daily sales}}$$

$$= \frac{15{,}000}{21{,}000 \div 91} \quad [1]$$

$$= 65 \text{ days}$$

= The average number of days which debtor accounts remain unpaid.

$$\frac{\text{Current level of material purchases per annum}}{\text{Creditors}}$$

$$= \frac{75{,}000}{13{,}250}$$

$$= 5{\cdot}66$$

This figure represents the 'turnover' of creditors in relation to an estimated twelve-month figure of purchases.[2] To convert this to a statement of the average period, in days, which creditor accounts remain unpaid, we have

$$\frac{365}{5{\cdot}66} = 65 \text{ days}$$

[1] The accounts in Exhibits 36 and 38 cover a period of three months. To ascertain the average daily sales, therefore, the actual sales in this period are divided by 91—the number of days in three months.

[2] Exhibit 36 shows purchases for the three months planning period as being £18,750. Assuming that this rate of material purchase continues throughout the year, then the annual level of material purchases = £18,750 × 4 = £75,000.

Review of ratio analysis

The story of ratio analysis of business accounts could continue with other very appropriate comparisons of financial data. However it was not intended to make this chapter into an extensive study of accounts interpretation. Its object is but an introduction to the ease with which a considerable amount of information can be gained from final accounts. The use to which this information is put, is far more important than the data itself. The suggested further reading list at the end of this chapter should enable a wider knowledge of the calculation and use of ratios to be obtained together with an appreciation of the ways in which the information should be used. The student is strongly advised to pursue the study of this subject, for the gains available in terms of an ever-growing understanding of financial reports, is considerable.

Evaluation of business worth

The main object in the analysis of business accounts is to be able to reach some assessment of the worth of the firm and the efficiency with which its management uses the corporate assets. Return on capital employed, turnover of stocks and the measurement of costs implicit in the sales mark up, etc., all have their uses in coming to a decision about the satisfactory conduct of a business. It is pointed out however that the accounts analyst will not always have the same viewpoint towards his analysis: the emphases which he portrays will depend upon the reasons for the investigation. If a company is being scrutinized on behalf of a bank or major financing organization in response to the firm's request for overdraft or loan, then the sort of information about the firm which would influence the potential lender will be

1 Security in the form of permanent assets, for the loan's liquidation.
2 Security in the form of income to meet loan charges.
3 Security in the form of a guaranteed management succession to ensure that the conditions under (1) and (2) continue to be safeguarded.

There are many other matters to consider beyond these but (1) to (3) above reflect an objective approach to a valuation of the firm's worth and viability, in the circumstances postulated.

An examination of the firm, on behalf of a potential creditor for supply of goods, would be greatly concerned with the liquidity state of the company. The trade creditor is worried not so much about the growth, development and continuance of the company over the next ten years as in the company's ability to pay its short-term debts in the next six to twelve months. Therefore whilst return on capital is of minor importance here, the adequacy and soundness of the firm's working capital is a prime factor in deciding whether to do business with the company.[1]

Another group of people who may be interested in the status of our company are potential shareholders. Now, in general, shareholders are hopeful of receiving continuing dividends, together with some increase in the rate paid plus a capital growth as shown in the share price quoted on the Stock Exchange. Many investors have little knowledge of company finance or management; the importance of working capital, the influence of depreciation charges upon return on capital employed do not create a financially meaningful impression upon the general body of shareholders. Their main interest is in income received. Therefore an investigation of company accounts which is executed on behalf of a potential investor will be directed to the net *earning* power of the company. An investor's concern with corporate net earning power is really a concern with the value of that earning power to *himself*. Before earnings can be translated into dividends or capital growth for the investor, however, such earnings (profit) must be affected by taxation—corporation tax. It is only after this levy that the residual net profit is available for shareholders' dividends and company growth. Whether retention of profits does in fact contribute to an increase in the value of a company depends on how the retentions are used. It is here that the importance of managerial skill and efficiency comes into the picture. Even so the student of business performance should not forget the influences of the firm's market, its buoyancy and economic development, upon the power of the company to prosper and grow in wealth. To continue the definition of an investor's share of corporate earning power, one

[1] The business man will always hope for the development and continuance of his customers' business, because such profitability portends further trade for himself in the future. Nevertheless he must look for the security of his own short-term debts.

does not stop at a consideration of the limiting power of corporation tax. Whilst the company suffers a charge called corporation tax, the individual similarly bears a levy upon his income. Thus when a dividend is declared, this total sum is reduced by income tax at the standard rate[1] before the investor can regard the payment as his own disposable income.

Moreover where retentions are used successfully by the company to promote profitable growth, such growth will result ultimately in an increase in the market value of its shares. Where this new market price rises above that paid by the investor when obtaining his shares, a capital gain is achieved.[2] Such a gain can be realized only when disposing of the shares—and that realized gain, determined in accordance with tax law and regulations, is taxable in the hands of the recipient, the shareholder. Now the point of this short discourse upon the taxation of investment income is that we all have different amounts and kinds of allowances to set against the final income upon which we pay tax. Many of us pay tax at different rates. For these reasons it is impossible to present a rate of return on income from shares which, net of all income and capital gains taxes, will apply to everyone. Therefore, in assessing the worth of a business, from the standpoint of a potential shareholder, it is necessary to consider the return on investment:

1 After corporation tax.
2 Before income and capital gains taxes.

Each individual can then apply his own personal taxation conditions to the income thus expressed. This is the approach which is used, by financial analysts and by the financial press, when expressing the dividends and earnings of public companies as a percentage return of the cost of investing in a share of those dividends and earnings.

The value of dividends

It was stated above that '. . . in general shareholders are hopeful of receiving continuing dividends, together with some increase in the

[1] This statement must be modified where the investor's own taxation circumstances result in his paying *less than* the standard rate of tax. On the other hand the surtax payer may be even further penalized up to his own higher personal taxation rate.

[2] In such a limited reference to taxation, particularly of capital gains, the writer does not pretend to offer a complete statement of the taxation problem. The object in tax examples is to show the impact of *taxes generally* upon an investor's returns and to give some indication of the power of taxation to reduce the monetary value of those returns, before they are received by a shareholder.

rate paid . . .'. The reader will remember that dividends are quoted at a percentage rate relating to the paid-up value of the shares, as the following example will show:

> One hundred Ordinary shares with a face value of £1 each have a total par, i.e. face, value of £100, provided that all of this sum has been demanded by the company, and paid to the firm by the shareholder. If a dividend of 10 per cent is declared, then the shareholder will receive £10—before deduction of income tax.

In view of the fact that the market price of a share is most often different from its face value, any dividend paid on a share needs to be related to its purchase price. In other words the dividend is compared with the current cost of getting that dividend—the price of a share on the Stock Exchange. By this calculation one can show the actual gross (pre income tax) return on the share's purchase price: this resultant percentage figure is termed the 'Gross Yield Per Cent'. The formula for the calculation is

$$\frac{\text{Dividend per share} \times 100}{\text{Market price per share}}$$

For the 100 shares given in the example above, assuming the share's price to be £2·50 each on the Stock Exchange, the gross yield will be (in decimal currency)

$$\frac{0{\cdot}10 \times 100^{1}}{2{\cdot}50} = 4 \text{ per cent}$$

It should be remembered that we are, in effect, valuing the company by looking at one aspect of its earning power and seeing how that compares with the market's appraisal of the firm's worth. Now there are many factors which will affect the share's market price. Basically these factors, which will always influence the demand for, and supply of, the shares, include

1 The general political and economic climate both for the firm's industry and for the economy as a whole.

[1] Care is needed here to ensure that numerator and denominator are both expressed in the same units—in this instance, in decimal currency. The dividend per share is obtained from 10 per cent of £1, the par value of the share. If the equation had been written in shillings, it would have been $\frac{2 \times 100}{50} = 4$ per cent.

2 The firm's prospects as expressed by the size of its order book.
3 The ability of its management to use the corporate assets efficiently.

The importance of earnings

However, dividends are not the sole return to the successful investor. The amount of total profits after tax is a much more valuable indicator of worth for it will reveal the *sum* of profits *available* to the company for expansion and development. To the extent that dividends are paid from this profit, expansion is restricted *but* from the standpoint of total power to produce a return on investment, the investor must look at the whole corporate post-corporation tax earnings. This is the value he buys when purchasing a share and the index of comparability which expresses the worth of a company's total earnings is called 'Gross Earnings Yield Per Cent'. The formula is

$$\frac{\text{Earnings per share} \times 100}{\text{Market price per share}}$$

These indices of investment worth refer predominantly to ordinary shares—the major risk-bearing section of a company's capital. Consequently when earnings after corporation tax have been determined, any sums due for dividends of the preference shareholders must be deducted. The remaining earnings are then divided by the *number* of ordinary shares *in issue*, to arrive at the available earnings per ordinary share.

If we now assume that the hypothetical company, whose £1 shares have been discussed, followed a dividend policy of paying out one half of its earnings to its shareholders, then the total post-tax earnings per share would have been 4s or 20 new pence. The gross earnings yield per cent, in these circumstances would be

$$\frac{0{\cdot}20 \times 100}{2{\cdot}50} = 8 \text{ per cent}$$

Here we have a means of comparison between different companies. It is a comparison based upon their individual post-tax earnings which is expressed as a percentage of the cost of buying a share of those earnings—the Stock Exchange share price. There is however a further point for the student of corporate worth to consider, and this refers to the definition of 'earnings'. In calculating the gross earnings yield per cent, financial analysts refer to '*maintainable* earnings'. In this context they mean the power of the company to continue generating the kind of earnings which are used in the ratio. Thus the earnings yield ratio should not be assessed on an historical basis only: attention should be paid to the firm's order book, its future cost structure and generally its ability to continue achieving its present earnings (at least) in the foreseeable future. Furthermore strict interpretation of maintainability of earnings always refers, as has been noted, to post-corporation tax earnings. It is therefore necessary to appreciate the potential variability of the taxation charge, and the sundry allowances which can operate to reduce that charge. Prominent amongst such tax reductions are capital allowances (and grants) which are given to a company on the purchase of certain fixed assets. These allowances and grants will vary from year to year according to the size of its expenditure on certain long-term fixed assets; they will also vary as the whims of successive Chancellors of the Exchequer cause changes in the taxation laws of the country. So, to arrive at the true maintainable corporate earnings, (the income earned by the company from its own *trading* activities) it is necessary to eliminate such non-trading increments from the taxation charge in order to leave an ultimate levy based solely upon the trading results. In this way those factors which tend to distort the year by year, and firm by firm, comparability of profits, are removed to give a more reliable appraisal of company worth.

Price/earnings ratio

For many years property valuers have used a method of property valuation which depends upon the earnings which the property can obtain. This method is of importance where the freehold land value portion of a leasehold property is sold. The sale price of the freehold, in these circumstances, is normally based upon an annual ground rent which is payable to the owner of the freehold. To calculate the price at which the freehold may change hands, such ground rent is then multiplied so many times—this multiplier being a specific number of years' expectation of continuance of the ground rent income. Thus, if a ground rent was £20, then a ten years' purchase would amount to a purchase price of £200 and the freehold could be sold, in those circumstances, at that figure. One would not expect that prices would be settled quite as easily as the example shows, for the time pattern for receipt of rent, the level of current and expected interest rates, would have to be taken into account. The reader will encounter the use of interest rates, when evaluating investment spendings, in the subsequent chapters on capital budgeting.

As regards the evaluation of company worth, the price earnings ratio is closely linked with the gross earnings yield. The P/E ratio (as it is termed) is found when the share price quoted on the Stock Exchange is divided by the earnings per share. Therefore, using the figures given in the gross earnings yield and applying the formula

$$\frac{\text{Market price per share}}{\text{Earnings per share}}$$

then the P/E ratio of our hypothetical company's shares will be

$$\frac{2{\cdot}50}{0{\cdot}20} = 12{\cdot}5$$

For the mathematically minded, the P/E ratio is but the reciprocal of the gross earnings yield, i.e.

$$\frac{1}{8 \text{ per cent}} = \frac{100}{8} = 12{\cdot}5$$

The value of the P/E ratio rests on the fact that it specifies the number of years within which a company's earnings per share will repay the present market price of buying that share. It is the time capitalization of a share's worth. Though it is a close relation of the gross earnings yield, the P/E ratio has an advantage over the yield index. 'Yield' connotes a value being received by the shareholder: but a shareholder does not *receive* the earnings of a company, he receives the dividend only and hopes that the retained earnings will produce eventually some other capital gain for him. Now the P/E ratio indicates the number of years which the shareholder must wait for dividends and growth to repay his capital outlay. It thus gives a value and a time scale to the relationship between earnings and shareprice.

R.E.A. Limited

The reader is now invited to refer to Exhibit 29 which shows a narrative profit and loss account as it would be affected by various rates of depreciation. Using the figures in the first column of that exhibit, and specifying certain other variable factors, it is now intended to show the relationship of dividend, dividend yield, earnings yield and price earnings ratio for R.E.A. Limited. The variable items are postulated below:

1 Share price	£3·00
2 Dividend declared	10 per cent
3 Previous highest share price in the current year	£3·75
4 Previous lowest share price in the current year	£2·00

DIVIDEND YIELD

This has been shown to be derived from the formula

$$\frac{\text{Dividend per share} \times 100}{\text{Market price per share}}$$

In the circumstances proposed in the previous paragraph, the dividend yield in respect of R.E.A. Limited's shares would be

$$\frac{0{\cdot}10 \times 100}{3{\cdot}00} = 3{\cdot}3 \text{ per cent}$$

Here we have the actual percentage revenue return an investor would secure if he bought the company's shares for £3 each, when a dividend of 10 per cent had been declared on the face value of those shares. Again, the gross earnings yield, using the formula on page 95, would be

$$\frac{0{\cdot}1375 \times 100^{1}}{3} = 4{\cdot}58 \text{ per cent}$$

The all important P/E ratio can also be calculated by the method already explained: it shows the number of years necessary for earnings, such as those given in Exhibit 29, to result in each shareholder recovering a capital cost of £3 per share.

$$\text{P/E ratio} = \frac{3}{0{\cdot}1375} = 21{\cdot}8$$

[1] Exhibit 29 shows the post tax earnings to be £1,375. As there are 10,000 ordinary shares of £1 each in issue, the earnings per share are therefore £0·1375. Note carefully that numerator *and* denominator are shown here in decimal units of £.

Information such as that produced above is given each day on the last two pages of the *Financial Times*. With one final item of dividend appraisal, the student will be able to construct his own *Financial Times* entry for R.E.A. Limited. The additional item of information refers to dividend cover, which gives an indication of the company's *present* power to repeat the dividends most recently declared. Dividend cover is quite a valuable index for it tells the investor of the extent to which retained earnings have exceeded the dividend allocation. It can also demonstrate whether the board of direct tors have had difficulty in declaring a dividend out of (meagre) earnings!

With reference to Exhibit 29, the profit and loss account shows post tax earnings of £1,375. A 10 per cent dividend would have cost £1,000 and could have been paid 1·37 times: the dividend cover would then be expressed as 1·4 which incidentally is a below average cover when compared with industrial and commercial norms around 1·5 to 2 times. Finally a specimen entry, relating to R.E.A. Limited, such as might appear in the *Financial Times* is given below.

High £	Low £	Stock	Closing Price £	+ or —	Div. % or amount	Times covered	Gross yield per cent	P/E ratio
3·75	2·00	R.E.A. Ltd.	3·00		10	1·4	3·3	21·8

The column '+ or —' gives the variation in market price of a share during that day's dealings on the Stock Exchange.

Chart of profitability

Exhibit 39 displays the various impacts upon the corporate return on capital employed. The chart sets out a few of the operating ratios and capital asset ratios which can be used to identify areas of investigation. By these means greater efficiencies and economies can be discovered.

EXHIBIT 39

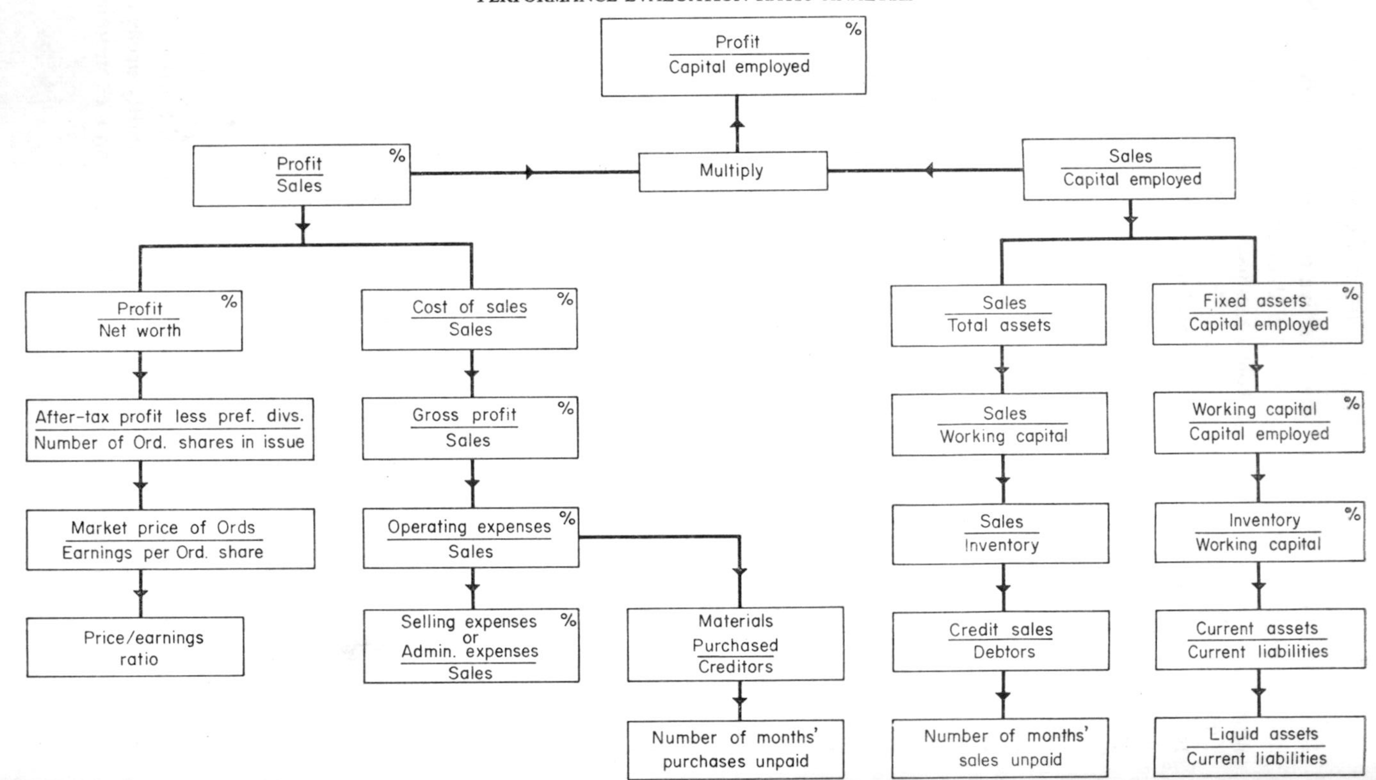

PERFORMANCE EVALUATION RATIO ANALYSIS
Profit / Capital employed %
Multiply
Profit / Sales %
Sales / Capital employed
Profit / Net worth %
After-tax profit less pref. divs. / Number of Ord. shares in issue
Market price of Ords / Earnings per Ord. share
Price/earnings ratio
Cost of sales / Sales %
Gross profit / Sales %
Operating expenses / Sales %
Selling expenses or Admin. expenses / Sales %
Materials Purchased / Creditors
Number of months' purchases unpaid
Sales / Total assets
Sales / Working capital
Sales / Inventory
Credit sales / Debtors
Number of months' sales unpaid
Fixed assets / Capital employed %
Working capital / Capital employed %
Inventory / Working capital %
Current assets / Current liabilities
Liquid assets / Current liabilities

Questions for discussion

1. What factors are likely to influence different classes of investors and creditors in their appraisals of company worth?
2. A weakness in ratio analysis of company performance is that it is a study of historical performance. How can this weakness be overcome?
3. How does the value of stock in trade affect the appraisal of liquidity when examining the size of working capital? Is this an important concept for all types of business?
4. What part does the management team's efficiency play in evaluation of company worth?
5. What do you understand by overtrading?
6. How would you appraise a company's dividend record? Do subjective influences enter into your assessments here?
7. What is the value of the P/E ratio when compared with the gross dividend yield?

Recommended reading

ROWLATT, J. and DAVENPORT, D., *The Pan Guide to Savings and Investment*, Pan Books, 1965.

JONES, F., *Guide to Company Balance Sheets and Profit and Loss Accounts*, Chapter 18, Heffer, Sixth edition 1964.

DAUTEN, C. A., *Business Finance: The Fundamentals of Financial Management*, Chapter 11, Prentice Hall, Second edition 1956.

FOULKE, R. A., *Practical Financial Statement Analysis*, McGraw-Hill, Fifth edition 1961.

CHAPTER 7 Break-even Analysis

Introduction

An analysis of the composition of product cost is a study of prime importance. Its conclusions can affect pricing policies, production and production mix policies and all decisions concerning capacity planning. Even before determining the cost of a product or service, the term 'cost' must itself be defined. To the accountant, cost represents the expenditure incurred on the goods and services which are consumed in producing an output of other goods or services. This output aims to meet the needs of the firm's forecast sales demand. Now the accountant's figures of expenditure (cost) will be found in the ledgers and other books of account which record the business' dealings: details of the sales will also be found there. Each of these recorded expenditures and incomes can be traced to a commercial transaction, which was completed at some point in the firm's history, and inevitably resulted in a transfer of cash, to or from the firm.[1]

The economist, on the other hand, regards cost as meaning *opportunity* cost. Opportunity cost refers to the gain, benefit or return which is given up when the decision-maker elects to make product A rather than product B. In this context the opportunity cost of product A would be the gains which could have been obtained by making product B. This is not to imply that product B's rejected gains are the only costs in the economist's eyes: it is the fundamental addition to all the other input costs of goods and services which are used to achieve an output—the turnover. The whole idea therefore adds to what may be termed the market cost of inputs, the net incomes which are surrendered when deciding to manufacture

[1] Notional charges, such as interest, made for the purposes of a theoretical total cost comparison have been ignored here.

product A instead of B.[1] The concept of opportunity cost can be applied to doing certain things at different times, e.g. the opportunity cost of postponing a venture to next year will be those gains which could have been achieved by doing that particular thing today.

Cost groups

It is intended that we should concern ourselves with accounting cost, at this stage. Now the total accounting costs of an operation or business can be divided into as many different groupings as the managers wish to have. By these means it is expected that an exact cost of some process or component can be found. Whatever the variety of cost groups which may be used, they each fall within three main categories. The common terminology for the main divisions of accounting cost comprises:

Variable cost.
Semi-variable cost.
Fixed cost.

Not all of these descriptive titles are going to be accepted here. Before criticizing the rigid group definitions, let the reader consider the cost sequence of engaging in manufacture, for example. As soon as production commences, some goods and services must be employed. A man working upon raw materials or components, and the material itself, are examples of input costs which must be incurred as soon as production is engaged. To this type of expense is given the name 'variable cost'; it describes those expenditures which must change in monetary size, whenever the level of production changes. Frequently called direct, or marginal costs, they are those costs of operation which cannot be avoided once production is engaged.

The 'fixed' group of costs concerns the environment within which production is undertaken. The machine operator is located within a factory building: his machine is ready and available for use: the business also provides services of administration and transport, etc. Now within the limits of a certain level of capacity, these buildings,

[1] The economists costs therefore are not all traceable to ultimate cash transactions in the books of the firm under examination. The services of an 'unpaid' manager or proprietor would not necessarily appear in the accountant's assessment of cost. However the economist *would* include, at an appropriate market price, the value of such a proprietor's services in the total input cost of obtaining the corresponding output.

machines and administrative services are needed to enable the firm to carry on its business. The expenditures which were incurred on setting up the firm's factory and administration, were incurred in consequence of a management decision which was taken sometime in the past. The *cash* was spent some time ago to provide a capacity structure. Most of capacity structure costs such as:

Administrative salaries.
Buildings, plant and machinery depreciation.
Works salaries.
Rent, rates and insurance.

are accumulated as time passes, *not* because production is engaged. For this reason therefore, the term fixed cost is inappropriate. Other more meaningful descriptions would be

1 CAPACITY COSTS—they are the costs of establishing the particular capacity for the firm.
2 PERIOD COSTS—they relate to a specific period, and it is the passage of time which largely determines their monetary cost.
3 DECISION COSTS—they are incurred because of some past management decision to enter into a business at a certain level of output.

One can of course insist that, however we may describe the above costs, they *are* fixed in fact. They are fixed in relation to a particular size of firm. Nevertheless, and this is vital, as soon as the firm changes its capacity size, then the so-called fixed costs must change to reflect the level of decisional costs implicit in the new physical capacity of the company. The so-called fixed costs will change, *not* in consequence of a change in the quantity of goods being produced, but because of a change in the power or capacity to produce.

The final category of costs, the semi-variable cost, relates to those goods and services whose market price is not linked solely to the consumption of individual items. The telephone bill consists of a standard quarterly expense plus a charge for each call that is made: power supplies may well consist of a standing charge relating to the potential demand of the firm's power load plus a sliding scale of charges for units of power consumed. Thus it can be said that such a kind of cost is not wholly fixed, nor is it wholly variable. It is therefore regarded as a semi-variable expense. One of the most difficult and time consuming tasks in the sphere of management accounting is the location of any item of cost into one of the three main divisions of cost. A careful precise analysis must be carried out in practical circumstances, of the effect upon individual expenditures, of changes in the level of production before cost data can be used in intelligent planning.

Break-even point

A most useful managerial planning tool which stems from an appreciation of the nature of variable and capacity costs, is the

EXHIBIT 40

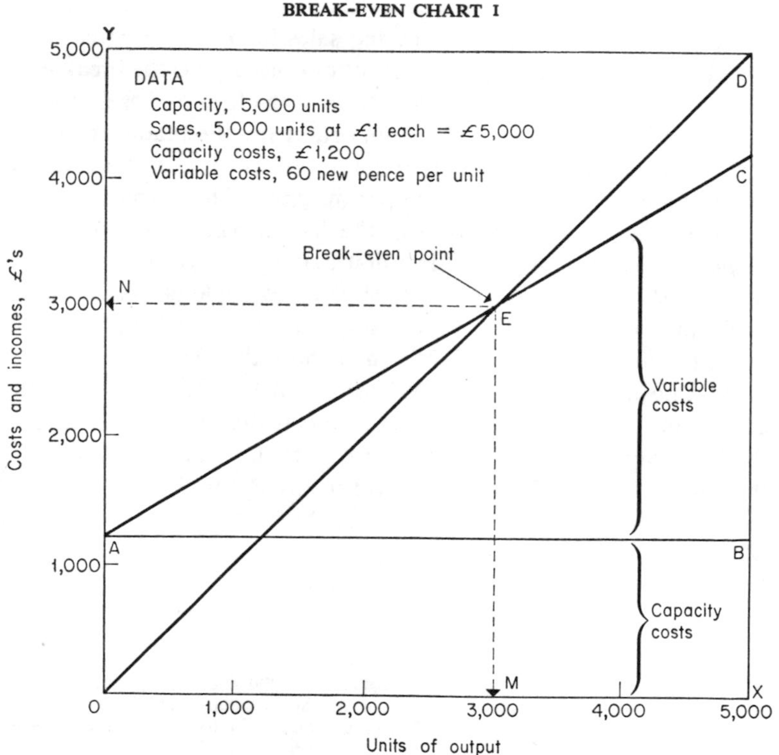

break-even chart (see Exhibit 40). The chart displays on its horizontal axis various levels of output up to the total capacity, whilst the vertical axis shows sizes of costs and incomes in units of £1. Capacity or decision costs for the firm are represented by the straight line AB: these costs apply to the maximum capacity of 5,000 units of output and are constant up to that level of production.[1] Those additions (to capacity costs) which we have called variable costs are shown by the area CAB. The reader will notice that these expenditures increase as the level of output in units increases. Therefore the *total* costs of producing the firm's output is represented by the line AC. Now any level of output on the horizontal axis can be related to a point on the total cost line AC: then this point on AC can be compared with the relevant level of cost as shown on the axis OY. Thus we can ascertain the costs of specific levels of output, up to 5,000 units.

If the line of expected sales income, OD, is then superimposed upon the graph, the reader will see that the point E gives the level of output/cost at which the expected sales income first equals, and then begins to exceed, the total cost of output. This is the break-even (B/E) point: it is the output level at which the firm makes no loss or profit but just *breaks even.* It is important for the reader to realize that the B/E graph is a series of static points—it is *not* a progress chart of a company's developing performance. The graph shows the expected cost/income situation of the firm *at each possible level of output:* it does *not* show the firm first making a loss, then making a profit *as it proceeds through the year.* Each example of output on the horizontal axis is a single static exposition of a possible production level: the lines on the graph can then show the firm's expected net income position should that level of output be achieved during the accounting period of the company.[2] When this precise function of the B/E graph is accepted, it can be seen that the area AEO enables the determination of operating loss for any output level up to OM. Similarly DEC indicates the area of profit for any output level from M up to maximum capacity.

[1] Here the analysis excludes rises in prices of capacity costs which may result from inflation or revaluation of capacity assets. In such circumstances the break-even graph would be redrawn to portray the new cost levels for the whole output potential.
[2] The level of capacity costs have been quoted at £1,200 and this figure relates to a specified period, i.e. the accounting period of the company. Therefore the cost/income relationships revealed by the B/E graph must refer to the firm's accounting period.

Contribution

Previously the nature of variable and capacity costs have been shown to be closely connected with their response to variations in output. For profitable business operations, sale price must be in excess of variable costs at least. Therefore the extent to which sales price exceeds variable cost will measure the amount earned, by each unit produced and sold, towards meeting the capacity costs of the firm. This amount earned in excess of variable cost is termed the product's 'Contribution' to the total capacity costs. Exhibit 41 which is based upon the same data as that used in Exhibit 40, is redrawn in order to emphasize the concept of 'Contribution'.

EXHIBIT 41

BREAK-EVEN CHART 2

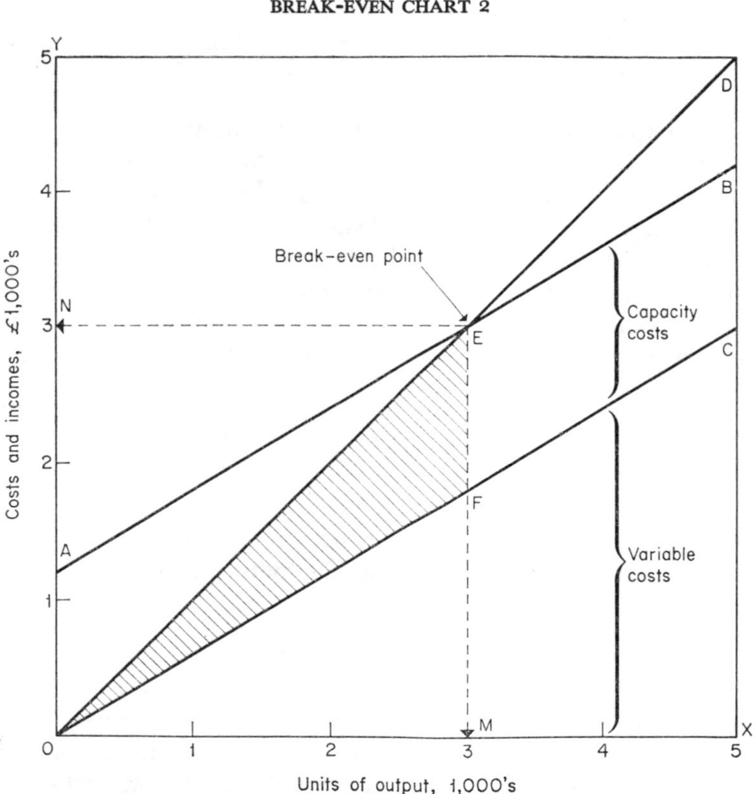

In this instance the total variable cost line OC compares with line AC in the previous chart, and the area COX represents the area of variable expenditures up to the total capacity of 5,000 units. Capacity costs are again portrayed by the line AB, so that the area of total capacity cost BAOC is equivalent to BAOX in Exhibit 40. The total cost, in Exhibit 41, is represented by the line AB. Now is must be observed that the total sales indicator OD again cuts the total cost line *at the same B/E point*, E. The important feature in presenting B/E analysis in this way concerns the line OE, and the shaded area EOF. This section shows the amount earned towards the total capacity costs, by each unit produced and sold at the various levels of output up to OM. At the output level OM, enough has been produced and sold so that the total earnings of the output will meet the expenses of:

1 The variable cost of each item.
2 The total capacity costs of the firm which is geared to a maximum output of 5,000 units.

For output performances above OM, therefore, the firm is in the profit making area. Now the situation of M in the axis OX is of material importance to the company's power to withstand a falling off in business. MX is termed the 'Margin of Safety'. In the instance shown in Exhibits 40 and 41, the saleable output of the company can fall from a maximum of 5,000 units to 3,000 units before the business begins to make a loss. The margin of safety is 40 per cent of total capacity.

Multiple break-even points

So far the graph has shown one simple break-even situation—a factor which can be calculated from the following formula:

$$\text{B/E} = \frac{C}{S - V} = \text{units of output at B/E point}$$

where C is the total capacity costs, S the sale price per unit and V the variable cost per unit. Using the data given in Exhibit 40, the formula confirms the B/E point as shown in Exhibits 40 and 41.

$$B/E = \frac{1{,}200}{1 - 0{\cdot}6}$$

$$= \frac{1{,}200}{0{\cdot}4}$$

$$= 3{,}000 \text{ units}$$

Thus an output of 3,000 units is the company's break-even production level: at a sales price of £1 per unit the sales value at B/E is £3,000.[1] The concept of a single break-even point represented in precise, linear graphical form must now be contested. Firstly the reader must consider the effect of a decision to double the capacity of the firm, and the impact of this decision upon the firm's capacity costs. This is shown in Exhibit 42; in drawing this chart it is assumed that doubling the capacity of the company will double the capacity costs. In practice this ratio may not apply since costs of administration, for example, have a considerable elasticity in meeting changes in output. However for purposes of emphasis, the variation in capacity costs from £1,200 to £2,400 is depicted in sharp outline. The additional of variable costs at a constant 60 new pence per unit portrays in a similar outline the consequent changes in total costs.[2]

Now if the line of total income is once more superimposed upon the graph, *two* B/E points emerge. The essential feature which is brought out in Exhibit 42 is that a business is not a rigid association: changes in the conditions of demand, or in the nature of costs,

[1] The formula given here will show the number of *units of output* which need to be produced and sold to achieve the B/E point. The sales total monetary volume can also be obtained by the formula

$$\frac{C}{1-(V/S)}$$

where V now equals *total* variable cost and S equals *total* sales income at the maximum output level. Again utilizing the data in Exhibit 40 we have

$$£\frac{1{,}200}{1-(3{,}000/5{,}000)}$$

$$= £\frac{1{,}200}{0{\cdot}4}$$

$$= £3{,}000$$

[2] It will be said that if the company doubles its capacity from 5,000 to 10,000 units, then the capacity costs will be £2,400 for *all* levels of output up to 10,000 units. The reason here for showing a level of capacity costs of £1,200 up to 5,000 units and *then* another level of £2,400 for output levels from 5,000 to 10,000 units, is to bring out clearly the effect on B/E of decisional costs. The firm does not have, in perpetuity, *one* break-even point.

EXHIBIT 42

BREAK-EVEN CHART 3

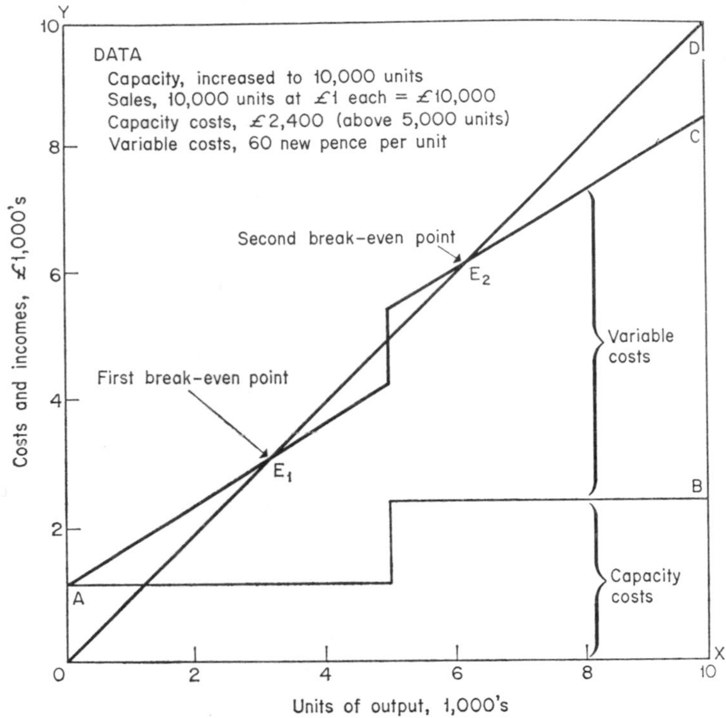

will produce new cost/profit situations for management to consider. In this instance the question to be asked is whether doubling the capacity of the firm will increase its net returns. Problems such as these are of frequent occurrence in a dynamic business and the effects of the expansion upon earnings per ordinary share and upon the ordinary share's P/E ratio (see pages 95–97) are examples of modern managements' approach to the impact of profit/capacity relationships.

Returning to a study of Exhibits 40 and 41, the reader can see that the net profit at the maximum output of 5,000 units is £800. If capacity is doubled, the company's sales must reach 8,000 units before any extra gain from the expansion can be expected. Above 8,000 units, provided that no additional ordinary share capital has to be issued to finance the expansion, earnings per ordinary share should increase. Consequently either the P/E ratio will be reduced or the market price of the company's shares will rise—both features being very acceptable to the company's top management. *All* of the above factors must be considered by the Board before it authorizes any expenditure on capacity increases. Thus can capacity costs be truly called 'decision' costs.

Criticisms of the orthodox break-even chart

A vital deficiency in the normal method of B/E presentation must now be discussed. In each of the Exhibits 40–42, the sales income line shows a progression which, after B/E point has been passed, portrays an ever widening gap between total cost and total income. As a demonstration of a perpetual relationship between total cost and total income, the hypothesis is fanciful. To maintain an ever growing sales volume requires, at the higher ranges of sales, additional expenses such as:

1 Incentive commissions to salesmen.
2 Extra discounts to tradesmen.
3 Eventually, price reductions to the buying public.
4 Possibly higher wage costs through overtime working or employment of less efficient labour (engaged to meet the need of increased production programmes).

The operation of any of the above constraints will result in a narrowing of the margin between total cost and total income: for these reasons the hypothetical chart's ever widening profit gap can be seen to be unrealistic. Even those products which are a household name[1] must eventually reach a plateau of sales income, at and beyond which net income will always have a tendency to decrease due to the costs of maintaining sales/production activity. The results of the effect of the limitations on an ever-growing profit margin are shown in Exhibit 43.

Here the impacts of the various cost increases and net sales decreases have been shown in a falling off in the income line OD_1. This has been done in order to present a graph which is as closely comparable

[1] So that they meet with less sales resistance.

EXHIBIT 43

BREAK-EVEN CHART 4

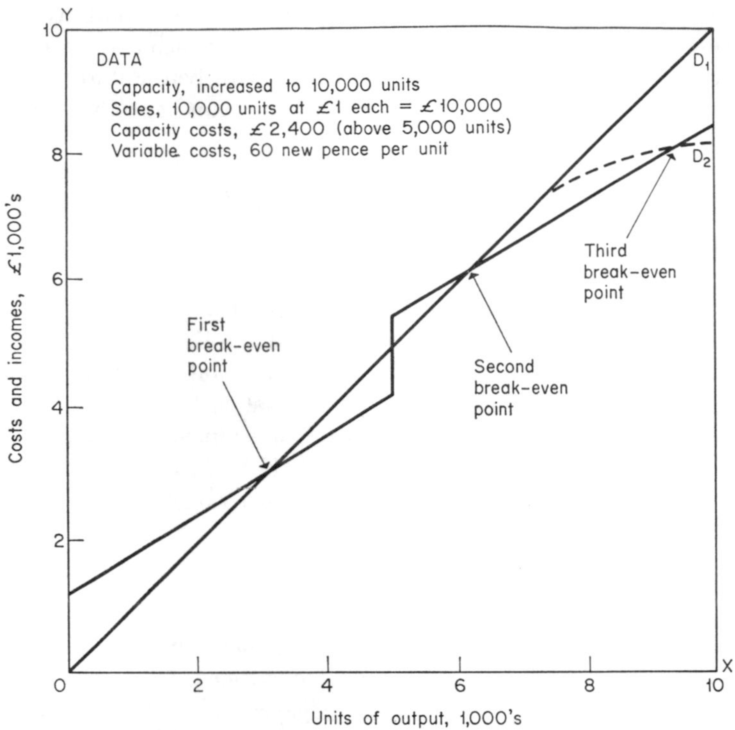

as possible with Exhibit 42. The main outlines of total cost and total income in the above exhibit are the same as those in the third break-even chart. The effect of the constraints, on both cost and income, which make it more and more difficult for the firm to obtain additional sales, is shown by the broken line D_2. The falling off of income thus can be seen to produce a potential third B/E point. The chart shows the possibility of a loss at a production level of 9,400 units. Nowhere does the increased capacity produce profits similar to those which were experienced when the firm's maximum output was limited to 5,000 units.

Profit/volume graph

The B/E graph is basically the chart of a company's profitability path. The reader has seen the effect of the different cost groups upon profit, and upon the margin of safety relevant to a particular cost/volume relationship. Now a principal objective of business operations must be profit and many different techniques are employed in the search for improved profitability. Some of these techniques and methods, such as plant modernization, will result in increased capacity costs. Such expenditures are incurred in the expectation that greater efficiency, better quality and more reliability will result in increased sales and increased net profit. Exhibit 44 demonstrates the profit/loss

EXHIBIT 44

PROFIT/VOLUME CHART

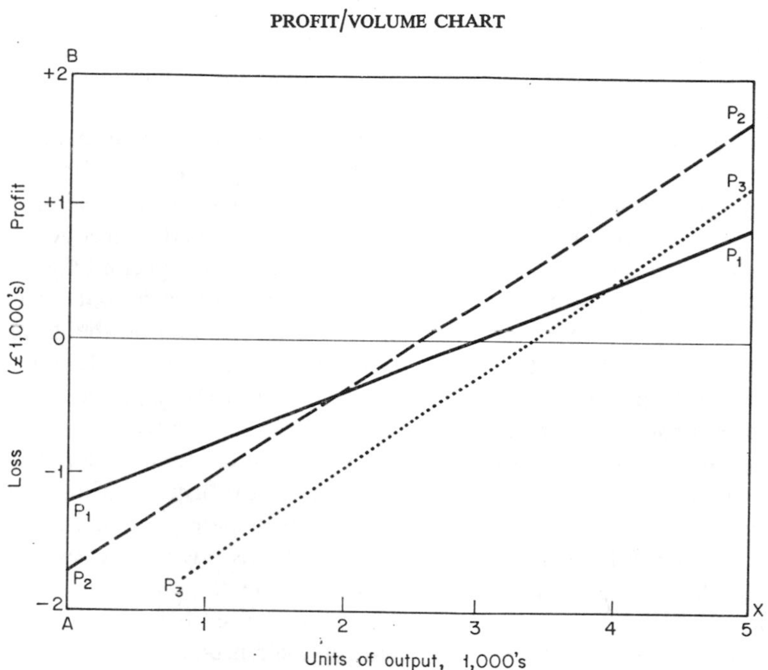

implications of a (hypothetical) production-flow reorganization, carried out in pursuit of greater efficiency and greater profit. Here the chart is concerned only with profit or loss (shown on axis AB) at the various levels of output given on AX. The continuous line P_1P_1 repeats the profit expectation revealed in Exhibits 40 and 41. At this stage it is to be assumed that wage increases are negotiated to stimulate greater productivity. These productivity agreements, together with other cost reduction studies, are planned to give an expected profit of £1,600, at maximum output. This profit potential is indicated by point P_2 on the chart.

Now, many of the increased costs which accrue from greater productivity policies have a rigidity which reacts unfavourably upon the company when production falls. Increased expenditure, such as higher *levels* of wages rates, sales commissions, distribution costs, etc., will remain with the company even though the demand for its products falls off. Therefore the impact upon the firm's profitability, as a result of the wage negotiations and cost-reduction studies, will be demonstrated by the broken line P_2P_2. It can be seen that whilst profit can be considerably increased at an output of 5,000 units, a corresponding increase in the loss incurred at an output of 1,000 units is to be expected—even though break-even point has been reduced.

A further hypothesis can now be introduced. Assume that management decides to replace old plant and machinery with more sophisticated equipment. The object of the exercise would be, for example, the production of better quality goods, a more reliable production flow with less wastage. It is furthermore assumed that, in consequence of the re-equipment, the expected profit at maximum output ought to be increased to £1,100. This amount is represented on the graph at P_3. Increased costs of plant will result in a higher B/E point, because capacity costs will be higher.[1] However the expected profit increase of £300 at maximum output is judged to be worth the risk of the re-equipment capacity costs. The essential point here is that such increased capacity costs are a feature of the firm's costing at *all* levels of output. Therefore whilst higher profits are possible beyond the higher B/E point, *greater losses* are just as possible below that new B/E point. The decision for management, in these cases of whether to modernize or not, must be influenced by their expectations of the future level of demand for their products. Though the profit/volume graph in Exhibit 44 is based upon hypothetical circumstances, the graph does represent a commonly found situation when profit and capacity planning is undertaken.

Marginal costing

Break-even analysis leads on naturally to a study of marginal costing. Marginal (or direct) costing enables the impact of business

[1] Assuming that the company has always calculated its depreciation charges on a historical, rather than a replacement basis.

EXHIBIT 45

SCHEMATIC DIAGRAM OF DIFFERENCES BETWEEN FULL-ABSORPTION AND DIRECT-MARGINAL COSTING

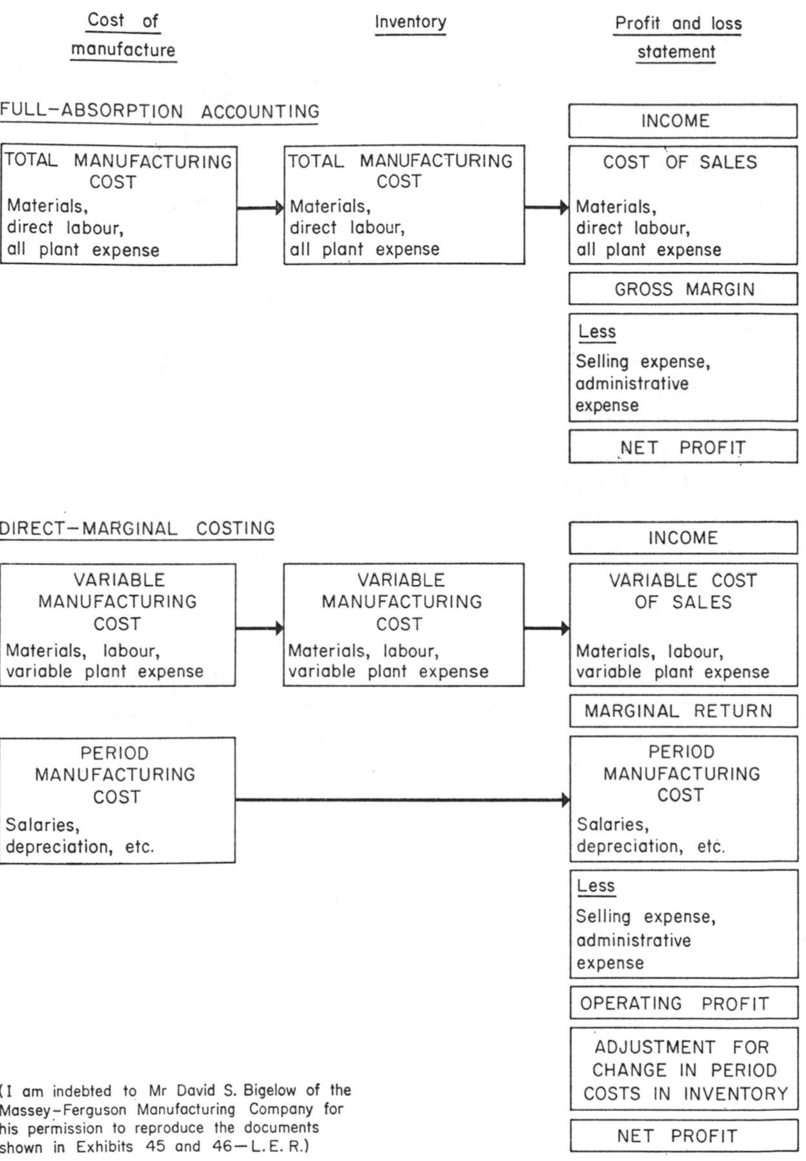

(I am indebted to Mr David S. Bigelow of the Massey-Ferguson Manufacturing Company for his permission to reproduce the documents shown in Exhibits 45 and 46—L. E. R.)

activity on production costs to be clarified, by locating those costs which are sensitive to production changes. While income in excess of *marginal* cost is not the final net gain to the company, because capacity costs have yet to be allocated, the marginal return can reveal areas of true profitability for the company. This arises from the fact that many capacity costs such as those relating to buildings, plant and machinery will have been paid for at some time in the past. They do not result in further similar cash cost outflows when the company's goods are manufactured. A study of marginal costing, therefore, will reveal the actual *current* cost of producing: it will show which of various products is the most profitable to make[1] from the standpoint of the *additional* costs involved in the product's manufacture.

Exhibit 45 above compares the reporting of cost information under a marginal cost system with that obtained with full-absorption costing. The latter system involves the aggregation of all costs of specific types, whether they be of a variable or capacity nature. Marginal cost reporting demonstrates the amount of *additional* expenditure, termed the 'variable cost of sales', which must be incurred when production is engaged. The marginal return, therefore, is the profit in terms of current cost accounting. It is applied in Exhibit 45 to the whole cost complex of a company's operations. Its relevance to product mix planning can be appreciated by studying Exhibit 46. In this exhibit the company has made an operating profit of £10,000 and a net profit of £6,000. The whole direct and indirect (capacity costs) cost of keeping the company in business was £94,000: it is this sum which has reduced the sales income of £100,000 to the net profit of £6,000. Information of this kind gives a hazy, over-all picture of the company's activities, whereas the marginal cost analysis, into groups of costs which are *caused by the manufacture* of each of the three products, provides more useful data for profit planning. The table shows that £11,500 of the total indirect decision i.e. capacity, costs are not influenced by the manufacture of any particular product. These expenditures have to be met whether the company is in business or not. Therefore, after recognizing that some portion of the total capacity cost will be affected by engaging in operations, the reader can see the true total variation in the cost of

[1] Other factors such as the marginal contribution per hour or per day are pertinent to this statement. Again the company's objectives in the field of business, such as growth of sales, may affect the decision. Whatever is decided, marginal costing can be of assistance in revealing the direct cost of the decision.

EXHIBIT 46

ANALYSIS OF INCOME STATEMENT BY PRODUCT GROUP

	Total	Common	Product A	Product B	Product C
	£	£	£	£	£
Net Sales.					
Home market					
Inter-Company					
Export and direct shipment					
TOTAL NET SALES	100,000		80,000	10,000	10,000
Direct Variable Costs					
Standard direct variable costs					
Cost allowances					
Freight, duty, insurance					
TOTAL DIRECT VARIABLE COSTS	60,000		48,000	6,000	6,000
DIRECT VARIABLE PROFIT	40,000		32,000	4,000	4,000
Direct Decision Costs					
Decision factory costs					
Production tooling					
Warehousing and machine storage					
Warranty and policy					
Rectification					
Obsolescence					
Product advertising and sales promotion					
Direct engineering expense					
TOTAL DIRECT DECISION COSTS	15,000		12,000	1,500	1,500
DIRECT PRODUCT PROFIT	25,000		20,000	2,500	2,500
Indirect Decision Costs					
Marketing expense	6,000	4,000	1,000	500	500
Marketing expense, Export	1,000	1,000			
General manufacturing administration	1,000	1,000			
Engineering administration	1,000	1,000			
General and administrative expense	2,000	1,000	500	400	100
Finance fees	1,000	1,000			
Miscellaneous income and expense	1,000	500	300	100	100
Provision for doubtful accounts	1,000	1,000			
Interest	1,000	1,000			
TOTAL INDIRECT DECISION COSTS	15,000	11,500	1,800	1,000	700
OPERATING PROFIT	10,000		18,200	1,500	1,800
Non-operating Impacts					
Change in decision costs in inventory	(500)				
Corporate expense	500				
Taxes	4,000				
TOTAL NON-OPERATING IMPACTS	4,000				
NET INCOME	£6,000				

manufacture of each of the three products. This variation in cost is shown by the line 'operating profit'. When operating profit is

EXHIBIT 47

ANALYSIS OF INCOME STATEMENT BY PRODUCT GROUP

Details	Totals	Product A	Product B	Product C
	£	£	£	£
Net Sales				
Home				
Inter company				
Export				
TOTAL NET SALES	100,000	75,000	10,000	15,000
Variable Cost of Sales				
Materials				
Labour				
Expense				
TOTAL VARIABLE COSTS	60,000	50,000	5,000	5,000
MARGINAL RETURN	40,000	25,000	5,000	10,000
MARGINAL RETURN AS PERCENTAGE OF SALES	40·0	33·3	50·0	66·3
Period or Capacity Costs				
Salaries	8,000			
General Administration	3,000			
Engineering Administration	2,000			
Financing Costs	1,000			
Bad Debts	1,000			
Depreciation	15,000			
TOTAL CAPACITY COSTS	30,000			
OPERATING PROFIT	10,000			
Non-operating Costs				
Corporate Expense	1,000			
Taxation	3,000			
TOTAL NON-OPERATING COSTS	4,000			
NET INCOME	£6,000			

expressed as a percentage return on sales, it can be seen that:

Product A gives a 22·8 per cent return.
Product B gives a 15 per cent return.
Product C gives an 18 per cent return.

This kind of information, coupled with data on market size for each product, will assist in the profitable planning of a manufacturing mix of products. Exhibit 47 presents a similar situation where no variation in any of the period costs is envisaged as being caused by varying levels of production.

The following simple example will show the reasoning behind the choice of a manufacturing mix, when a marginal cost approach is employed. The problem which is posed assumes that materials, etc., will be available to meet any variety of production programme which may be decided upon.

PROBLEM—The XYZ Manufacturing Company, Limited, makes three products. Product A sells for £22, product B £26, and product C £35. The marginal costs of sales are £7, £14 and £28 for A, B and C, respectively. The company's machining capacity available for production is 20,000 hours. The machining time for each unit is

A 3 hours
B 2 hours
C 1 hour

The attainable market share for each product is assessed as follows:

A 10,000 units
B 2,000 units
C 1,000 units

What is the best mix of products for profitable operations?

ANSWER

Products	A	B	C
	£	£	£
Sales price	22	26	35
Variable costs	7	14	28
Marginal return, i.e. contribution	£15	12	7
Machine hours per unit	3	2	1
Marginal return per hour	£ 5	6	7

PRODUCTION PROGRAMME	*Marginal return*
C 1,000 units × 1 hr = 1,000 machine hours × £7 =	7,000
B 2,000 units × 2 hr = 4,000 machine hours × £6 =	24,000
A 5,000 units × 3 hr = 15,000 machine hours × £5 =	75,000
Total marginal return	£106,000

In the above programme the whole available 20,000 hours of machining capacity has been allocated. From the resultant sales of £197,000, a direct return of £106,000 is expected. The reader should now remember that the capacity costs should now be deducted from the £106,000 in order to arrive at the final net profit. The above example is a simple one and problems of whether to buy in some components, rather than make them, have not been introduced. The basic worth of marginal costing, and the importance of contribution as a planning tool are however demonstrated.

Questions for discussion

1. How would you define opportunity cost?
2. Break-even analysis looks to the future and can show what level of output is necessary before the firm can become profit earning. What kind of information system would you establish in order to know whether a company's current performance was likely to meet the forecast B/E target?
3. Why do break-even points change?
4. Why is it more meaningful to plot capacity costs *above* variable costs on the break-even chart?
5. What is the margin of safety? What would be the importance of this margin to a highly automated company, in a period of declining business?
6. How can British Rail justify their policy of cheap mid-week fares for holidaygoers? Which sort of cost analysis will justify the policy?
7. If an economist prepared a break-even chart for a company, how would it differ from a similar chart prepared by the company's accountant?

Recommended reading

GARDNER, F. V., *Profit Management and Control*, McGraw-Hill, 1955.

SIDEBOTHAM, R., *Accounting for Industrial Management*, Pergamon Press, 1964.

HORNGREN, C. T., *Cost Accounting: A Managerial Emphasis*, Prentice Hall, 1962. (Initial studies should be limited to Chapters 1–3 and 9–10).

NATIONAL ASSOCIATION OF ACCOUNTANTS (USA), 'Current applications of direct costing,' *Research Report No.* 37.

CHAPTER 8 Capital Expenditure Evaluation

Introduction

The reader has seen how a company's accounts can reveal information on a business's performance. Furthermore it has been shown how forecasting and a study of the relationships between specific groups of *operating* costs can aid the planner to guide and control performance in the future. At this point it becomes necessary to consider how the business manager can improve his decisions concerning expenditure on long term assets—the *capacity* costs of break-even analysis. Capital expenditure concerns money spent with the knowledge that the gain therefrom will not accrue immediately or even within a few months. More often it implies that such expenditure is buying a stake in the future and, as capital assets are usually of limited specific use,[1] the needs of the future must be carefully assessed. Once capital expenditure is engaged, it is most difficult to change the course of the firm spending the money—at least without considerable cost. This considerable cost could stem from having to sell the capital assets at unfavourable prices, or from having to spend further sums on altering and modifying the assets retained. Either of which happenings would mean a loss which could have been avoided if the original capital expenditure proposed had been properly assessed and the decision thus taken on better informed bases.

Business management is concerned with decision making. In the capital asset sphere it frequently involves the making of a choice between several possible alternatives. There may be different ways in which a company can proceed to manufacture a particular commodity. Various types of machinery are available: such choices of

[1] If a shoe-making plant is set up, the machinery involved could not be used to manufacture motor cars, or shirts, or bearings. It is vital therefore that the correct choice is made before expenditure is incurred.

machines could be influenced by their running costs, their purchase costs, the quality of work produced and so on. Again there are various commodities that a company might decide to produce: it could buy, lease or rent the equipment and buildings which it would need to complete its manufacturing programme. The extent of the possible alternative opportunities open to a dynamic business are much wider in scope and greater in number than those instanced above. Therefore it becomes essential to be sure about the means of measurement of the worth of alternatives, when a manager is planning his firm's capital expenditures. These plans will determine the future direction, profitability and growth of his business. Finally, the concept of choice between available alternative investments in capital assets must always consider the consequences of *not* investing at all. In this way a complete picture of the consequences of a decision-maker's actions is obtained, and the future of his company is the better evaluated and influenced.

Techniques of appraisal

Now the choice criterion, the yardstick by which investment in capital assets is assessed, involves measuring future incomes which will arise from operating an asset, against its purchase and installation costs. In all cases this is a calculation of the effects of change; thus it is the costs and incomes relating from change which are relevant, and these are termed incremental costs and incomes.[1] Any yardstick of measurement must present a means of identifying acceptable and unacceptable investment proposals. It must also be a means of choosing between alternatives, and this is of utmost importance where there are two ways of achieving one end. Furthermore the capital planner will find it helpful if the criterion of choice gives not only a 'go' or 'no go' answer, but also presents a ranking of projects in an order of desirability. This latter quality in the evaluation technique is not easy to achieve and the examples given below show why the business planner should approach with care his selection of a criterion of investment choice.

[1] The notion of incremental costs and incomes refers to those costs and incomes which arise as a result of doing something, e.g. of capital investment. It has its comparisons with the variable costs in break-even analysis and is frequently referred to as the marginal cost of doing something or the marginal saving from *not* doing that something.

PAYBACK

The most widely used method of investment evaluation is payback. Its popularity derives from its simplicity and cheapness of operation. This technique gives forth a ratio which is a simple expression of the length of time it takes for a project to return to a firm the cash outlays involved in the original investment. It indicates the speed with which the corporate treasury is replenished by the incomes generated from the activity of the capital expenditure. Payback looks no further than the time necessary for a project to re-finance its initial cost, and therefore has no regard for subsequent receipts, or for the length of economic life of the investment.

Exhibit 48 demonstrates three different investments and their related annual cash flows and costs. Each investment has the same grade in the payback index—two years, i.e. it takes exactly two years for the several projects to return the cash cost of the original capital investment to the investor.[1] No regard is paid to the varying distributions of cash flows, although the time of receipt could well be of importance to the firm's liquidity position. To emphasize the time factor of cash flowback, the percentage column in the table indicates the proportion of the original cost represented by each separate year's net cash flows. These cash flow comparisons tend to emphasize the inequality of the three investments, at least from the liquidity point of view. The use of payback therefore should be questioned as to its reliability and this specific point will be exemplified below.

However the method is frequently used as a first hurdle in an investment approval screening system. Here a maximum number of years' payback is necessary for a proposal to proceed to a more precise form of capital expenditure assessment. In the table above it should be noted that when comparing the alternative prospects of A and B, the *additional* capital cost of B, £2,500, returns *additional* cash to the corporate funds of £3,000 in the first year alone. This first year incremental receipt gives a payback of 5/6ths of a year to the incremental capital cost. So though the calculation of payback

[1] The reader will have noticed that comparisons of *profit* with investment cost are not being made in these appraisals of the worth of capital expenditure proposals. In earlier chapters the impact of asset valuation upon profit calculation has been examined, and the potential distortion of the profit figure has been clearly shown. In capital investment analysis we must compare like with like—cash going out upon payment of investment cost is compared with the cash flow return resulting from the operation of the investment. To refresh the mind upon cash flow, it would be useful to refer to page 59.

EXHIBIT 48

EVALUATION OF INVESTMENTS BY PAYBACK

Details	Project A		Project B		Project C	
Cost of investment	£5,000		£7,500		£10,000	
Cash flows	£	Percentage of original cost	£	Percentage of original cost	£	Percentage of original cost
Year 1	2,000	40	5,000	66·7	6,000	60
Year 2	3,000	60	2,500	33·3	4,000	40
Year 3	1,000	20	1,500	20·0	2,000	20
TOTAL CASH FLOWS	£6,000	120	£9,000	120·0	£12,000	120
PAYBACK	2 years		2 years		2 years	

is simple, easy to understand and its costs of calculation are inexpensive in operation, its use poses problems of choice. It does not solve problems of choice in a reliable fashion. Nevertheless perhaps it could be said that for a company which is short of liquid funds, payback has some value. Such value could lie in its use as an initial screening tool, where a maximum payback is specified as a first requirement for all capital expenditure proposals to satisfy before passing on to a more stringent test. It is a practice frequently used in industry; it may seem short-sighted for it does not take note of *all* factors affecting the investment situation.

RATES OF RETURN ON BOOK COST

There are several expressions of the simple rate of return method of investment evaluation. When formulating this rate of return index therefore, it is necessary to be precise in the descriptions of the data to be used in the evaluation. The ratio or percentage rate of return figure which is intended to be a demonstration of an investment's profitability should be used consistently to enable effective comparison of alternative proposals to be made. That the rate of return should also indicate a preferential ranking of those alternatives is also desirable. Now the simple return criteria are to be criticized for ignoring the importance of the yearly flow of cash receipts. In general, early replenishment of investment outgoings is to be preferred to a later recoupment, if only because it may enable advantage to be taken of possible opportunities for re-investment. In favour of the various returns on book cost is the fact that a projection of earnings *over investment* life should be calculated,[1] whereas payback is concerned with those years of life up to the time of capital cost replenishment only. Simple book rates of return are as easy to calculate as payback: they are equally popular because of this, but their effectiveness in locating the profitable investment, in presenting a ranking of investments in order of profitability, is dubious.

[1] My examinations of business practices have shown that many companies express the first full year's net receipts *only* as a percentage of capital investment cost. This may be acceptable if the yearly gains from the investment are expected to be constant. In other cases forecasts are made for the first 4 years of a project's (say) 20-year life: the years 5–20 are then just a repetitive extension of the expectations of the 4th year. Much of this short-cut policy stems from a lack of experience and/or lack of confidence in practical long term planning—L.E.R.

1 RETURN PER £ INVESTED—This variant of ROR (rate of return) gives a desirability index by dividing the cost of the investment into the total net cash flows. The resulting factor, while ignoring the time period of the receipts, purports to give a measure of investment assessment. Lack of consideration for the timing of the proceeds is however a major fault in this measure of investment worth. Applying the return per £ invested criterion to the investments shown in Exhibit 48 will produce the indices of investment worth shown in Exhibit 49.

EXHIBIT 49

EVALUATION OF INVESTMENTS BY RETURN PER £ INVESTED

Details	Project A	Project B	Project C
Total cash flows	£6,000	£9,000	£12,000
Investment cost	£5,000	£7,500	£10,000
Desirability index	1·2	1·2	1·2

By this method also each of the proposed capital spendings appear to be of equal worth. Yet the analyst must wonder how this can be so, especially when project B returns 66·7 per cent of its capital cost in *the first year of its life*.

2 AVERAGE ANNUAL INCOME PER £ INVESTED—Here an assessment is made by calculating the annual average of the total net cash flows and dividing that sum by the initial cost of the investment. *Some* credit must be given to these evaluating criteria because they are concerned with the whole life of the project. Applying this method to the proposals in Exhibit 48 demonstrates desirability indices for each of the proposals (see Exhibit 50). Similar doubts (to those already quoted for payback and return per £ invested) arise concerning the acceptability of this criterion as an indicator of investment worth. Each project still has a common appraisal of desirability.

3 AVERAGE ANNUAL INCOME AS A PERCENTAGE OF THE BOOK VALUE OF INVESTMENT—There are numerous variants of this measure of return: the average annual income may be calculated before or after depreciation, before or after tax, for

EXHIBIT 50

EVALUATION OF INVESTMENTS BY AVERAGE ANNUAL INCOME PER £ INVESTED

Details	Project A	Project B	Project C
Total cash flows	£6,000	£9,000	£12,000
Average per year	£2,000	£3,000	£4,000
Investment cost	£5,000	£7,500	£10,000
Desirability index	0·4	0·4	0·4

example. Such inconsistencies reflect the lack of uniformity of many expressions used in accounting, for the 'book rates of return' are based upon accounting concepts and accounting statements.[1] For the purposes of this publication, however, it is intended to use the term 'income' to indicate profit after depreciation charges have been levied. Now after the average annual income has been determined, the resultant sum is then expressed as a percentage of the capital investment cost as shown in Exhibit 51.

EXHIBIT 51

EVALUATION OF INVESTMENTS BY AVERAGE ANNUAL INCOME EXPRESSED AS A PERCENTAGE OF INVESTMENT BOOK VALUE

Details	Average income	Deprecia-tion*	Net income	Investment cost	Percentage return index
Project A	£2,000	£1,667	£333	£5,000	6·7
Project B	£3,000	£2,500	£500	£7,500	6·7
Project C	£4,000	£3,333	£667	£10,000	6·7

* Straight-line depreciation.

A further variant of this rate of return is introduced by presenting the average annual income as a percentage of the *average* book value

[1] See Exhibit 30.

of the capital asset. Average book value (on straight-line depreciation) means one half of the original cost. The result upon the rate of return index is simply to double the percentages shown in the above table. Thus again it must be emphasized that consistency of treatment of the data in calculating the rate of return is of prime importance. Book rates of return are widely used in view of their simplicity. The major criticism to be directed against their operation is once more the lack of consideration given to the timing of the proceeds of innovation.

DISCOUNTED CASH FLOW METHOD (DCF)

Several methods of capital expenditure evaluation have now been presented. Each one has the fundamental drawback of its complete lack of consideration for the timing of cash returns. Furthermore in the hypothetical projects given in the above tables, none of the criteria so far examined has been able to present a positive tool of choice to the investor. In every instance the previously studied measures of return give identical assessments to the several projects. What is required therefore is some positive indicator of desirability, some rating index which can be regarded as a reliable guide for the analysis of investment worth. In this context investment worth will be taken to apply to proposals where profitability can be measured and is furthermore the desirable objective.[1]

Time adjusted rates of return give emphasis to the incidence of cash returns in each year of a proposed investment's expected economic life. The emphasis is given by applying, to the forecast returns, an interest discounting factor which has the effect of levying a rate of interest *charge* on each year's budgeted cash receipts. This charge reduces, i.e. discounts, the cash flows of the future years to an amount which represents their worth at the present time. The investor is then able to compare the cost today of the proposed

[1] Some investment proposals may be undertaken in order to improve welfare and medical facilities for the company's employees. Assessing the profitability of this type of capital expenditure is practically impossible. Again, all proposed capital investment must be considered in the light of the company's business objectives. It may be that the policy maker's plans are being directed to the achievement of a certain growth in sales, or growth in the asset value of the company. In such circumstances there could be occasions where *profitable* investment opportunities would not satisfy the objectives set out in the corporate long-term plan: these proposals, though profitable might well be rejected where the firm's directing managers considered the long-term strategy to be of greater importance than short-term profitability.

capital expenditure, with the evaluation—also in present day terms—of the related future cash receipts. Like is being compared with like and the assessment becomes more meaningful.[1]

There are three forms of time-adjusted return, which are finding increasing acceptance for the evaluation of industrial capital expenditure. The three DCF return indices are:

1 The yield method.
2 The net present value method.
3 The annual value method.

Before studying the impacts of these time adjusted rates of return upon the assessment of the projects shown in Exhibits 48 to 51, it is advisable that the simple mathematics of discounting and compounding are understood. For this purpose the reader is referred to Appendix C 'Discounting Techniques Explained'.

I THE YIELD METHOD—The object of the yield method of investment appraisal is to ascertain the rate of interest which, when applied to the future cash flows, will reduce, i.e. discount, their monetary size until, in total, they are equal to the initial cost of the investment. Frequently referred to as the internal rate of return or the marginal efficiency of capital, yield presents a percentage rating which can be used as a tool of choice by the investment analyst; it answers the question—'What rate of interest could the company pay to finance the project yet still enable the investment to break even?' The following calculations demonstrate the application of the technique to the projects already evaluated by other criteria of desirability (see Exhibits 52 and 53). By taking the discount factor[2] of 10 per cent the present value of £5,047 shows that the cash flows of the investment can bear an even higher rate before they are brought down to £5,000, the investment cost. A higher rate is therefore tried. The required rate is found by interpolation to be 10·6 per cent.[3] Utilizing similar processes on B and C will show their DCF yield rating to be 12·3 and 11·9 per cent, respectively.

[1] The different worths attributed here to £1 today and £1 at a specified future time is a function of the rate of interest. This function, which is fully explained in Appendix C, has *nothing* to do with prices rising in the future because of a monetary inflation.
[2] See the interest tables at Appendix D for the factors used.
[3] The method of interpolation takes the difference between the present value totals (£5,047 − 4,666 = 381), divides this resultant sum into the excess present value of the lower percentage factor (£5,047 − 5,000 = 47) and then multiplies by the percentage gap (15 − 10 = 5) of the two discounting factors.

EXHIBIT 52

YIELD EVALUATION OF PROJECT A

Year	Cash flows £		Discount factor 10%		Present value £
1	2,000	×	0·909	=	1,818
2	3,000	×	0·826	=	2,478
3	1,000	×	0·751	=	751
	£6,000				£5,047

EXHIBIT 53

YIELD EVALUATION OF PROJECT A

Year	Cash flows £		Discount factor 15%		Present value £
1	2,000	×	0·870	=	1,740
2	3,000	×	0·756	=	2,268
3	1,000	×	0·658	=	658
	£6,000				£4,666

2 THE PRESENT VALUE METHOD—This method shows the monetary difference between the original cost, and the total future cash flows when they are *discounted at a specific percentage rate*. On the other hand yield seeks the rate of interest which will discount the future cash flows until they equal capital costs; it does not therefore specify the rate for discounting. Once the yield rate is found it can be used as an indicator of investment worth. The decision-maker would be prepared to accept proposals where yield is above a certain minimum rate which he considers may have to be paid in order to raise finance for the

project. Now net present value specifies in advance a minimum percentage interest factor at which the future cash flows must be discounted. Then the difference between the capital cost and the total discounted sum of the future cash flows is termed the net present value. If this sum is positive the investment is *prima facie* acceptable; if the net present value calculated in this way is negative, the investment should be rejected. The present value of project A is given in Exhibit 52 as £5,047, using an interest factor of 10 per cent. Subtracting the capital cost £5,000, the *net* present value of the investment is £47, at a 10 per cent cost of financing.

Comparisons of yield and net present value

In the same way one can ascertain the net present values of projects B and C to be £236·5 and £260, respectively. Thus these two time adjusted rates of return have both given ratings which have been affected by the time distributions of the cash receipts. Nevertheless they do not agree on the order of preference to be accorded to the several investment opportunities. Both yield and net present value are sound measures to employ when seeking a 'yes' or 'no' answer to the question of whether to invest or not. Furthermore, which (of several) investments to undertake first is an additional problem to which the business planner needs to know the solution. This ranking of projects in the order of their desirability is wanted especially in those instances where a company may have a limited quantity of funds but a goodly supply of investment needs and ideas. Any ranking of projects is considerably affected by the cost of capital finance and the importance of this concept to sound capital planning will be discussed in the next chapter.

Now discounted rates of return just compare input (cost of all capital resource use caused by the investment) with output (cash earnings). It is essential, *after this comparison has been made*, that the calculated return index should be related to the cost of capital financing. Net present value does this automatically where the discount rate chosen is in fact the investor's cost of capital. It has been noted (see above) that where the net present value is positive, i.e. gives a gain in excess of the financing cost, the project may be accepted (subject to any other limitations imposed by corporate objectives).

On the other hand the yield percentage arises as a result of averaging the returns implicit in the cash flows of each of a series of years. The percentage index has then to be compared with the cost of financing and if the yield is *above* the cost of financing, the project may be accepted. So, whilst the yield method demonstrates a percentage *rate of growth*, net present value reveals an absolute *quantity* of growth in money terms. This latter measure indicates the extent of the growth in wealth which would accrue to the firm if the related investment is undertaken. Furthermore where the firm has several investment opportunities open to its choosing, the sum of the NPV's of the investments selected will indicate the probable total increase in corporate wealth resulting from that selection. This assumes that the capital expenditure proposals have equal risks, or that each NPV has been determined after an analysis of the inherent risks and uncertainties. No such conclusion could be drawn from an aggregation of yield percentages, each of which would simply reveal the rate of interest at which the relevant investment could be financed without incurring a loss or making a gain.[1] Yield is the break-even cost of capital rate for the investment.

Finally to complete a brief comparison of these two methods of appraisal, it must be pointed out that assessment of yield index can produce somewhat disturbing results. Certain combinations of cash flows will give forth no yield result at all. Another series will present *two* measures of return. Whilst these results stem from the mathematical relationships involved in the calculations, they do not give comfort in the practical situation where it is necessary to make a choice between various available projects. Several writers point out[2] how the problem, presented by two rates, may be overcome: they also assert that the conditions which give rise to uncommon results (two rates of return for one project) are themselves uncommon. The reader is encouraged to study the methods suggested for rationalizing the apparent paradox of double rates of return. However the fact remains that such results can happen: the measures to be taken to solve the problem present further complications to the unsophisticated user of indices of investment worth. For these and other

[1] The situation is best expressed by imagining that the investment is financed by a loan *from the company* to the investing department. The earnings from the project must then repay principal and interest to the company before being able to contribute to corporate profits.

[2] MERRETT, A. J. and SYKES, A., *The Finance and Analysis of Capital Projects*, Longmans, 1963.

reasons the writer's preference rests on the use of net present value for evaluation of investment worth. This statement should not be regarded as a recommendation to be applied on all occasions, however, and it will be necessary to return to this problem in a later chapter. For the moment it must be re-emphasized that corporate long-term planning and/or short-term liquidity will certainly affect some capital spending decisions. It could be that two or more indices of worth should be used to obtain a *comprehensive* view of any single investment. Here the decision-maker might use a liquidity index (payback), a growth index (net present value) or a long-term earnings rate (yield).[1]

ANNUAL VALUE METHOD

Whilst the writer's clear preference for net present value as a criterion of investment worth has been stated, the picture of indices of worth would not be complete without a study of the annual value method of appraisal. Nearly all the discussions surrounding the appraisal of capital expenditures, refer to the assessment of proposals as projects. The constituents of the proposals are frequently overlooked and it must be remarked that most investment opportunities involve the purchase and use of assets. Many proposals consist of a mixture of different types of assets such as land, buildings, machinery, equipment or vehicles. Now whilst the project may have an extensive life, it could be that the assets themselves will have lives different from the proposal life. Machinery, plant and vehicles would need to be changed during the life of the proposal. In the determination of cash flows to be used in a DCF evaluation such periodic outflows would be shown, either by reduction of the operations' cash inflow or as a discounted part of the whole capital cost of the project. Thus the problem is not new, but the annual value protagonists deal with the situation in a different way.

Much academic argument has surrounded the choice of method and choice of index to be used in capital investment planning. It is not intended here to join the debate on the wearisome subject of the mathematical proofs of the various indices of return. Nevertheless

[1] An improvement to the simple payback index would be the *discounted* payback where the number of years for the project to repay its capital cost is not assessed by aggregating the absolute sums of annual cash flows but by aggregating the *discounted* values of the annual cash flows.

annual value evaluation must be discussed for it contains the ingredients of an acceptable criterion: the extent to which it satisfies the need for a time adjusted evaluation of future returns will be considered.

In practical commercial conditions, forecasting the future earnings of an investment proposal is a tedious and difficult business. Firms report that they estimate a project's earnings for 5, 10 or even 20 years ahead. A closer study shows, however, that many of these so called forecasts are projected to the 3rd, 4th or 5th year only: then where the project is expected to have a life in excess of these periods, the expected earnings of the following years up to the end of the project life are merely repetitions of the estimated cash flows of that 3rd, 4th or 5th year. Annual value uses this practice, to some extent, when it evaluates capital expenditure proposals by comparing investment cost with future earnings by expressing each of these two factors as uniform annual sums. If the annual value of expected earnings is greater than the annual cost, the investment is worth considering.

Recognizing that the future of an investment proposal rarely can be accurately determined, and that different proposals can have different actual lives, it is suggested that an evaluation of alternatives should be based upon their continuance into perpetuity. Thus the valuation of future cash flows expressed in terms of a permanent annual, i.e. annuity, income can be compared with the investment's annual (or annuity) cost. In order to ascertain a proposal's annuity cost, the Annual Value Method uses the accountant's sinking fund. This is a concept which purports to show how much should be set aside each year:

1 For the replacement of fixed assets at a specified future date.

or

2 In order to accumulate a sufficient amount for the discharge of a debt, e.g. debenture, at a specified future date.

All that needs to be known in assessing the annual cost is the required ultimate size of the sinking fund, the period during which it will operate, and the rate of interest at which the annual contributions to the fund are expected to grow. Now a sinking fund is a useful method of arriving at *some* evaluation of an annual cost. At least it produces a uniform annual charge in each year's accounts, when planning for such contingencies as those stated in (1) and (2) above.

However that uniformity is achieved by assuming the funds growth at a regular, unvarying, annual rate of interest and if such a fund were set up in practice this factor alone would hardly ever be obtained without some parallel capital variation in the size of the fund.

MECHANICS OF ANNUAL VALUE CALCULATIONS

Exhibit 54 shows the capital cost and relevant net cash flows of a proposed capital investment having an estimated five year life.

EXHIBIT 54

WEIGHTED ANNUAL AVERAGE NET CASH FLOWS—I
INVESTMENT COST £15,000

Year	Interest factor, 10%	Cash flows	PV of cash flows at 10%
		£	£
1	0·9091	3,000	2,727·3
2	0·8264	(2,000)	(1,652·8)
3	0·7513	5,000	3,756·5
4	0·6830	6,000	4,098·0
5	0·6209	7,000	4,346·3
TOTALS	3·7907	£19,000	£13,275·3
Unweighted annual average		£3,800	
Discounted annual average[1]			£3,502

The conventional appraisal criteria would give payback as $4\frac{3}{7}$ years, a net present value of £1,724·7 and a DCF yield of 6·5 per cent. The net cash flows have been expressed as a weighted (or discounted) average in order to prepare the reader for an eventual annual value assessment of investment worth (as it is the discounted average of the net cash flows which annual value uses to compare with an annual cost in order to determine project worth).

Exhibit 55 now assumes that the cash flows of the final year of the

[1] The discounted average is achieved from dividing the total PV of the cash flows by the total PV of the interest factors. Dividing by the PV of the interest factors is the same as multiplying by its reciprocal, i.e. ×0·2638. This reciprocal represents the annuity (for 5 years) which £ today would purchase at a 10 per cent interest rate.

EXHIBIT 55

WEIGHTED ANNUAL AVERAGE NET CASH FLOWS—II
INVESTMENT COST £15,000

Year	Interest factor, 10%	Cash flows	PV of cash flows at 10%
		£	£
1	0·9091	3,000	2,727·3
2	0·8264	(2,000)	(1,652·8)
3	0·7513	5,000	3,756·5
4	0·6830	6,000	4,098·0
5–10	2·9747[1]	7,000	20,822·9
TOTALS	6·1445	£54,000	£29,751·9
Unweighted annual average		£5,400	
Discounted annual average			£4,842

forecast period are continued for a further five years. An assumption such as this would be made where it was desired to compare two projects, one of 5 years' duration with another of 10 years' duration. The assumed projection is frequently recommended in order to bring such alternative projects to a fairer basis of comparison.[2] The effect on the discounted annual average of arbitrary extensions of income life can be seen in the new weighted average of £4,842 which is an increase of £1,340 for the 5-year period.

[1] The interest factor for 5–10 year period is ascertained from either

1 Sum of PV's of £ in each of years 5 to 10,

or

2 PV of £ p.a. for 10 years—£ p.a. for 4 years.

or

3 PV of £ at year 4 × PV of £ p.a. for 6 years.

[2] The suggested projections of investment life are made to put alternative proposals—with discrete lives—on a better basis of comparison. Annual value has never demanded this approach: it *accepts* that projects will have different lives and to this extent the method is questionable. Where the problem of varying lives arises, it must be quantified in some way. Otherwise most long life projects would be in a favourable position by virtue of their longer earning periods. (See also Bierman and Smidt *The Capital Budgeting Decision*, for the concept of a chain of investments, where the whole of a project's net cash flows are discounted into perpetuity.)

The next Exhibit, 56, shows the additional impact of projecting the investment's life into perpetuity: this notion is suggested for all proposals being evaluated in order that each may be considered on the basis of a common income life. Thus it is hoped that an even better comparability can be assured between all investment alternatives which may be competing for corporate funds. These limited

EXHIBIT 56

WEIGHTED ANNUAL AVERAGE NET CASH FLOWS—III
INVESTMENT COST £15,000

Year	Interest factor, 10%	Cash flows	PV of cash flows at 10%
		£	£
1	0·9091	3,000	2,727·3
2	0·8264	(2,000)	(1,652·8)
3	0·7513	5,000	3,756·5
4	0·6830	6,000	4,098·0
5 onwards to perpetuity	6·8301*	7,000	47,810·7
TOTALS	9·9999		£56·739·7
Discounted annual average			£5,674·02

* Ascertained from
1 The PV of a £ a year in perpetuity (calculated from the reciprocal of 10 per cent) less the present value of a £ a year for 4 years (= 10 − 3·1699 = 6·8301).

or

2 The PV of a £ at the 4th year × the PV of £ a year in perpetuity.

demonstrations of the effect, upon forecasted cash flows, of arbitrary extensions of their estimated economic lives would be incomplete without considering the impacts of such extensions of life upon a variety of cash flow patterns. Exhibits 57 and 58 present three alternative investments—each with a different pattern of cash flows. The continuance into perpetuity of the net cash flows of the final year results in the value ranking of the discounted annual averages changing from C:B:A in Exhibit 57 to A:B:C in Exhibit 58. Clearly the acceptance of the concept of discounting a final year's estimated

EXHIBIT 57

WEIGHTED ANNUAL AVERAGE NET CASH FLOWS—IV
INVESTMENT COST £15,000

INVESTMENT		A		B		C	
TYPE OF FLOW		RISING		UNIFORM		FALLING	
Year	Interest factor, 10%	Cash flows	PV of cash flows at 10%	Cash flows	PV of cash flows at 10%	Cash flows	PV of cash flows at 10%
		£	£	£	£	£	£
1	0·9091	3,000	2,727·3	5,000	4,545·5	7,000	6,363·7
2	0·8264	4,000	3,305·6	5,000	4,132·0	6,000	4,958·4
3	0·7513	5,000	3,756·5	5,000	3,756·5	5,000	3,756·5
4	0·6830	6,000	4,098·0	5,000	3,415·0	4,000	2,732·0
5	0·6209	7,000	4,346·3	5,000	3,104·5	3,000	1,862·7
TOTALS	3·7907	£25,000	£18,233·7	£25,000	£18,953·5	£25,000	£19,673·3
Unweighted annual average		£5,000		£5,000		£5,000	
Discounted annual average			£4,810·1		£5,000		£5,189·9

EXHIBIT 58

WEIGHTED ANNUAL AVERAGE NET CASH FLOWS—V
INVESTMENT COST £15,000

INVESTMENT		A		B		C	
TYPE OF FLOW		RISING		UNIFORM		FALLING	
Year	Interest factor, 10%	Cash flows	PV of cash flows at 10%	Cash flows	PV of cash flows at 10%	Cash flows	PV of cash flows at 10%
		£	£	£	£	£	£
1	0·9091	3,000	2,727·3	5,000	4,545·5	7,000	6,363·7
2	0·8264	4,000	3,305·6	5,000	4,132·0	6,000	4,958·4
3	0·7513	5,000	3,756·5	5,000	3,756·5	5,000	3,756·5
4	0·6830	6,000	4,098·0	5,000	3,415·0	4,000	2,732·0
5 On to perpetuity	6·8301	7,000	47,810·7	5,000	34,150·5	3,000	20,490·3
TOTALS	0·9999		£61,698·1		£49,999·5		£38,300·9
Discounted annual average			£6,169·9		£5,000		£3,830·1

net cash flow into perpetuity is of considerable importance. It will change completely the comparative income values of alternative capital expenditure proposals. The reader is reminded that the method of discounting into perpetuity has been proposed in view of the fact that it is most difficult to forecast the actual economic life of an investment.[1] In consequence of the (theoretical) extension of the lives of all proposals being considered, the influence of discrete lives amongst the alternatives is limited.

To complete an annual value appraisal of the investments referred to in Exhibits 57 and 58, the capital expenditure initial cost must be expressed as an annual cost or annual charge. Here the annual value method charges interest on the total capital outlay plus a cost of amortization, i.e. renewal or depreciation charge, of the assets. The amortization charge is assessed as though a sinking fund were set up to provide sufficient funds to repay the initial capital cost at the end of the assets' lives.[2] A simple example (see Exhibit 59) will serve to illustrate the operation of the method.

EXHIBIT 59

CALCULATION OF THE ANNUAL CAPITAL CHARGE—I
INVESTMENT COST £15,000

Depreciation or Amortization	
£15,000 at £0·1638 per £	= 2,457
Interest	
£15,000 at 10%	= 1,500
ANNUAL CAPITAL CHARGE	£3,957

[1] For this reason, amongst others, the analysis of risk and uncertainty is important to the whole problem of investment appraisal. Whilst the quantification of risk is dealt with in Chapter 11, it is essential at this stage to point out that the uncertainty of project life (together with other relevant uncertainties) can be dealt with very effectively in other ways—see pages 199–208.

[2] As implied earlier, the sinking fund charge can be calculated as if the fund required at the end of the assets' lives was to be used to replace the assets at that time. Thus the impact of inflation can be countered by introducing a *replacement cost* annual charge.

[3] *a* The sinking fund is arrived at by taking the PV of a £ p.a. at 5 years (3·7908) and calculating its reciprocal. This factor 0·2638 is the annuity factor: deduct the interest rate 0·10 to arrive at the sinking fund factor which, therefore, is 0·1638.

b The annual capital charge represents the annuity which would be received over a period of 5 years when £15,000 is invested at 10 per cent.

c If the cash flows of Exhibit 56 are regarded as the future estimated earnings of the investment, then the annual value of the investment is derived from the annual income —the annual charge, i.e. £5,674 − 3,957 = £1,717.

In the above exhibit the amortization sum is shown as an equal annual charge derived from the initial investment cost of £15,000. To present the calculations more appropriately it will be necessary to import an asset content to the £15,000. Therefore the annual charge calculation is shown again in Exhibit 60 where the capital expenditure cost is assumed to be made up of:

1 A machine with a 20-year life, costing £10,000.
2 Equipment with a 5-year life, costing £5,000.

EXHIBIT 60

CALCULATION OF THE ANNUAL CAPITAL CHARGE—II

Depreciation or Amortization	
Machine: £10,000 at £0·0175 per £*	£175
Equipment: £5,000 at £0·1638 per £	819
Interest	
£15,000 at 10 per cent	1,500
ANNUAL CAPITAL CHARGE	£2,494

* Sinking fund calculation:

Reciprocal of PV of £ p.a. for 20 years at 10 per cent	= 0·1175
Less interest factor at 10 per cent	= 0·1
Sinking fund factor	= 0·0175

Comparing the above annual cost of the investment proposal with the discounted annual average of the net cash flows as shown in Exhibit 56, the net annual gains for the investments will be £5,674 − £2,494 = £3,180.

The reader should note that the above comparisons have been made after assuming that the £15,000 capital cost for each investment proposal consisted of a similar mixture of equipment and machinery. Such an assumption was made with the object of showing the calculation of an annual value rating.

Questions for discussion

1. In what way does the 'return' in a return on capital employed calculation differ from the 'return', i.e. net cash flows, used in a time adjusted yield calculation?

2. What do you understand by *incremental* cash flows and by *incremental* capital cost?
3. What are the advantages and disadvantages of the payback criterion in investment evaluation?
4. What is the importance of a corporate long-term plan in influencing the assessment of the worth of alternate investment opportunities?
5. What are the main features of the annual value method of investment appraisal?

Recommended reading

ROCKLEY, L. E., *Capital Investment Decisions*, Business Books, 1968.

BIERMAN, H. and SMIDT, S., *The Capital Budgeting Decision*, Collier-MacMillan, 1966.

BROSTER, E. J., *Appraising Capital Works*, Longmans, 1968.

ARCHER, S. H. and D'AMBROSIO, C. A., *Business Finance Theory and Management*, Collier-MacMillan, 1966.

CHAPTER 9 The Cost of Capital

Introduction

The examination of time-adjusted rates of return and net present values in the previous chapter has been presented as a means of indicating those investments which could be accepted where acceptance implied their being judged from the point of view of profitability. Profitability was measured by a yield of a certain percentage—a rate of return above the minimum requirement laid down by the company's planners. Similarly a positive net present value, when calculated by using a minimum rate of discount, revealed a desirable project whereas a negative net present value showed a project which should be rejected. However, it must be pointed out that to judge proposed capital investments *solely* upon their profitability *rate* is to take a narrow view of corporate development. All investment proposals must be considered in the light of long-term strategic plans for the firm's progress, its future markets and future products. This topic will be discussed in later chapters. It is mentioned here to ensure that the reader does not attribute to the index of choice more than its own intrinsic value. A rate of return is a part only of the whole concept of capital expenditure planning.

The supply of capital

Thus we come to the determination of a minimum cut-off rate for DCF yield or a minimum discounting percentage to be used in an NPV calculation. It is here that we are concerned with what is called the cost of capital. Now a company has many sources of finance; it can, for example:

1 Borrow from the bank.
2 Issue debentures.

3 Increase trade creditors (delay payments).
4 Sell assets.
5 Issue more Ordinary shares.
and/or
6 Use funds generated by profitable operations.

Each of these sources of money can have a different cost. That cost may also change with time, according to the stability or instability of the economy or of trade. Some of the above types of finance have a well defined cost. A loan or overdraft from the bank will carry an interest charge which is fixed having regard, amongst other things, to the current level of the Central Bank rate. Again the level of debenture interest will be affected by the current market rate for long-term loans whilst funds obtained from profitable operations have a lower cost than that of a new issue of shares.[1] These comments indicate that there could be a wildly fluctuating cost of capital over a period of years. On the other hand the cost could well vary even within a short period of *one* year, where it was considered that different investments were being financed by specific allocations of these different types of capital. Nevertheless it is reasonable to suggest that the whole of the corporate financial base should be deemed to be available for each branch of the corporate activities. Thus with certain exceptions[2] the definition of the cost of capital must rest upon some average rate which takes into account the differing costs of the major groups of capital finance.

Before examining the concept of an average cost of capital, two items need to be settled. They are:

1 What is the 'cost' of Ordinary shares?
2 What mix of the total capital supply ought to be used in the calculation?

The cost of Ordinary shares is the reward which must be provided to the Ordinary shareholder to induce him to buy those shares. It has been shown[3] that over the period 1919 to 1966 shareholders would have received a discounted rate of return post-tax of about 6 per cent from a continuous annual investment during this period.

[1] For the influence of tax upon the net cost of loan finance, see page 148.
[2] See pages 152–155.
[3] MERRETT, A. J., and SYKES, A., Return on equities and fixed interest securities, 1919–1963, *District Bank Review*, December 1963. See also *Capital Budgeting and Company Finance* by the same authors, published by Longmans, 1966.

If the shareholder had invested a lump sum then his discounted rate of return would have been about 8 per cent. Furthermore, throughout the period 1919 to 1966 the Ordinary shareholder's real return for 75 per cent of the 10-year cycles was 7 per cent per annum both for the continuous investment and the lump sum investment. The question which begs an answer is whether this kind of performance can be expected to continue. Opinion generally favours the continuance of an 8 per cent *real post-tax* return to shareholders, at least over the next 10 or 20 years. During this coming time the financial manager will need to study the general movement of, for example, share prices and dividends in order to test the maintenance of the Ordinary shareholder's expected rate of return. The reader should remember when studying this concept that the Ordinary shareholder's reward is made up of two elements, namely annual dividends plus a capital growth in terms of an increasing share price. It is this combined return requirement that must be met by the user of subscribed share capital (the company); the better the investing public is served in this way, the easier it will be to raise further capital for future corporate development. A capital investment cut-off rate therefore needs to be set at that level which will ensure a corporate earning power capable of sustaining the Ordinary shareholders' continuing expectance of future rewards of around 8 per cent after tax.[1]

But Ordinary shares do not constitute the whole of the capital supply. Neither do they form the largest element in the total capital structure of companies.[2] Retained earnings, long- and short-term debts such as debentures, bank loans and overdrafts also play a large part in financing business development. Each of these will have a different cost and it is the proportions of these different costs, as

[1] The growth of unit trust and other institutional investment has undoubtedly led to a greater quantity of competitive research into company performance and potential. When this is followed by competitive dealing in shares, it is most likely that the market for shares will stand higher than it otherwise would: the future is more often already discounted. The result of these actions may well be that capital can be raised more cheaply by businesses wishing to expand especially where their market rating, forced up by institutional and research action, portends *profitable* expansion. See *Investment: Art, Science or What?* by Basil Taylor, Lloyds Bank Review (January, 1969).

[2] British companies have found more than two thirds of the capital needed to finance their own growth internally in recent years. In the period 1954–1959 some 70 per cent of the growth of net assets was financed internally: from 1959 to 1963 companies still found 67 per cent of their growth capital.

Amongst the sources of outside finance, issues of Ordinary shares were much the most important of the decade 1954–63 inclusive. 1960 was the best year for Ordinary shares (86 per cent of outside finance) whilst 1962 was the peak year for loan finance (just under 57 per cent). (*Foonote continued on page 147*)

parts of the whole capital supply, that need to be considered. Clearly a company's long term capital structure will change from year to year if only from the growth of retained earnings resulting from each succeeding year's profitable operations. Furthermore, it will be necessary for the company to take up additional permanent capital or long-term loans, from time to time, because its business growth

(Footnote continued from previous page)

Receipts in cash from the issue of loan and share capital (less redemptions)

	Long-term loans, %	Preference shares %	Ordinary shares %
1954	55·1	14·2	30·7
1955	33·7	11·8	54·4
1956	44·1	3·2	52·7
1957	42·9	4·0	53·0
1958	40·7	3·8	55·4
1959	33·4	6·1	60·5
1960	10·2	4·1	85·7
1960[a]	7·7	4·7	87·6
1961[a]	22·9	1·0	76·0
1962[a]	56·9	4·3	38·8
1963[a]	49·0	3·9	47·1

[a] Quoted companies with net assets of £0·5 million or more, or income of £50,000 or more, 1960.
Source: the Financial Times, 1 March, 1966 and Economic Trends. (Reprinted by Permission of Financial Times.)

Subsequent years' figures show the pattern of company external financing to be undergoing a decisive change. Retained earnings have continued to provide between 70 and 75 per cent of the finance required but the impact of the dividend withholding tax (in the Finance Act of 1965) on external financing is shown below:

Receipts in cash from the issue of loan and share capital (less redemptions)

	Long-term loans %	Preference shares %	Ordinary shares %
1963	61·2	3·0	35·8
1964	59·2	2·0	38·8
1965	87·7	—3·5	15·8
1966	74·3	4·2	21·5
1966 (6 months)	67·9	4·2	27·9
1967 (6 months)	89·7	—1·5	11·8

demands further injections of liquid funds in excess of the cash generated by operations. Such expansions of capital finance are rarely effected by the issue of several kinds of share or debt certificates at the same time. It is generally found that a company's financial structure will change by periodic issues of different kinds of long-term capital. Thus the corporate capital structure is not made up of precisely the same proportions of each type of finance in each year. The long-term trend may well present an average picture. Whilst this average picture will vary from trade to trade because of the ability of some businesses to raise a greater proportion of loan money,[1] the concept of a normal capital structure for an individual company is not unreasonable. The question that arises therefore is whether the cost of capital should be calculated having regard to the *long term* intentions of the firm's planners for corporate financing.

Before this question is answered the impact of the various forms of capital upon the whole corporate capital cost must be considered. So long as dividends distributed by a company suffer a withholding tax before payment to the shareholder, then profits not distributed, i.e. retained earnings, will constitute a cheaper form of equity money than new issues of shares. This arises because a shareholder who invests in a new share issue does so out of income which has suffered a tax charge of so much in the £1. Retained earnings do not have to bear this further imposition. For example, if an investor wishes to buy £1,000 worth of shares in a company which is going to use the money, say, for capital expansion, the cost of these shares to the ordinary shareholder would be £1,000 of his income *after tax*. If, however, the shareholder provides this finance by going without dividends, or by receiving lower dividends, the capital expansion will be financed from retained earnings. In this case the cost to the shareholder of financing the expansion will be the £1,000 left with the company less the tax he would have paid on the £1,000 if it had been distributed as dividend. With a tax rate of 8/3d in the £ the shareholder would be surrendering a net receipt of £587·5[2] in order

[1] 'Firms with relatively low risk can afford to secure much, if not most, of their total capital requirements from creditors . . . Firms with higher relative variance in expected earnings must have larger equity contributions. Thus business firms as a group average about 65% equity . . .' ARCHER, S. H., and D'AMBROSIO, C. A., *Business Finance: Theory and Management*, page 521, Collier-MacMillan, 1966.

The reader should consider also the availability of capital assets for mortgaging as security for debt issues. See BIERMAN, H., and SMIDT, S., *The Capital Budgeting Decision*, pages 165–68, Collier-Macmillan, 1966.

[2] £1,000 less 8/3d in the £ means a tax deduction of £412·5 leaving a net receipt of £587·5.

to enable the company to invest £1,000 in corporate expansions. On the other hand if retained earnings are not used for the proposed capital development, then the shareholder would have to receive a gross sum of £1,702 in order to invest, after tax deduction, £1,000 in the company's shares. For this reason retained earnings are able to generate the required 8 per cent (see page 146) return for the company's Ordinary shareholders even though the return demanded from the employment of retained earnings is set lower than that required from the employment of new issue money.

Similar considerations apply to the use of fixed interest loan capital. Whilst the cost of borrowing money has risen considerably in recent years, it is estimated that the gross interest cost of loan financing will be about 6½ to 7 per cent in the long term. The reader will remember (see page 75) that interest on debt is a cost which is charged in the profit and loss account before the determination of profit. Whilst dividends are paid out of *taxed* profits, loan interest is a cost *allowed before the tax on those profits is assessed.* The net cost of loan interest to the company therefore is not 7 per cent but 7 per cent less the tax rate levied on company profits, which gives a net-of-tax cost of 4·025 per cent.[1] Each of these various impacts upon the return a company must seek from its investments needs to be taken into account when considering what has been termed the weighted cost of capital. This concept will now be examined by the calculation of a weighted cost of capital for a hypothetical capital structure.

Weighted cost of capital

For the purpose of the cost of capital assessment it is necessary to postulate a long term capital structure, so that the cost of each type of capital can be given its due influence in calculating the cost of the whole. The assumed capital structure for use in the following examples will be

Ordinary shares, 30 per cent.
Reserves, 50 per cent.
Debentures, 20 per cent.

[1] With corporation tax levied at 42·5 per cent of profits, the net cost of debenture and loan interest is the total interest rate, e.g. 7 per cent, less the reduction which arises because the interest paid will reduce the sum of profit upon which corporation tax is assessed. The tax saving on a 7 per cent interest rate is $7 \times 42{\cdot}5 = 2{\cdot}975$ per cent giving a net cost of $7 - 2{\cdot}975 = 4{\cdot}025$ per cent.

ORDINARY SHARES

Several factors affect the rate to be earned upon this type of capital. Firstly the costs of issue of the shares will be around 3 per cent of the issue price, and in some cases it may be higher even than this. Therefore the share proceeds actually received and employed by the company must gain a return capable of satisfying the *whole* subscription, not just that 97 per cent which is received by the firm after deduction of the issue costs. Furthermore, because dividends payable to shareholders are subjected to a further tax deduction, companies must justify new share issues by earning a return thereon higher than that demanded of retained earnings. This higher rate required of Ordinary shares brings the Ordinary share capital cost into line with the cost to be attributed to retained earnings. In other words the minimum rate required, around 8 per cent, needs to be increased for Ordinary share capital by the net-of-tax percentage which is applied to the income from which the shareholder finances his subscriptions to new share issues. Thus the cost of Ordinary share capital finance is derived from the following.

1 The basic minimum requirement, which is taken to be 8 per cent in real terms.
2 Because of issue costs, the capital actually subscribed will be greater than that received by the firm: assuming the issue costs to be 3 per cent, then the equity must earn 8 × 1·03 = 8·24 per cent in order to cover an 8 per cent return on the gross capital subscribed.
3 The influence of tax upon a shareholder's income results in a company having to justify its equity issues by earnings in excess of the above 8·24 per cent: the increased level of earnings is determined by dividing 8·24 per cent by 0·5875—the net-of-tax rate for shareholder income: this raises the required rate to 14·03 per cent.[1]
4 Finally with a continuous inflation of about 2–3 per cent per annum the shareholder's *real* return can be preserved only if the 14·03 per cent requirement above is increased by the expected future inflation rate: thus if the expected inflation rate is 3 per cent per annum, the final cost of ordinary share capital will be 114·03 × 1·03 − 100 = 17·4 per cent: the reader must realize

[1] With tax at the standard rate of 8/3 in the £.

that 17·4 per cent is the *money* return which Ordinary share capital needs to earn in order to give the shareholder a *real* return after tax of 8 per cent.

RETAINED EARNINGS

1 Again the basic minimum requirement for all forms of equity is taken to be 8 per cent in real terms.
2 As inflation will affect the return to retained earnings in the same way as that for Ordinary shares, the expected money rate of return requirement will be $108 \times 1{\cdot}03 - 100 = 11{\cdot}24$ per cent.[1]

LONG-TERM DEBT

Here the expected interest rate for long-term lenders will be set at 7 per cent per annum and in consequence the cost of capital will be based on that percentage. It must be remembered that 7 per cent is the *money* cost of loan capital and the following calculations determine the *real* cost of debt financing:

1 As with equity issues the cost of issuing debentures will be about 3 per cent of the issue price and the influence of issue costs upon the return required will be $7 \times 1{\cdot}03 = 7{\cdot}21$ per cent.
2 The reader will remember that debenture interest is an expense which is allowed in assessing the amount of the firm's tax liability; therefore the firm will bear 57·5 per cent[2] only of the gross money cost and the net cost will be $7{\cdot}21 \times 57{\cdot}5 = 4{\cdot}15$ per cent. It must be emphasized that this is still a *money* cost of loan capital.

[1] Retained earnings measure the growth in value of a company's equity shares. To the extent that retained earnings are used efficiently and profitably, so will they result in increased Ordinary share prices. Thus with the presence of a Capital Gains Tax those returns produced by retained earnings will contribute to the emergence of a capital gains tax liability when shares are sold at a price higher than their initial cost. For this reason some writers suggest that the minimum cost of retained earnings should be raised by 1·5 per cent to cover this increased liability for tax. Other writers suggest that the market prices of shares have already discounted future tax liabilities for capital gains and that no further variation in the rate requirement should be made.

[2] With Corporation Tax at 42·5 per cent.

3 The impact of inflation must be considered in the same way as for equity capital: to convert this money cost of loan interest to a *real* cost (post tax) for the company 4·15 per cent is divided by the 3 per cent inflation rate, thus 104·15 ÷ 1·03 − 100 = 1·11 per cent.

TOTAL WEIGHTED COST OF CAPITAL

The incorporation of the above factor costs into the total costs of the whole capital supply is demonstrated below:

Type of capital	Real cost %	Money cost %	Weighting	Weighted real cost %	Weighted money cost %
Ordinary shares	14·03	17·40	0·3	4·2	5·22
Retained earnings	8·00	11·24	0·5	4·0	5·62
Loan capital	1·11	4·15	0·2	0·2	0·83
Total weighted cost				8·4	11·67*

* The calculations of the cost of capital to the second decimal place have been done for precise demonstration only. In practical business circumstances no company would specify its cost of capital cut-off rate in these terms. A higher whole figure should be specified.

Cost of capital application

The relevance of the post-tax weighted money costs and weighted real costs of capital concerns the method of forecasting. The various influences of inflation on cost and income groups is dealt with more fully in Chapter 10 but it will be sufficient for the moment to emphasize the following:

1 The money cost of capital should be used where forecasts are compiled in money terms.

2 The real cost of capital should be used where forecasts are compiled having regard to the influences of inflation on the

various factor cost and income groups which are the determinants of a project's expected future performance.

Now the question was put on page 148 asking whether the costs of capital should be calculated on the basis of a planned long-term capital structure, or whether the cost of capital should be determined so as to reflect every change in the proportions of the whole capital supply. It is to be expected that a company would have a planned pattern of growth and that it would be always enlarging its long-term finance within the planned growth pattern. If this is so then the weighted costs of capital should be based upon that planned capital structure even though there will be periodic divergences from the precise pattern as the firm develops from one level of capital size to the next higher level. This is a view which is expressed frequently on the subject of the corporate costs of capital.

However, practice has its own divergences. The writer has discussed with many financial managers the problems of capital supply and the measurement of corporate efficiency. Several of the best growth companies in the UK take the view that the cost of capital must be based upon the cost of equity shares only: any method of financing which ensures a lower cost of capital just increases the profitability of operations. Thus whilst the cost of Ordinary share capital determined as above is used as the firm's cost of capital, any project-financing that utilizes loan capital or retained earnings still has to meet the minimum earning rate required by equity shares. A further restriction on the use of the weighted cost of capital refers to the situation where a project being appraised is so large as to need a special supply of finance to support it. In such cases, and particularly where the project is of such a size as to bring about a considerable change in the firm's total asset structure, then the cost of capital should be the cost of that finance specially raised to meet the cost of establishing the project.

Other reservations concerning the use of the weighted cost must now be referred to. It is suggested that such weighted costs should be reserved for *relatively* risk free investments. The basic 8 per cent which started the whole calculation is based upon *average* returns to the ordinary shareholder over a period of 47 years and it must therefore reflect an *average* experience of risk. Consequently, where a project is thought to have inherent risks greater than the average it is suggested that a premium should be added to the weighted cost of capital requirement to cover that risk. Here the capital planner departs from the facts of

1 A historical rate of return received by Ordinary shareholders.
2 The current level of taxation on incomes.
3 The recent historical experience of the annual rates of inflation.

which have been used in the assessment of the weighted cost of capital. Upon a reasonable basis of fact is superimposed an element of judgement. In many cases the experienced businessman's judgement will be the most valuable factor in investment appraisal. However, the application of practices for the analysis of risk and uncertainty will show more clearly (see Chapter 11) the potential risk element in that a *probability* of loss or gain can be quantified. Here at least the decision-maker can see the measured extent of the risks involved and can compare them with the expected most likely returns for the project. In this way the presence of risk can be brought into the decision and can affect a choice between alternative investments.

Again there are circumstances where the aim of best available profitability from alternative business opportunities may be set aside where it is considered that other objectives are temporarily paramount. These other objectives may include the desire for a specific rate of growth[1] or a larger market share or may refer to the provision of welfare amenities for company employees, etc. On the other hand a higher return than the weighted cost of capital may be necessary when the company does not intend to raise capital (or cannot) to satisfy the demands of all available investment opportunities. These circumstances will be found where the proprietors or directors do not wish to go to the market for money because they fear that they may suffer some loss of control of their business—an experience of numerous private limited companies.[2] Finally the power of all

[1] The form of growth is not specified here but may include growth of asset size, sales, share price or earnings per share, etc.

[2] The writer has encountered, recently, several private limited companies which were operating quite efficiently. The demand for the products, both for the home market and abroad, was strong. It appeared that output could be increased, with profit, if the necessary finance for expansion had been forthcoming. The directors could not subscribe the necessary finance themselves because '. . . the high level of taxation did not leave enough money for the individual . . .' to enable them to invest the *total* quantity of finance required. At the same time they did not intend going to the equity issues market because they could see that such action would weaken *their* control of *their* '*own*' company.

companies to make profit from capital investment must rest with its managerial ability to *manage* their projects *profitably*. Any shortage of the right management calibre will limit the company's ability to run its affairs at the most efficient level: such a limitation will therefore restrict the company's power to expand through accepting all the investment opportunities which come its way. It should undertake those projects only which it can effectively and efficiently manage, no matter what returns are forecast.

Objects of cost-of-capital determination

Any discussion of the cost of capital would be inadequate without some reference to the object of the calculations. Business activity must be directed to profitability, for profitability is necessary for corporate continuance and for all the other non-profitable activities to be sustained. Whilst operational incomes and costs can be identified, within the limits of the power to forecast events, it must be remembered that a normal profitability statement does not include the costs of dividends or of loan interest. Therefore the rate of profit generation which is forecasted for a proposal needs to be sufficient to pay the costs of financing at least. It is for this reason that a cost-of-capital yardstick is assessed to show how a proposal's expected rate of return matches with the cost of getting the money to finance that proposal. The financial manager should be concerned with assessing the right cost of capital and choosing the right criteria of investment evaluation. His advice on these topics needs to be well informed advice in order that the directing managers can choose that investment pattern which will enable the company to achieve the objectives of its long-term plans. It is in this context that the cost of capital is so important: it is for this reason that its impact on investment worth must be studied.

Exhibit 61 shows a profile of net present values of the net cash flows of a project. The net present values are calculated at varying rates of discount from 5 to 25 per cent.

At the point where the profile crosses (A) the line of investment cost, the yield is given by the corresponding discount rate on the horizontal axis OX. If at this stage the cost of capital is assumed to be 10 per cent, then the NPV of the proposal is measured by the line BC. The financial value of the NPV, shown on the OY axis, represents the

EXHIBIT 61

PROFILE OF NET PRESENT VALUES—I

Rates	5% £	10% £	15% £	20% £	25% £
Discounted NCFs.	2,723	2,487	2,283	2,107	1,952
Investment cost	2,200	2,200	2,200	2,200	2,200
Net present values	523	287	83	−93	−248

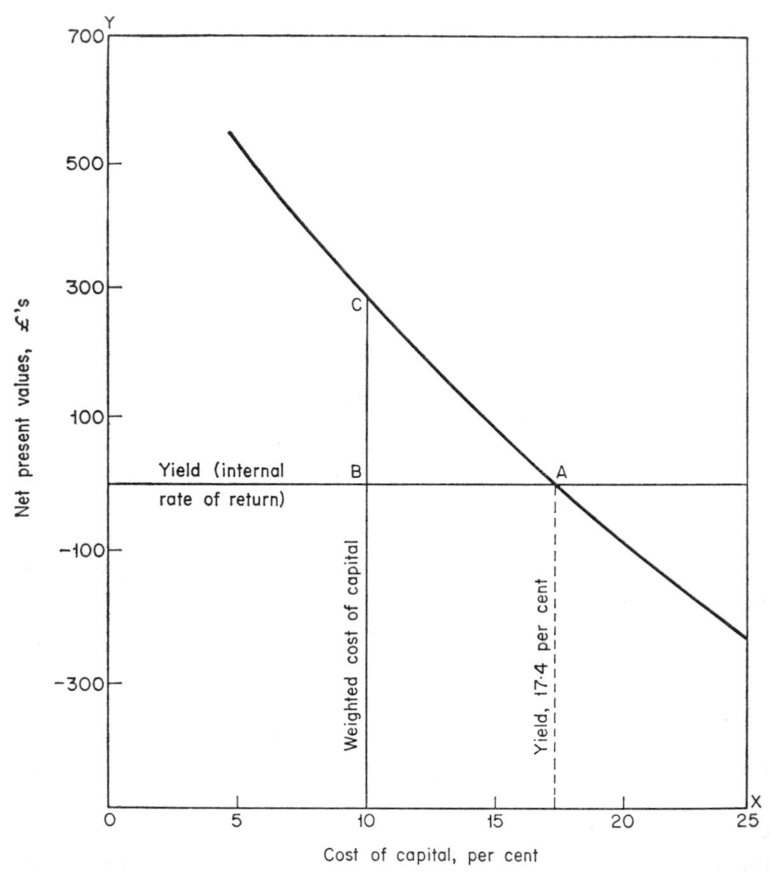

growth in wealth which would accrue to the firm as a result of implementing the investment.

Exhibit 62 gives details of the discounted net cash flows, initial investment costs and net present values of three separate investment proposals. These data of project returns have again been discounted at varying rates from 5 to 25 per cent. The resultant profiles of net present worths are then displayed on the graph in Exhibit 63. Here

EXHIBIT 62

PROJECT RETURNS WITH VARYING COSTS OF CAPITAL—I

Project	Details	Cost of capital				
		5%	10%	15%	20%	25%
		£	£	£	£	£
A	Discounted NCF's	15,443	12,289	10,038	8,385	7,141
	Investment cost	10,000	10,000	10,000	10,000	10,000
	Net present values	5,443	2,289	38	−1,615	−2,859
B	Discounted NCF's	23,165	18,434	15,056	12,578	10,712
	Investment cost	13,000	13,000	13,000	13,000	13,000
	Net present values	10,165	5,434	2,056	−422	−2,288
C	Discounted NCF's	30,887	24,578	20,075	16,770	14,282
	Investment cost	16,000	16,000	16,000	16,000	16,000
	Net present values	14,887	8,578	4,075	770	−1,718

the reader can see the discounted cash flow yield and the net present value for each project (if the cost of capital remains at 10 per cent). Clearly project C has a higher value, for both yield and NPV, than B: furthermore B has higher values than A. Whichever cost of capital is chosen or calculated for the company, the above order of preference will be maintained. The only feature to vary will be the net present values, because these emerge from the application of different discounting, i.e. cost of capital, rates.

Two further examples are examined in Exhibit 64 where future cash flows of two potential investments are discounted at rates varying from 5 to 30 per cent. Again the sequence of net present values are represented in profile form on a graph in Exhibit 65. The importance of correct determination of the cost of financing is emphasized here when yields and NPV's are calculated. The yields of A and B are shown to be 28·1 and 23·4 per cent, respectively. By

EXHIBIT 63

PROFILES OF NET PRESENT VALUES—II

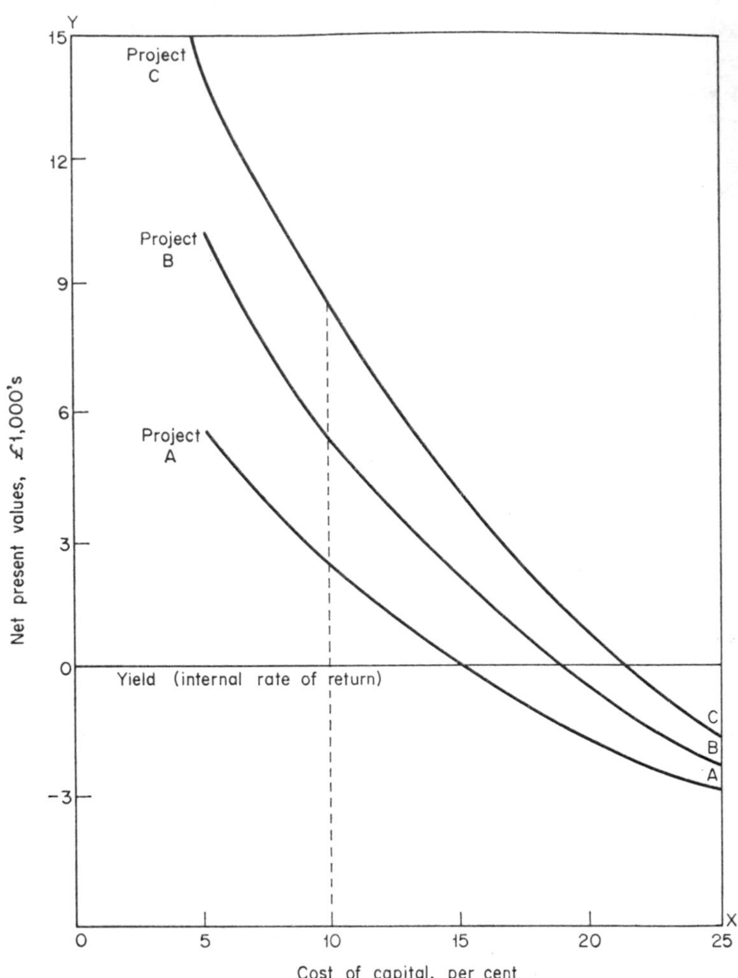

this criterion of measurement, A is shown to be superior to B when the constraints of corporate policy are removed from a comparative evaluation.

In these circumstances project A would be chosen rather than project B. However, if the cost of capital is assessed at 10 per cent,

EXHIBIT 64

PROJECT RETURNS WITH VARYING COSTS OF CAPITAL—II

		Cost of capital					
Project	Details	5%	10%	15%	20%	25%	30%
		£	£	£	£	£	£
	Discounted NCF's	2,749	2,538	2,360	2,205	2,072	1,954
A	Investment cost	2,000	2,000	2,000	2,000	2,000	2,000
	Net present values	749	538	360	205	72	−46
	Discounted NCF's	3,379	2,888	2,496	2,177	1,917	1,699
B	Investment cost	2,000	2,000	2,000	2,000	2,000	2,000
	Net present values	1,379	888	496	177	−83	−301

then from the graph and from the data in Exhibit 64 it can be seen that the NPV of A is £538 whilst that of B is £888. On *this* basis project B will generate a greater growth in wealth for the company than A: B ought therefore to be chosen rather than A, when the cost of capital is 10 per cent.

EXHIBIT 65

PROFILES OF NET PRESENT VALUES—III

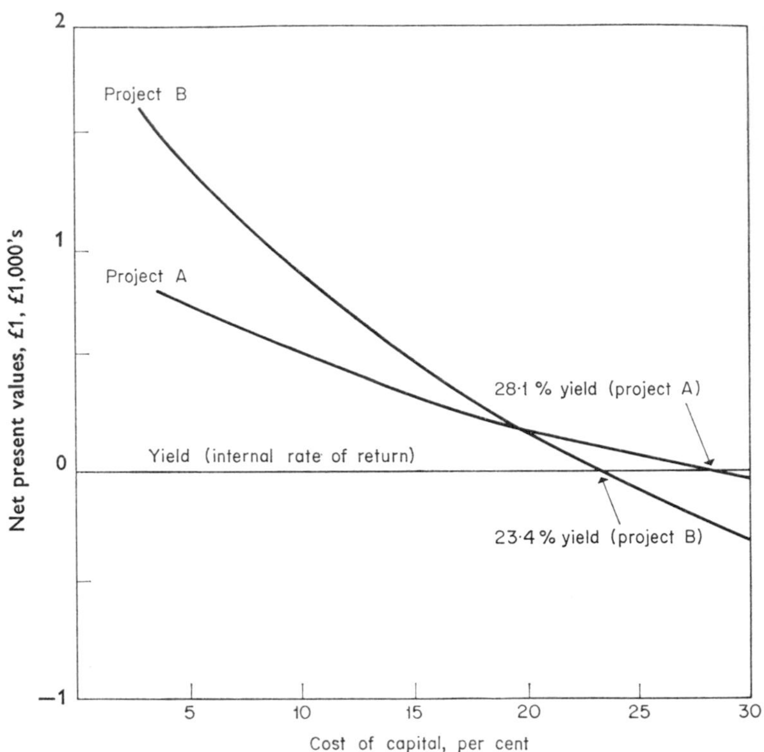

In fact, for any cost of capital up to 19 per cent, project B is superior to A: beyond that discounting rate the reverse position arises. The changing fortunes of these two investment proposals arise from the nature of their cash flows, which are given in Exhibit 66. These time periods of cash flows show that it takes four years before A and B are roughly equal in total cash receipts: for years 1, 2 and 3 project A

EXHIBIT 66

PROJECT NET CASH FLOWS

Project	Investment cost Year 0	Net cash flows Year 1	2	3	4	5
	£	£	£	£	£	£
A	2,000	2,000	250	250	250	250
B	2,000	400	600	800	1,000	1,200

earns higher aggregate cash returns than B. Such a pattern of returns will always be influenced to a lesser extent by the higher discount rates than by lower rates. Thus at rates in excess of 19 per cent, proposal A is more acceptable than B.

Cut-off rates

The lesson involved in Exhibits 64 and 65 concerns not the importance of the cost of capital only, but also the criterion of choice. It is pointed out that both criteria (yield and NPV) give the same answer to a question of whether or not to invest. The answer would be 'yes' in both cases assuming that the cost of capital was set at any rate of discount up to 23 per cent. From the point of ranking the investments in order of preference, however, NPV has the advantage: the growth *sum* is revealed and the *rate* of growth can be determined. The appreciation of NPV's value stems from a clear knowledge and understanding of the cost of capital. It is this concept which has forced the issue of choosing between yield and NPV.

Perhaps the main use of the cost-of-capital rate for each firm relates to the policy of identifying acceptable investment projects. It is suggested that the cost of finance must represent the minimum level of return for a project, if it is to receive the 'go ahead' from the firm's directing managers. Whilst the minimum return may be set in this way, it does not necessarily mean that enough projects will be sought and approved in each year, until the marginal project just covers its cost of financing as promulgated in the cut-off rate. This is because the net cash flows of investment proposals are the final outcomes of numerous estimates of incomes and costs. Many of these estimates will be based on very sound premises: others may well be pure aspirations.[1] The point is that the forecasted rate of return will rarely be achieved so precisely. Thus to safeguard against losses which could arise from imperfect forecasts, investment approval procedures frequently propound a cut-off rate higher than the arithmetically determined cost of finance.[2] The point at which the company's policy makers fix the cut-off rate will depend upon the cost of finance and upon other matters of policy also. For example, the available time of top management is limited: if managerial time is dispersed over too many projects, the efficiency of control and direction will eventually decline. Therefore the company's directing managers recognize the need to use top management's time to the best advantage. This best advantage will not be secured if too much time and thought is concerned with an overlarge investment programme.[3]

A high cut-off rate may also be adopted because of limited liquid resources but at the same time it may discourage profitable proposals which do not attain the required exalted return. The higher is set the ante for investment proposals to overcome, the greater will be the danger that proposals of real urgency relating to the improvement of existing operations may be postponed. For management to be constantly delaying capital expenditures until the *high* return is obtained might result in investments being postponed until present equipment is so inefficient that the profitability of any investment must rise considerably. To reach this stage, however, the years of operating inefficient assets will have caused reduced profits and increasingly uncompetitive outputs.

On the other hand, a low cut-off rate needs to be examined within the context of opportunity cost—can the company use some of its cash resources on more profitable ventures elsewhere on the industrial scene? While a low cut-off rate for proposed investments should not cause the company to suffer from a stifling of new ideas or

[1] See Chapter 11 on the analysis of risk and uncertainty.

[2] Rockley, L. E., *Capital Investment Decisions*, pages 56–7, Business Books, 1968.

[3] Especially if that programme is made overlarge by accepting projects of low returns, even if these low returns are still just above the cost of capital. If managerial control declines, so eventually will the total return on capital employed. A decline in the total return may eventually result in a reduction of the dividend paid to shareholders or at least it will affect the growth of the total shareholders' interest. Results such as these would cause the market price of the company's shares to fall and up will go the cost of capital.

proposals for capital spending, it becomes much more important that capital expenditure proposals should be subjected to a precise appraisal of expected benefits. The margin of error is reduced when the cut-off rate is reduced. The determination and use of an investment proposal cut-off rate needs continual re-assessment. It should be used mainly as a moderator between investment opportunities coming forward, the availability of funds to meet those opportunities, and the quantity and quality of management capable of directing the projects during and after installation. It is here that data on the cost of capital is so pertinent to policy making.

Questions for discussion

1. What are the various sources of finance available to a public limited company?
2. What do you understand by the term 'capital' when it is used in the context of business financing?
3. What determines the cost of capital for a company?
4. Does debt-financing lower the cost of capital?
5. Would you use the cost of capital as a cut-off rate in proposal evaluation? In what circumstances would you vary the cut-off rate?
6. Is there a case for using the cost of equity capital only (rather than a weighted cost of capital) in evaluating investment proposals?
7. To what extent do you consider that: (*a*) a stable dividend policy; (*b*) a rising P/E ratio, will influence the cost of capital of a firm and consequently its future investment programme?

Recommended reading

HOWE, M., British company finance: a panoramic view, *Certified Accountant's Journal*, November and December 1968.

WRIGHT, F. K., Investment criteria and the cost of capital, *Journal of Management Studies*, Volume 4, No. 3, October 1967.

PANNI, A. K., The realities of capital budgeting, *Business Management (UK)*, September 1967.

ALLEN, F. B., Does going into debt lower the cost of capital?, *The Analyst's Journal*, August 1954.

DEAN, J., *Capital Budgeting*, Chapters 3 and 4, Columbia University Press, 1951.

CHAPTER 10 Analysis of Project Returns

Introduction

The application of discounting techniques to the appraisal of capital expenditure proposals will now be displayed in a series of examples. Each case studied shows the net present value of the proposal using 10 per cent as the firm's cost of capital: yield ratings are also shown and the reader should remember that a project can be regarded as acceptable provided that:

1 The net cash flows give a positive net present value when they are discounted at the given cost of capital.

and/or

2 The yield rating is in excess of the cost of capital percentage.

Again the importance of corporate long term objectives must be stressed. All investments, whatever their NPV or yield, need to be directed towards fulfilling the company's strategic plans. The appraisal indices, which are used to indicate the worthwhileness of a proposal, do not of themselves select those proposals which are to be implemented. The criteria of investment appraisal are only aids for the decision-maker when he faces problems of choice between, and preferential ordering of, a selection of available investment opportunities.

Investment profiles

Three investment projects A, B and C are detailed in Exhibits 67, 68 and 69, respectively. By using the discounting tables at pages 241–249 the reader will be able to verify the calculations of yield and NPV for

EXHIBIT 67—PROJECT A

INVESTMENT COST £15,000

Year of life	NCF's	Interest factor, 10%	Present value of NCF's	Interest factor, 15%	Present value of NCF's	Interest factor, 20%	Present value of NCF's
	£		£		£		£
1	2,000	0·9091	1,818·2	0·8696	1,739·2	0·8333	1,666·6
2	3,000	0·8264	2,479·2	0·7561	2,268·3	0·6944	2,083·2
3	4,000	0·7513	3,005·2	0·6575	2,630·0	0·5787	2,314·8
4	5,000	0,6830	3,415·0	0·5718	2,859·0	0·4823	2,411·5
5	6,000	0·6209	3,725·4	0·4972	2,983·2	0·4019	2,411·4
6	7,000	0·5645	3,951·5	0·4323	3,026·1	0·3349	2·344·3
TOTALS	£27,000		£18,394·5		£15,505·8		£13,231·8

Net present value at 10% cost of capital = £3,394·5

Yield, by interpolation $= 15 + \left(\frac{505{\cdot}8}{2{,}274} \times \frac{5}{100}\right) =$ 16·1 per cent

EXHIBIT 68—PROJECT B

INVESTMENT COST £15,000

Year of life	NCF's	Interest factor, 10%	Present value of NCF's	Interest factor, 20%	Present value of NCF's	Interest factor, 30%	Present value of NCF's
	£		£		£		£
1	7,000	0·9091	6,363·7	0·8333	5,833·1	0·7692	5,384·4
2	6,000	0·8264	4,958·4	0·6944	4,166·4	0·5917	3,550·2
3	5,000	0·7513	3,756·5	0·5787	2,893·5	0·4552	2,276·0
4	4,000	0·6830	2,732·0	0·4823	1,929·2	0·3501	1,400·4
5	3,000	0·6209	1,862·7	0·4019	1,205·7	0·2693	807·9
6	2,000	0·5645	1,129·0	0·3349	669·8	0·2072	414·4
TOTALS	£27,000		£20,802·3		£16,697·7		£13,833·3

Net present value at 10% cost of capital = £5802·3

Yield, by interpolation $= 20 + \left(\frac{1697{\cdot}7}{2864{\cdot}4} \times \frac{10}{100}\right) =$ 25·9 per cent

EXHIBIT 69—PROJECT C

INVESTMENT COST £15,000

Year of life	NCF's per year	Interest factor, 10%	Present value of NCF's	Interest factor, 15%	Present value of NCF's	Interest factor, 20%	Present value of NCF's
	£		£		£		£
6	4,500	4·3553	19,598·8	3·7845	18,030·2	3·3255	14,964·7

Net present value at 10% cost of capital = £4598·8

Yield, by interpolation $= 15 + \left(\frac{3030\cdot2}{3065\cdot5} \times \frac{5}{100}\right) =$ 19·9 per cent

each of the three proposals. Their net cash flows have been discounted at the percentage rate shown at the head of the 'Interest factor' column. Now for determination of a yield rating, the object of discounting is to find that percentage discount which will reduce the future net cash flows until they equal the capital cost of the investment (see Appendix C). For project A, it is evident that a 15 per cent rate of discount is not a high enough *rate of charge*, for the present value of the future cash flows is greater than the initial investment outlay.[1] Therefore a higher rate must be chosen and at 20 per cent the resultant present value total is lower than the cost of the investment, showing that 20 per cent is too high a rate of charge. In these circumstances DCF yield must fall between the two rates tested and interpolation reveals the result to be 16·1 per cent. In each of the Exhibits, the future cash flows have been discounted at a 10 per cent rate (the cost of capital) in order to ascertain the NPV for each proposal.

Project C earns net cash returns of £4,500 in each year of its life. With uniform cash flows, such as those found in C, it is not necessary to calculate *separately* the present value of *each year's* flows in order to determine the total present value of the whole cash flows of the project. A single interest factor, which represents the present worth of £1 per year for each of the six years, is used in this case. Reference to the interest tables on page 246 shows that the factor for a six-year life at 10 per cent discount is 4·3553. Now this single interest factor equals the sum of the individual factors for each of the years during which the proposal is expected to generate net cash flows of £4,500. Thus for investments producing equal annual cash flows, the calculations are greatly reduced. Furthermore, location of the yield percentage is easier. A DCF yield rating results from a comparison of an investment's initial cost with its net cash flow returns. It is determined by finding out the value for r in the following equation:

$$C = \frac{A_1}{(1+r)} + \frac{A_2}{(1+r)^2} + \frac{A_3}{(1+r)^3} + \ldots + \frac{A_n}{(1+r)^n}$$

where C is the investment cost,

A the net cash flows in each year up to n years,

r the rate of discount and

n the number of years.

[1] Another way of explaining this point would be to say that the returns to the investment can support a higher interest charge in order to finance the project.

If the net cash flows are the same amount in every year of the proposal's operating life, the equation can be written as

$$\frac{C}{A} = \frac{1}{(1+r)} + \frac{1}{(1+r)^2} + \frac{1}{(1+r)^3} + \ldots + \frac{1}{(1+r)^n}$$

Now the answer to the right-hand side of the equation produces that interest factor which is equal to the sum derived from dividing the investment's initial cost by its uniform annual net cash flow amount. Applying the method to project C above we have

$$\frac{15{,}000}{4{,}500} = 3{\cdot}3333$$

This solution represents the factor of interest for a six-year life, where a project's future net cash flows are equated with its original cost of installation. By examining Table B (pages 247–248) and looking along the line of interest factors for a six-year life, the reader will see that the amount 3·3333 falls between interest rates of 18 and 20 per cent. It follows therefore that the yield will fall between 18 and 20 per cent: in fact the calculations at the foot of Exhibit 69 show the yield to be 19·9 per cent.

The work involved in finding out the percentage yield can be simplified in another way. Exhibit 70 is a form which can be used by clerical staff to ascertain a yield rating. Discount factors for percentages from 4 to 30 are printed on the form: in the second column under the heading 'actual' should be entered:

1 The capital cost in year 0.
2 The estimated future net cash flows in years 1 to 6.

Interest factors shown under the various percentages must be multiplied by the forcasted flows. Thereby present values of the project's net cash flows in each year of its forecast life are produced. It is then a simple matter to ascertain the NPV's of the investment at given costs of capital. The squared section of the form is provided for drawing a profile line of the NPV's which were produced by the calculations in the top half of the document. A vertical scale must be devised for the NPV data of the investment proposal which is being studied. When the profile is drawn on the graph, the point at which it intersects the horizontal line of a nil NPV can be read on the horizontal scale as the DCF yield.

EXHIBIT 70

PROJECT APPRAISAL BY DCF YIELD

PROJECT ....

Year	Net cash flow, £										
	Actual	4%		10%		15%		20%		30%	
		Factor	Present value	Factor	Present value	Factor	Present value	Factor	Present value	Factor	Present value
0		1.00		1.00		1.00		1.00		1.00	
1		0.962		0.909		0.870		0.833		0.769	
2		0.925		0.826		0.756		0.694		0.592	
3		0.889		0.751		0.658		0.579		0.455	
4		0.855		0.683		0.572		0.482		0.350	
5		0.822		0.621		0.497		0.402		0.269	
6		0.790		0.565		0.432		0.335		0.207	
NPV											

PRESENT VALUE PROFILE

Net present values, £

0 10 15 20 30

Discount, %

Exhibit 71 below shows a form completed in respect of project A.

A study of project worth can be greatly aided by the profile method. Exhibit 72 displays net present value profiles for each of

EXHIBIT 71

PROJECT APPRAISAL BY DCF YIELD

PROJECT ....

Year	Net cash flow, £											
	Actual	4%		10%		15%		20%		30%	
		Factor	Present value	Factor	Present value	Factor	Present value	Factor	Present value	Factor	Present value
0	(15,000)	1.00		1.00	(15,000)	1.00	(15,000)	1.00	(15,000	1.00	
1	2,000	0.962		0.909	1,818	0.870	1,740	0.833	1,666	0.769	
2	3,000	0.925		0.826	2,478	0.756	2,268	0.694	2,082	0.592	
3	4,000	0.889		0.751	3,004	0.658	2,632	0.579	2,316	0.455	
4	5,000	0.855		0.683	3,415	0.572	2,860	0.482	2,410	0.350	
5	6,000	0.822		0.621	3,726	0.497	2,982	0.402	2,412	0.269	
6	7,000	0.790		0.565	3,955	0.432	3,024	0.335	2,345	0.207	
NPV					£3,396		£506		(£1,769)		

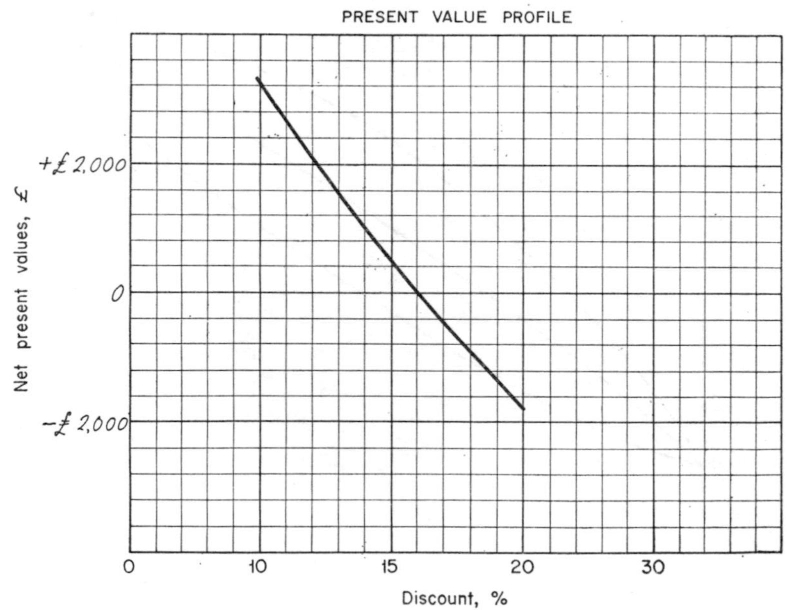

the projects A, B and C which have been discussed in this chapter. Each profile is based on the data in the table at the head of the

EXHIBIT 72

PROJECTS A, B, AND C YEARLY NPV PROFILES

Years	A	B	C
	£	£	£
1	(13,182)	(8,636)	(10,909)
2	(10,703)	(3,678)	(7,190)
3	(7,698)	78	(3,809)
4	(4,283)	2,810	(736)
5	(558)	4,673	2,058
6	3,393	5,802	4,598
YIELDS	16·1%	25·9%	19·9%

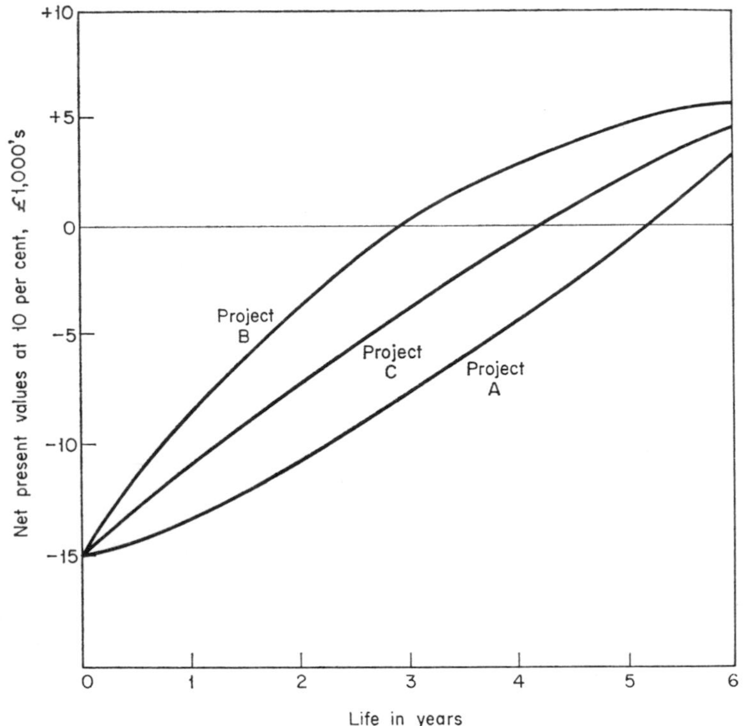

exhibit: the table shows the NPV of each investment at the *end of each year* of its expected economic life. Clearly the figures given for year 6 must equal the NPV for each investment, and the reader can verify this by referring to the exhibits on pages 165–167. The table of data also records the expected DCF yield for each project. The important element revealed by *these* NPV profiles concerns the point of intersection of the zero line by the profile line. When related to the horizontal scale, the point of intersection shows the discounted payback period in years for each project. Conclusions which can be drawn from the exhibit include:

1 Project B has a risk period of approximately 3 years: its net present value up to that point is a negative quantity.
2 Project C has a risk period of approximately 4·3 years.
3 Project A has a risk period of approximately 5·2 years.
4 At the time when project B passes from being a wholly risk project into the profit-making stage, project A still has over £7,600 of unrecovered capital expenditure at risk.

Influence of taxation and other allowances

Projects A, B and C were easy proposals to assess, and ranking them in an order of desirability presents few problems—if they are to be graded according to their respective profitabilities. The evaluation of an investment's net cash flows is not always so straightforward, however. Net cash flows refer to the cash flow *changes* resulting from implementing a proposal and it is essential that the *cash flow changes remaining with the company* are used in the investment appraisal. Therefore it is the *after-tax* gains of an investment which are vital to correct evaluation. This means that where grants are received towards the cost of a project, the amount of the grant and the timing of its receipt should be brought into the appraisal. Similarly annual capital allowances[1] which are given in consequence of certain capital expenditures and which operate to reduce the amount of tax on company profits, must be included in the assessment of an investment's expected rate of return.

Thus in the next series of investment examples, the influence of grants and writing down allowances will be studied. The reader must recognize that taxation rates, allowances and grants change frequently. The important point is that the influence, on investment worth, of net cash flows after tax is appreciated. When these after tax, after grant influences on net cash flows are fully understood

[1] Now called writing-down allowances.

and when the methods by which these allowances are brought to the investment appraisal are followed, then future variations in investment incentives, i.e. tax allowances, can be brought to the account also.

Project D

The Alpha Manufacturing Company, Limited, has decided to make a new product which is expected to have a marketable life of six years. The life of this product should be adequate, for it will enable the development of longer term plans in this particular field. Other products should be fully tested in time for their release to the public in about six years' time. Machinery and equipment for production are estimated to cost £32,000 whilst the net cash flows arising from the project should be £7,000 in each of the six years of the expected life of the investment. An investment grant of 20 per cent will be received in consequence of expenditure on machinery and equipment. This machinery should have a disposable value of £3,000 at the end of its life. Taxation writing down allowances for the plant will be at the rate of 20 per cent per annum and corporation tax is currently levied at 42·5 per cent. The company assesses its cost of capital at 12 per cent and the board would like to know if the project is worth implementing on the basis of its forecast profitability.

In order to emphasize the importance of grants and allowances in the final outcome of a proposal's profitability rating, it is proposed in the first instance to evaluate the project *without* considering these incentives.

EVALUATION I

		£
Capital cost of investment proposal:		32,000
Net cash flows: present values at 10 per cent discount rate:		
Years 1 to 6: £7,000 × 4·355	=	30,485
Year 6: £3,000 × 0·565	=	1,695
Total present value of future NCF's at 10 per cent		£32,180

Net cash flows: present values at 15 per cent discount rate:

			£
Years 1 to 6:	£7,000 × 3·785	=	26,495
Year 6:	£3,000 × 0·432	=	1,296

Total present value of future NCF's at 15 per cent £27,791

By interpolation the yeild is found to be

$$10 + \left(\frac{180}{4{,}389} \times \frac{5}{100}\right) = \underline{10{\cdot}2 \text{ per cent}}$$

With a result showing a yield which is less than the assessed cost of capital, the proposal should be rejected (on grounds of insufficient profitability). Each of the above interest factors can be verified from the interest tables on pages 241–249. Here the reader will notice that the expected scrap sale value of the machinery is shown as a cash receipt at the end of the expected life of the project. To introduce the grant element to an evaluation, the next appraisal will reduce the capital cost to the company by £6,400—the value of the grant which was stated to be 20 per cent of the machinery, etc., cost.

EVALUATION 2

	£
Capital cost of the investment proposal:	32,000
Less, investment grant of 20 per cent:	6,400
Net cost of the investment	£25,600

Net cash flows: present values at 15 per cent discount rate:

See Evaluation 1; total present values £27,791

Net cash flows: present values at 24 per cent discount rate:

			£
Years 1 to 6:	£7,000 × 3·021	=	21,147
Year 6:	£3,000 × 0·275	=	825
			£21,972

By interpolation the yield is found to be

$$15 + \left(\frac{2,191}{5,819} \times \frac{9}{100}\right) = \underline{18{\cdot}4 \text{ per cent}}$$

The mere fact of introducing a grant has increased the yield calculation by 80 per cent. The evaluation method is still open to criticism however for the grant of £6,400 will not be received until approximately 1 year after installation of the machinery. To achieve a satisfactory comparison of future net cash flows with investment cost, all incomes and costs must be expressed in present day values. The grant sum should therefore be discounted at the cost of capital for one year. Furthermore the net capital expenditure on plant and equipment will attract further allowances which will operate to reduce the company's profits assessable to tax. Finally the income gained from installing the project represents an increase of profit upon which corporation tax at 42·5 per cent will be payable. The next evaluation of the worthwhileness of project D will take all of these factors into account.

EVALUATION 3

	£
Capital cost of the investment proposal:	32,000
Less, 20 per cent grant received after one year: discounted at the cost of capital = £6,400 × 0·893:	5,715
	£26,285

After-tax returns

The process of determining the proposal's after-tax net cash flows, and their timing is demonstrated in Exhibits 73 and 74. The first of these two exhibits deals with writing-down allowances. Now revenue expenses of running a business and earning a profit are accepted as a proper charge against income *in the year in which the revenue expense is incurred.* On the other hand, costs of capital goods are not allowed in this way. Expenses of buying capital assets are accepted as proper charges against income *over the years of life of the asset.*[1] This means

[1] The tax effects upon a company's net profit are dealt with here in the simplest possible way. The reader will recognize that a detailed explanation of a tax assessment on company profits would be out of place in this book. Furthermore it would not add much to the general understanding of the *principles of investment evaluation,* which are being presented in the ensuing examples.

that a part of the total capital cost is allowed against profit in each year of the asset's economic life. Calculation of each year's portion of the capital cost is completed by using certain percentage allowances specified by Inland Revenue. Exhibit 73 shows how these allowances are assessed where the approved rate of depreciation is 20 per cent: column 4, the annual allowance for the year is calculated by taking 20 per cent of the amount shown in column 3.

EXHIBIT 73

WRITTEN-DOWN VALUES AND WRITING-DOWN ALLOWANCES (WITH 20 PER CENT INVESTMENT GRANT)

Year (1)	Details (2)	Written-down values at 1 January (3)	Annual writing-down allowances for each year (4)	Tax saved by annual allowances (Corporation Tax 42·5%) (5)
		£	£	£
1	Capital cost, net of investment grant, i.e. £32,000 – £6,400	25,600	5,120	2,176
2	Calculation of year's allowances	20,480*	4,096	1,741
3	ditto	16,384	3,277	1,393
4	ditto	13,107	2,621	1,114
5	ditto	10,486	2,097	891
6	ditto	8,389	1,678	713
	Balancing allowance £3,711, i.e. written down value £6,711 less scrap value £3,000	6,711	3,711	1,577
	TOTALS		£22,600	£9,605

* Written-down values in any year result from the reduction of the *previous year's* capital allowance from *that year's* commencing balance.

Because these writing-down allowances are accepted as proper reductions of profit assessable to tax, so there will be a reduction of the amount of Corporation Tax to be paid. The precise amount of tax relief is found by multiplying the capital allowance figure by the Corporation Tax rate and column 5 gives the answer. Exhibit 74 below brings together the extra tax charges on the additional income (net cash flows), and the tax reductions resulting from the capital allowances: Exhibit 75 then completes the evaluation of project profitability.

EXHIBIT 74

CALCULATION OF POST-TAX NET CASH FLOWS
(CORPORATION TAX: 42·5 PER CENT)

Year (1)	NCF's (2)	Corporation Tax on previous year's NCF's (3)	Tax saved by annual allowances (4)	Post-tax NCF's (5)
	£	£	£	£
1	7,000	—	—	7,000
2	7,000	(2,975)	2,176	6,201
3	7,000	(2,975)	1,741	5,766
4	7,000	(2,975)	1,393	5,418
5	7,000	(2,975)	1,114	5,139
6	7,000 3,000*	(2,975)	891	7,916
7		(2,975)	731 1,577	(685)
TOTALS	£45,000	£(17,850)	£9,605	£36,755

* This amount represents the forecasted receipts from sale of the proposal's assets at the end of life. Such sums are capital receipts and although not shown as bearing tax in column 3, £3,000 has been taken into account in assessing the balancing allowance of £3,711 in Exhibit 73.

With a capital cost of £26,285 (see page 176) the yield is found, by interpolation, to be

$$10 + \left(\frac{543}{3{,}441} \times \frac{5}{100}\right) = 10{\cdot}8 \text{ per cent}$$

Whilst the post-tax return is shown to be 10·8 per cent it must be remembered that this return is calculated where Corporation Tax is levied at 42·5 per cent. With a tax level of 45 per cent the return becomes 10·3 per cent. Now many companies have factories in various regions of the United Kingdom; in these circumstances the

EXHIBIT 75

EVALUATION OF INVESTMENT POST-TAX RETURNS
(CORPORATION TAX 42·5 PER CENT)

Year (1)	Post-tax NCF's (2)	Interest factor, 10% (3)	Present value of net cash flows (4)	Interest factor, 15% (5)	Present value of NCF's (6)
	£		£		£
1	7,000	0·909	6,363	0·870	6,090
2	6,201	0·826	5,122	0·756	4,688
3	5,766	0·751	4,330	0·658	3,794
4	5,418	0·683	3,700	0·572	3,099
5	5,139	0·621	3,191	0·497	2,554
6	7,916	0·565	4,473	0·432	3,420
7	(685)	0·513	(351)	0·376	(258)
TOTALS	£36,755		£26,828		£23,387

question of whether it would be profitable to instal the machinery in one of the company's development area locations ought to be considered. If this action was proposed the investment grant would be increased from 20 to 40 per cent of the installed cost of the machinery. The effect of the increased grant would produce a return of 17·9 per cent for the project, and the company's management might well reconsider their capital spending programme for the development areas, in which their other factories are situated. A project that would have been rejected in its original location becomes a viable proposition, in terms of profitability, in another (development area) location.

Project E

The Beta Milling Company Limited has a group of machine tools which are manually operated. The Works Manager has been considering whether to install numerically controlled machines. The new machines cost £20,000, including all installation costs and the expenses of re-arranging the shop floor layout. An investment grant of 40 per cent would be received towards the total initial cost. Furthermore the machines would attract annual writing-down allowances of 15 per cent on the £20,000 less grant of £8,000. The economic life of the numerically controlled machines is put at 9 years; no scrap value is expected to be received when the equipment is retired from use. If the machines are installed in January of year 1, the operating cost savings are forecasted to be

	£
Year 1	1,800
Year 2	2,000
Year 3	2,500
Year 4	3,000
Year 5	3,000
Year 6	3,500
Year 7	4,000
Year 8	5,000
Year 9	2,000

It is proposed that the machines would be taken out of service in year 10, thus allowing for their uninterrupted use throughout year 9. With a cost of capital of 10 per cent, the Managing Director would like to know whether the proposal should be implemented.

EXHIBIT 76

EVALUATION OF CAPITAL COST: PROJECT E

	£
Capital cost of the investment proposal:	20,000
Less 40 per cent grant, assumed to be received after one year: discounted at the cost of capital = £8,000 × 0·909	7,272
	£12,728

Again it is the post-tax returns which are relevant and therefore Exhibit 77 demonstrates the annual writing down allowances and the tax saved on those allowances.

As in the previous example (Project D) it is assumed that the tax effects of the cost reductions will be assessed to Corporation Tax in

EXHIBIT 77

WRITTEN-DOWN VALUES AND WRITING-DOWN ALLOWANCES (WITH 40 PER CENT INVESTMENT GRANT)

Year	Details	Written-down values at 1 January	Annual writing-down allowances for each year	Tax saved by annual allowances (Corporation Tax 42·5%)
(1)	(2)	(3)	(4)	(5)
		£	£	£
1	Capital cost, net of investment grant, i.e. £20,000 – £8,000	12,000	1,800	765
2	Calculation of year's allowances	10,200	1,530	650
3	ditto	8,670	1,300	553
4	ditto	7,370	1,106	470
5	ditto	6,264	940	399
6	ditto	5,324	799	340
7	ditto	4,525	679	289
8	ditto	3,846	577	245
9	ditto	3,269	490	208
10	Balancing allowance	2,779	2,779	1,181
	TOTALS		£12,000	£5,100

the year following those cost reductions. In the same way, tax savings brought about by the writing-down allowances are deemed to influence tax payments in the year following the capital expenditure (or its written down amount). With these comments in mind the reader can see in Exhibit 78 the present value of the project's post-tax cash flows. When these cash flows are discounted at a cost of capital, a net present value of £191 is revealed.

Theoretically a positive net present value of £191, calculated at the company's cost of capital, indicates an acceptable project. It must be remembered however that this result stems from *forecasts* covering a period of nine years—each of these forecasted cost savings being presented as a single possible outcome. Without an analysis of the risks and uncertainties, without some further study of the company's long term plans and other investment needs, such a small net present value must be treated with some reserve. The writer's action on such an evaluation (NPV = £191) would be to consider the other implications of the forecasts *and* the corporate strategy before accepting the proposal.

EXHIBIT 78

EVALUATION OF INVESTMENTS POST-TAX RETURNS
(CORPORATION TAX 42·5 PER CENT)

Year (1)	Pre-tax NCF's (2)	Tax on NCF's* (3)	Post Corporation tax cash flows (4)	Writing-down allowances (5)	Tax saved by annual allowances (6)	Post-tax NCF's, i.e. columns 4 + 6 (7)	Interest factor, 10% (8)	Present value of post-tax NCF's (9)
	£	£	£	£	£	£		£
1	1,800		1,800			1,800	0·909	1,636
2	2,000	765	1,235	1,800	765	2,000	0·826	1,652
3	2,500	850	1,650	1,530	650	2,300	0·751	1,727
4	3,000	1,062	1,938	1,300	553	2,491	0·683	1,701
5	3,000	1,275	1,725	1,106	470	2,195	0·621	1,363
6	3,500	1,275	2,225	940	399	2,624	0·565	1,483
7	4,000	1,488	2,512	799	340	2,852	0·513	1,463
8	5,000	1,700	3,300	679	289	3,589	0·467	1,676
9	2,000	2,125	(125)	577	245	120	0·424	51
10	—	850	(850)	490	208	(642)	0·386	(248)
11				2,779	1,181	1,181	0·351	415
TOTALS	£26,800	£11,390	£15,410	£12,000	£5,100	£20,510	—	£12,919

* 42·5 per cent of the previous year's NCF's shown in column 2.

Project evaluation at Courtaulds Limited

The use of present value profiles in calculating DCF yield will be demonstrated again in the next series of exhibits. The forms used in Exhibits 79 to 82 are reproduced by permission of Courtaulds Limited.[1] Exhibit 79, which is Form No. 1 in the firm's documentation is completed with details of expenditure on plant, buildings and working capital etc. The fact that it may take several years for some projects to be installed is recognized by the provision of five year/lines on the chart. The importance of this fact and its impact on the calculations will be shown when Form 3 is examined. Data from Form 1 is transferred to Form 2 (Exhibit 80) in order to assess the net tax saved as a result of the writing-down allowances which are given in consequence of the capital expenditure.

The next stage in the evaluation involves the transfer of data from Forms 1 and 2 (Exhibits 79 and 80) to Form 3 (Exhibit 81) where the information is matched with the project's forecasted income as shown in column 3. As in Exhibit 70 the pre-printed form contains discounting factors for several rates of interest from 5 to 40 per cent and thus the calculations can be completed easily by a clerical assistant using a desk calculator. Reference has been made already to the five year-lines, shown on Form 1, in order to accommodate those projects which take more than one year to be fully installed. The totals from table B on Form 1 (Exhibit 79) are transferred to table A on Form 3 (Exhibit 81). The time-adjusted cost of the investment's cash outflow can then be expressed in present value terms in readiness for comparison with the present value of the project's cash inflows.

When the ratios of outflow to inflow, for several discount rates are plotted on the interpolation chart, the DCF yield is shown to be 11·5 per cent.[2]

A further simplification of the calculations involved for the assessment of post-tax values of writing down allowances is given Exhibit 83.

The percentage figures shown in the table, when multiplied by the net capital cost of an investment will give a figure of tax savings

[1] Reference should be made to *Appraisal of Investment Projects by Discounted Cash Flow* by A. M. Alfred and J. B. Evans (Chapman and Hall) for a complete study of the evaluation techniques used by Courtaulds Limited. I am indebted to the company for permission to use these forms in my examples—L.E.R.

[2] Precise calculations will give the return of 11·8 per cent.

EXHIBIT 79

SCHEDULE OF EXPENDITURE AND GRANTS

FORM 1

A EXPENDITURE FOR TAX PURPOSES

PROJECT YEAR	(1)	(2)	(3)	(4)	(5)	(6)	(7)	(8)	(9)	(10)
	Expenditure before deducting grants				Net expenditure for tax purposes				ALLIED REVENUE EXPENDITURE	WORKING CAPITAL
	PLANT			BUILDINGS	PLANT			BUILDINGS (c)		
	eligible for grant		not eligible for grant		eligible for grant (a)		not eligible for grant (b)			
	with wear and tear allowance of				with wear and tear allowance of					
	15 %	20 %	15 %		15 %	20 %	15 %			
0	£20,000				£12,000					
1										
2										
3										
4										

(*a*) 80% of columns 1 and 2 *outside* a Development Area, 60% *within* a Development Area

(*b*) repeat figures from column 3

(*c*) the same as in column 4 if *outside* a Development Area, if *within* a Development Area, normally 75% of column 4

B ESTIMATED CASH OUTFLOW

PROJECT YEAR	(11)	(12)	(13)	(14)	(15)	(16)	(17)	(18)
	Expenditure before deducting grants			GRANTS receivable		ALLIED REVENUE EXPENDITURE	WORKING CAPITAL	TOTALS to Form 3 11 + 12 + 13 + 16 + 17 − 14 − 15
	PLANT		BUILDINGS (f)	PLANT (g)	BUILDINGS (h)			
	eligible for grant (d)	not eligible for grant (e)						
0	£20,000			—	—			£20,000
1				£8,000				£8000
2								
3								
4								

(d) the sum of columns 1 and 2 above

(e) the same as column 3 above

(f) the same as column 4 above

(g) 20% of column 11 of *the previous year* if the project is *outside* a Development Area, 40% if the project is *within* a development Area

(h) nil if the project is *outside* a Development Area, normally 25% of column 13 if the project is *within* a Development Area

Note: The grants are not lagged in part A, but are lagged one year in part B

SCHEDULE OF TAX ALLOWANCES AND RECOVERIES*

FORM 2

PROJECT YEAR	(1)	(2)	(3)	(4)	(5)	(6)	(7)	(8)	(9)	(10)	(11)	(12)	(13)	(14)	(15)	(16)	(17)	(18)	(19)	(20)
	NET EXPENDITURE (from Cols. 5–10 of form 1)						NET TAX SAVED RESULTING FROM EXPENDITURE													
	PLANT			BUILDINGS	ALLIED REVENUE EXPENDITURE	WORKING CAPITAL	PLANT PURCHASED (a)									BUILDINGS PURCHASED (b)			ALLIED REVENUE EX-PENDITURE (c)	TOTALS to Form 3 col. 5
							Year 0			Year 1			Year 2			Year 0	Year 1	Year 2		
	eligible for grant		not eligible for grant				eligible for grant		not eligible for grant	eligible for grant		not eligible for grant	eligible for grant		not eligible for grant					
	with wear and tear allowance of						with wear and tear allowance of													
	15%	20%	15%				15%	20%	15%	15%	20%	15%	15%	20%	15%					
0							–	–	–	–	–	–	–	–	–	–	–	–	–	–
1	£12,000									–	–	–	–	–	–		–	–		
2							765						–	–	–			–		765
3							650													650
4							553													553
5							470													470
6							399													399
7							340													340
8							289													289
9							245													245
10							208													208
11							1,181													1,181
12																				
13																				
14																				
15																				
16																				
17																				
18																				
19																				
20																				

* Recoveries (i.e. scrap and residual values of plant and buildings and recoveries of working capital) should be entered as appropriate in columns 1–6 in the final year of the project

(a) To be completed from Tax Table 1(a) in the case of eligible plant, and Tax Table 1(b) in the case of non-eligible plant
(b) To be completed from Tax Table 11
(c) 42½% of column 5 lagged one year

In this example the project expenditure has been stated to be incurred on 1 January of the first year of operation. To avoid any confusion, the expenditure has been shown to be incurred in year 0; the effect for discounting purposes is the same in both cases. The annual writing-down allowances will be received during that year of account *after* the year of account in which the expenditure was incurred however. Therefore they are shown, in this particular case, as being received in year 2, though year 2 is only one accounting period subsequent to the period of the expenditure.

EXHIBIT 81

FORM 3

CASH FLOW SCHEDULE

A: CASH OUTFLOW

YEAR	CASH OUTFLOW from Form 1 col. 18		DISCOUNTED AT 5%		DISCOUNTED AT 10%		DISCOUNTED AT 15%		DISCOUNTED AT 20%		DISCOUNTED AT 40%	
			Factor	Resultant	Factor	Resultant	Factor	Resultant	Factor	Resultant	Factor	Resultant
0	20,000		1.0	20,000	1.0	20,000	1.0	20,000	1.0		1.0	
1	(8,000)		.952	(7,616)	.909	(7,272)	.870	(6,960)	.833		.714	
2			.907		.826		.756		.694		.510	
3			.864		.751		.658		.579		.364	
		TOTALS [A]		12,384		12,728		13,040				

B: CASH INFLOW

YEAR	(1) Profit	(2) Depreciation	(3) PROFIT BEFORE DEPRECIATION	(4) TAX at 42 1/2 % on previous year of col. 3	(5) TAX SAVED on allowances (from Form 2 col. 20)	(6) Recovery of capital (from final year of cols. 1–6 Form 2)	(7) NET CASH INFLOW 3+5+6−4	DISCOUNTED AT 5% Factor	DISCOUNTED AT 5% Resultant	DISCOUNTED AT 10% Factor	DISCOUNTED AT 10% Resultant	DISCOUNTED AT 15% Factor	DISCOUNTED AT 15% Resultant	DISCOUNTED AT 20% Factor	DISCOUNTED AT 20% Resultant	DISCOUNTED AT 40% Factor	DISCOUNTED AT 40% Resultant
0								1.0		1.0		1.0		1.0		1.0	
1			1,800				1,800	.952	1,714	.909	1,636	.870	1,566	.833		.714	
2			2,000	765	765		2,000	.907	1,814	.826	1,652	.756	3,304	.694		.510	
3			2,500	850	650		2,300	.864	1,987	.751	1,727	.658	1,513	.579		.364	
4			3,000	1,062	553		2,491	.823	2,060	.683	1,701	.572	1,425	.482		.260	
5			3,000	1,275	470		2,195	.784	1,721	.621	1,363	.497	1,091	.402		.186	
6			3,500	1,275	399		2,624	.746	1,958	.564	1,483	.432	1,134	.335		.133	
7			4,000	1,488	340		2,852	.711	2,028	.513	1,463	.376	1,072	.279		.095	
8			5,000	1,700	289		3,589	.677	2,430	.467	1,676	.327	1,174	.233		.068	
9			2,000	2,125	245		120	.645	77	.424	51	.284	34	.194		.048	
10				850	208		(642)	.614	(394)	.386	(248)	.247	(159)	.162		.035	
11					1181		1,181	.585	691	.350	415	.215	254	.135		.025	
12								.557		.319		.187		.112		.018	
13								.530		.290		.163		.093		.013	
14								.505		.263		.141		.078		.009	
15								.481		.239		.123		.065		.006	
16								.458		.218		.107		.054		.005	
17								.436		.198		.093		.045		.003	
18								.416		.180		.081		.038		.002	
19								.396		.164		.070		.031		.002	
20								.377		.149		.061		.026		.001	
							TOTALS [B]		16,086		12,919		12,408				
							RATIOS A/B		0.77		0.98		1.05				

D.C.F. SOLUTION RATE is where ratio A/B = 1.0: by interpolation from graph = 11.5%

EXHIBIT 82

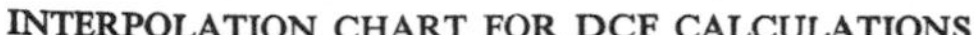

INTERPOLATION CHART FOR DCF CALCULATIONS

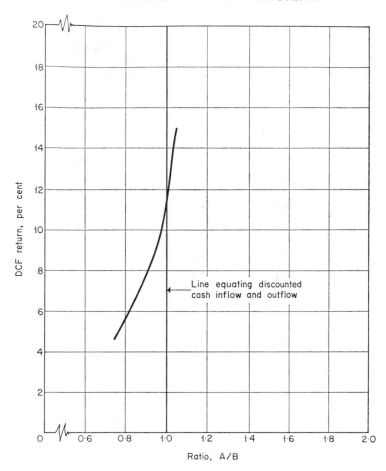

resulting from that investment's writing-down allowances. The reader will observe that the tax savings entered on Form 2 are those which were previously calculated in Exhibit 77. They differ slightly from the results obtained by using the above percentages[1] because of the

[1] For example: £12,000 × 6·4% = £768 for the first year after purchase. This compares with the tax saving shown on Form 2 of £765 in year 2, year 1 being the actual year of purchase—see footnote on page 185.

(The information in Exhibit 83 was supplied by Courtaulds Limited.)

EXHIBIT 83

CAPITAL ALLOWANCES ON PLANT
TAX SAVED AS PER CENT OF NET COST (AFTER DEDUCTING GRANTS): 42½ PER CENT TAX RATE

Number of years after purchase	Table 1a		Table 1b	
	Eligible for grant		Not eligible	
			(Initial allowance 30%)	
	15% writing-down allowances	20% writing-down allowances	15% writing-down allowances	20% writing-down allowances
	%	%	%	%
1	6·4	8·5	19·1	21·3
2	5·5	6·8	3·5	4·3
3	4·5	5·5	3·0	3·4
4	3·9	4·4	2·6	2·7
5	3·3	3·5	2·2	2·2
6	2·8	2·8	1·8	1·7
7	2·4	2·2	1·5	1·4
8	2·0	1·9	1·3	1·1
9	1·7	1·5	1·1	0·9
10	1·5	1·2	1·0	0·7
11	1·2	0·9	0·8	0·6
12	1·1	0·7	0·7	0·5
13	0·9	0·5	0·6	0·4
14	0·8	0·4	0·5	0·3
15	0·7	0·4	0·4	0·2
16	0·5	0·3	0·3	0·2
17	0·4	0·3	0·3	0·2
18	0·4	0·3	0·3	0·1
19	0·4	0·1	0·2	0·1
20	0·3	0·1	0·2	0·1
21	0·3	0·1	0·2	0·1
22	0·3	0·1	0·1	—
23	0·1	—	0·1	—
24	0·1	—	0·1	—
25	0·1	—	0·1	—
26 onwards	0·9	—	0·5	—
	42·5%	42·5%	42·5%	42·5%

approximations involved in the percentages themselves. The extent of approximation in the table can be demonstrated by the basis of the calculations and this is shown below.

Year 1: tax saved

= 42·5 per cent of 15 per cent writing-down allowance

$= 0{\cdot}425 \times 0{\cdot}15$

$= 0{\cdot}06375$

= 6·4 per cent

Year 2: tax saved

= 42·5 per cent of 15 per cent writing-down allowance (i.e. 15 per cent of 85 per cent)

$= 0{\cdot}425 \times (0{\cdot}85 \times 0{\cdot}15)$

$= 0{\cdot}425 \times 0{\cdot}1275$

$= 0{\cdot}0541875$

= 5·4 per cent

Project F

The Gamma Machine Company Limited, is considering extending its range of products by producing a line of high-quality tools for the export market. The cost of new machinery and equipment would be £75,000, but this expenditure would rank for a grant of 20 per cent: annual writing-down allowances in respect of the net expenditure would be at the rate of 15 per cent. It is anticipated furthermore that extra working capital of £5,000 a year would be necessary to finance additional stocks of materials and some increase in the amount of debtors. This increase in working capital would be needed from the first year of operations.

The incremental income (net cash flows) stemming from the project are anticipated to be £12,000 per annum for 10 years. No scrap value is expected to accrue from the machinery and equipment when it is retired from use, but the working capital of £5,000 will be released to other operations of the company by the end of year 11. Corporation tax is levied at 42·5 per cent.

If the cost of capital is given as 10 per cent, should the investment be undertaken?

EVALUATION

A new factor for investment appraisal arises in this proposal—the requirement for additional working capital. Clearly working capital must be regarded as a part of the investment's total cost. It is needed to finance the business growth which will stem from the new range of tools. Therefore the present value of the future net cash flows must be compared with the present value of the cost of machinery and equipment *plus* working capital, *for the period that additional finance is required for this project.* Again it is emphasized that it is the after-tax, after-grant, cash flows which should be brought to account in the appraisal. Method 1 below shows an incorrect evaluation where the full after tax implications of the proposal are not measured

Method 1. Incorrect evaluation, ignoring taxation allowances on machinery and taxation charges on increased profit.

	£
Capital cost of the investment proposal—machinery and equipment	75,000
Add: Working capital increase from year 1: £5,000 × 0·909	4,545
	79,545
Less: 20 per cent grant received after one year: discounted at the cost of capital: £15,000 × 0·909	13,635
	£65,910
Net cash flows, discounted at cost of capital:	
£12,000 per annum for years 1 to 10: £12,000 × 6·145	73,740
release of working capital in year 11: £5,000 × 0·351	1,755
Present value of future net cash flows	£75,495

A net present value of £9,585, rendering the proposal acceptable in terms of profitability, is revealed by the above appraisal.

Method 2. Exhibits 84 to 87 now demonstrate a comprehensive evaluation of the Gamma Company's investment project. The interpolation chart and cash flow schedule reveal a DCF yield of 8·9 per cent and a net present value (at 10 per cent cost of capital)

EXHIBIT 84

SCHEDULE OF EXPENDITURE AND GRANTS FORM 1

A EXPENDITURE FOR TAX PURPOSES

PROJECT YEAR	(1)	(2)	(3)	(4)	(5)	(6)	(7)	(8)	(9)	(10)
	Expenditure before deducting grants				Net expenditure for tax purposes				ALLIED REVENUE EXPENDITURE	WORKING CAPITAL
	PLANT			BUILDINGS	PLANT			BUILDINGS		
	eligible for grant		not eligible for grant		eligible for grant (a)		not eligible for grant (b)			
	with wear and tear allowance of				with wear and tear allowance of					
	15 %	20 %	15 %		15 %	20 %	15 %	(c)		
0	75,000				60,000					
1										5,000
2										
3										
4										

(a) 80 % of columns 1 and 2 *outside* a Development Area, 60 % *within* a Development Area
(b) repeat figures from column 3
(c) the same as in column 4 if *outside* a Development Area, if *within* a Development Area, normally 75 % of column 4

B ESTIMATED CASH OUTFLOW

PROJECT YEAR	(11)	(12)	(13)	(14)	(15)	(16)	(17)	(18)
	Expenditure before deducting grants			GRANTS receivable		ALLIED REVENUE EXPENDITURE	WORKING CAPITAL	TOTALS to Form 3 11 + 12 + 13 + 16 + 17 − 14 − 15
	PLANT							
	eligible for grant (d)	not eligible for grant (e)	BUILDINGS (f)	PLANT (g)	BUILDINGS (h)			
0	75,000			—	—			75,000
1				15,000			5,000	10,000
2								
3								
4								

(d) the sum of colums 1 and 2 above
(e) the same as column 3 above
(f) the same as column 4 above
(g) 20 % of column 11 of *the previous year* if the project is *outside* a Development Area, 40 % if the project is *within* a Development Area
(h) nil if the project is *outside* a Development Area, normally 25 % of column 13 if the project is *within* a Development Area

Note: The grants are not lagged in part A, but are lagged one year in part B

EXHIBIT 85

SCHEDULE OF TAX ALLOWANCES AND RECOVERIES*

FORM 2

	(1)	(2)	(3)	(4)	(5)	(6)	(7)	(8)	(9)	(10)	(11)	(12)	(13)	(14)	(15)	(16)	(17)	(18)	(19)	(20)
PROJECT YEAR	NET EXPENDITURE (from Cols. 5–10 of form 1)						NET TAX SAVED RESULTING FROM EXPENDITURE													
	PLANT			BUILDINGS	ALLIED REVENUE EXPENDITURE	WORKING CAPITAL	PLANT PURCHASED (a)									BUILDINGS PURCHASED (b)			ALLIED REVENUE EX-PENDITURE (c)	TOTALS to Form 3 col. 5
	eligible for grant		not eligible for grant				Year 0			Year 1			Year 2			Year 0	Year 1	Year 2		
	with wear and tear allowance of						eligible for grant		not eligible for grant	eligible for grant		not eligible for grant	eligible for grant		not eligible for grant					
							with wear and tear allowance of													
	15%	20%	15%				15%	20%	15%	15%	20%	15%	15%	20%	15%					
0	60,000						—	—	—	—	—	—	—	—	—	—	—	—	—	—
1						5,000	3,840			—	—	—	—	—	—		—	—		3,840
2							3,300						—	—	—			—		3,300
3							2,700													2,700
4							2,340													2,340
5							1,980													1,980
6							1,680													1,680
7							1,440													1,440
8							1,200													1,200
9							1,020													1,020
10							900													900
11							5,100													5,100
12																				
13																				
14																				
15																				
16																				
17																				
18																				
19																				
20																				

* Recoveries (i.e. scrap and residual values of plant and buildings and recoveries of working capital) should be entered as appropriate in columns 1–6 in the final year of the project

(a) To be completed from Tax Table 1(a) in the case of eligible plant, and Tax Table 1(b) in the case of non-eligible plant
(b) To be completed from Tax Table 11
(c) 40% of column 5 lagged one year

NB The net tax saved, which is shown in column 7, is derived from multiplying the net capital expenditure shown in column 1 by the percentage amounts given in Table 1a of Exhibit 83

EXHIBIT 80

CASH FLOW SCHEDULE

FORM 3

A: CASH OUTFLOW

YEAR	CASH OUTFLOW from Form 1 col. 18	DISCOUNTED AT 5% Factor	DISCOUNTED AT 5% Resultant	DISCOUNTED AT 10% Factor	DISCOUNTED AT 10% Resultant	DISCOUNTED AT 15% Factor	DISCOUNTED AT 15% Resultant	DISCOUNTED AT 20% Factor	DISCOUNTED AT 20% Resultant	DISCOUNTED AT 40% Factor	DISCOUNTED AT 40% Resultant
0	75,000	1.0	75,000	1.0	75,000	1.0	75,000	1.0		1.0	
1	(10,000)	.952	(9,520)	.909	(9,090)	.870	(8,700)	.833		.714	
2		.907		.826		.756		.694		.510	
3		.864		.751		.658		.579		.364	
TOTALS [A]			65,480		65,910		66,300				

B: CASH INFLOW

YEAR	(1) Profit	(2) Depreciation	(3) PROFIT BEFORE DEPRECIATION	(4) TAX at 42½% on previous year of col. 3	(5) TAX SAVED on allowances (from Form 2 col. 20)	(6) Recovery of capital (from final year of cols. 1–6 Form 2)	(7) NET CASH INFLOW 3+5+6−4	DISCOUNTED AT 5% Factor	DISCOUNTED AT 5% Resultant	DISCOUNTED AT 10% Factor	DISCOUNTED AT 10% Resultant	DISCOUNTED AT 15% Factor	DISCOUNTED AT 15% Resultant	DISCOUNTED AT 20% Factor	DISCOUNTED AT 20% Resultant	DISCOUNTED AT 40% Factor	DISCOUNTED AT 40% Resultant
0								1.0		1.0		1.0		1.0		1.0	
1			12,000		3,840		15,840	.952	15,080	.909	14,399	.870	13,781	.833		.714	
2			12,000	5,100	3,300		10,200	.907	9,251	.826	8,425	.756	7,711	.694		.510	
3			12,000	5,100	2,700		9,600	.864	8,294	.751	7,210	.658	6,317	.579		.364	
4			12,000	5,100	2,340		9,240	.823	7,605	.683	6,311	.572	5,285	.482		.260	
5			12,000	5,100	1,980		8,880	.784	6,962	.621	5,514	.497	4,413	.402		.186	
6			12,000	5,100	1,680		8,580	.746	6,401	.564	4,839	.432	3,707	.335		.133	
7			12,000	5,100	1,440		8,340	.711	5,930	.513	4,278	.376	3,136	.279		.095	
8			12,000	5,100	1,200		8,100	.677	5,484	.467	3,783	.327	2,649	.233		.068	
9			12,000	5,100	1,020		7,920	.645	5,108	.424	3,358	.284	2,249	.194		.048	
10			12,000	5,100	900		7,800	.614	4,789	.386	3,011	.247	1,927	.162		.035	
11				5,100	5,100	5,000	5,000	.585	2,925	.350	1,750	.215	1,075	.135		.025	
12								.557		.319		.187		.112		.018	
13								.530		.290		.163		.093		.013	
14								.505		.263		.141		.078		.009	
15								.481		.239		.123		.065		.006	
16								.458		.218		.107		.054		.005	
17								.436		.198		.093		.045		.003	
18								.416		.180		.081		.038		.002	
19								.396		.164		.070		.031		.002	
20								.377		.149		.061		.026		.001	
						TOTALS [B]			71,829		62,878		52,250				
						RATIOS A/B			0.84		1.05		1.27				

D.C.F. SOLUTION RATE is where ratio A/B = 1.0: by interpolation from graph = 8.9%

EXHIBIT 87

INTERPOLATION CHART FOR DCF CALCULATIONS

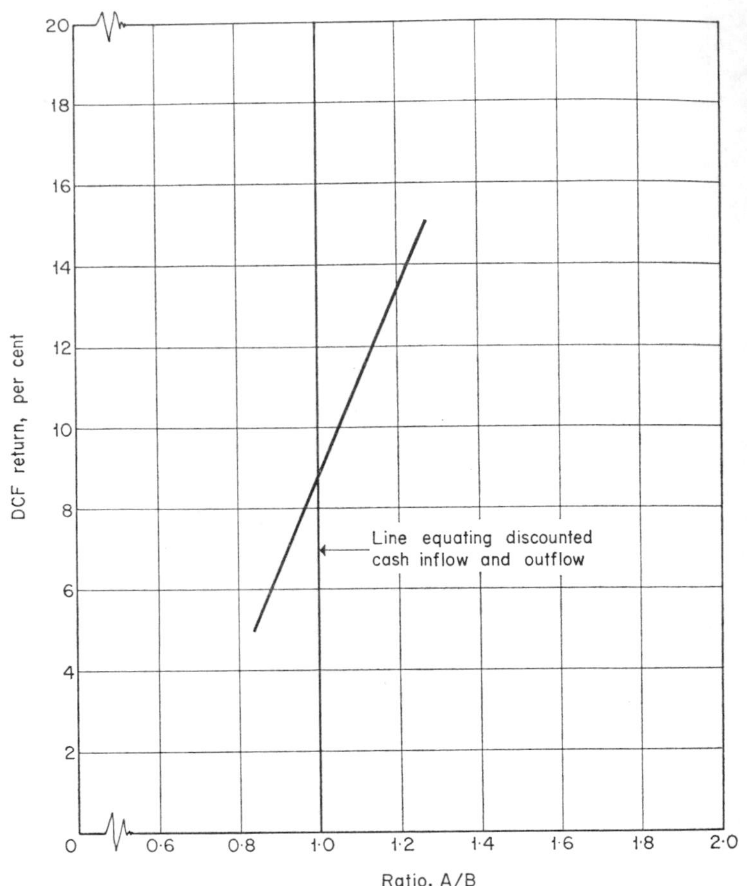

of—£3,032. Both of these criteria of project assessment give the same answer—the proposal is unacceptable when judged in terms of profitability.

Questions for discussion

1. Of what importance is the criterion of evaluation in a company's investment appraisal procedures?

2. What do you understand by a project's 'risk period'?
3. To what extent should investment decisions be determined by project profitability?
4. How should a proposal's cash outflows and inflows be calculated for correct investment appraisal?
5. How do project profiles (of net present values) aid the study of potential investment opportunities?

Recommended reading

ALFRED, A. M. and EVANS, J. B., *Appraisal of Investment Projects by Discounted Cash Flow*, Chapman & Hall, 1965.

MOCK, E. J., *Financial Decision Making*, International Textbook Co., 1967.

CHILDS, J. F., *Profit Goals and Capital Management*, Prentice Hall, 1968.

KINGSHOTT, A. L., *Investment Appraisal*, Ford Business Library, 1967.

HENRICI, S. B., Eyeing the R.O.I., *Harvard Business Review*, Volume 46, No. 3, 1968.

BURSK, E. G. and CHAPMAN, J. F. (Editors), *New Decision-making Tools for Managers*, Mentor Executive Library, 1963.

CHAPTER 11 Risk and Uncertainty

Introduction

Capital investment decisions have been portrayed, up to this stage, as though they were based invariably upon accurate statements of future costs and incomes. From these figures a forecasted rate of return for a particular proposal has then emerged. In examples demonstrated in the previous chapters, investment lives varied from 5 to 10 years, whilst industrial forecasters can instance investments where much longer lives are being forecast. Few investment projects are limited to the precise lives quoted in their original forecast information, because any capital expenditure decision is always subject to unknown developments in the future. Such developments may affect an investment's initial cost, its running costs, the size of the market and thus the ultimate sales volume, price at which the output can be sold and the life of the project itself. No single table of DCF calculations can bring together all of the imponderables which may affect a project's outcome, yet business decisions are being based upon the type of single estimated rate of return which has been demonstrated in the earlier chapters.

The place of judgement

This is not to say that the evaluation criteria used in Chapter 10 are badly conceived. They make the best use of the information upon which they are based. They represent a conventional approach to investment appraisal—assessing future outcomes as a result of 'best guesses' of the timing of future events, of the level of future costs and incomes. With such best guess forecasted single rates of return, a business manager can then apply his own judgement of the proposed expenditure's chances of survival or of profit. In other words, hunch still plays a vital part in investment choice. Nevertheless it is true to say that investment decision-making has experienced considerable improvements, in the method and technique of proposal evaluation, during the last ten years. Not the least of these improvements concerns the use of time adjusted rates of return which take into account the time value of money. However these changes in method are not enough, by themselves, for ensuring the best decisional aids in the investment analysis of the future. Even if it is accepted that the experienced manager's judgement (of a future cash flow's potential) can be a viable criterion in selecting between alternative investment choices, it is still not enough to enable him to assess an average value of his hunch appraisal. This can be achieved only with considerable experience of specific investment types. A sufficient historical experience of certain capital expenditure proposals may well form a judgement base for appraising similar projects in the future. Where a company undertakes frequent small investment projects, it is likely that the ultimate variations between forecasted and actual returns will average out over the whole range of such projects. In these instances the single best guess indicator of project desirability may well be sufficient.

On the other hand, where a capital expenditure project is expected to have considerable impact on a firm's existing capital and asset structure, the same conclusions about the sufficiency of the single best guess criterion cannot be supported. It is very probable that a poor actual performance of the large project would have a significant influence upon the firm's total rate of return. In consequence the company's dividend potential and market rating (P/E ratio) could be

EXHIBIT 88

FORECAST DATA OF INVESTMENT PROPOSAL

Sales price of product	£10 each
Sales volume	36,000 units per annum
Running costs	£250,000 per annum
Economic life	12 years
Investment cost	£75,000
Net cash flows per annum	£360,000 − £250,000 = £110,000
Present value of net cash flows at 15 per cent cost of capital	£110,000 × 5·4206 = £596,266
Net present value	£596,266 − £75,000 = £521,266

adversely affected, and therefore its power to raise further long-term capital for expansion severely restricted. With the relatively large capital expenditure proposal, more information on possible future outcomes for a project's returns is essential for better corporate long term planning. Exhibits 88, 89 and 90 below show the problems a decision maker might have to face when he has to apply his judgement to the question of whether or not to accept a particular investment proposal.

The results in Exhibit 88 were obtained by the single best guess approach and look attractive: they represent a growth in wealth which should accrue to the company *after charging a* 15 *per cent cost of capital rate of interest*. However a closer examination of the proposal's prospects reveal quite a range of potential outcomes for the various factors affecting the proposal's whole performance. The additional information is given in Exhibit 89.

EXHIBIT 89

LIKELY RANGES OF FUTURE OUTCOMES FOR PROPOSAL DATA

Sale price of product	£9 to £12 each
Sales volume	32,000 to 40,000 units per annum
Running costs	£240,000 to £270,000 per annum
Economic life	10 to 20 years
Investment cost	£70,000 to £100,000.

EXHIBIT 90

BEST AND WORST OUTCOMES FROM FORECAST DATA

	Best result	*Worst result*
Sales price of product	£12	£9
Sales volume	40,000 units	32,000 units
Running costs	£240,000	£270,000
Economic life	20 years	10 years
Investment cost	£70,000	£100,000
Sales income	£480,000	£288,000
Running costs	£240,000	£270,000
Net cash flows per annum	£240,000	£18,000
PV of net cash flows at 15 per cent	£1,502,160	£90,342
Net present value	£1,432,160	−£9,658

In order to assess the limits of the risks attaching to the investment proposal, a decision maker may now calculate a most optimistic and a most pessimistic rate of return. These returns are based upon the likely extremes of the values shown for the various factors affecting the proposal. Exhibit 90 shows how this concept is applied. These two extremes of *possible* net present values of the proposal should be compared with the single best guess result of £521,266. It then becomes very obvious that such widely varying estimates of future returns present the decision maker with totally inadequate information for reliable investment forecasting. The question which must be answered is—'How can the basic data be improved to make the ultimate evaluation of a project more meaningful?'

Improving decisional data

A first priority should be the improvement of forecasts. In so far as errors and uncertainties can be removed by, for example, an extension of market research or extrapolation of cost trends from internal cost data, this should be done. However, just as the cost of costing has always been a major point of concern for management accountants, so should the costs of forecasting be weighed against the additional benefit which it produces. Where a considerable expenditure is necessary to achieve a minimal increase in forecasting accuracy, it may well prove to be not worth the expense.

Again most managers can cite instances of the optimistic and the pessimistic estimator. The writer has met instances where decision makers have known of a certain manager's propensity for over confidence. Where these circumstances have produced estimates which were, say, 10 to 15 per cent in excess of the actual outcomes for 90 per cent of the time, then clearly a specific adjustment of such future forecasts ought to be made. A more frequently used method for countering hidden risks and uncertainties arises where the decision maker demands a higher return for a proposal which *he considers* is risky. Where it seems that sizeable uncertainties could be hidden in the many variable factors which determine a projects profitability, then the raising of the cut off rate for proposal acceptance may provide some 'cover' for taking on the uncertainty. It is suggested however that the method is somewhat weak because the decision maker can never know the size of the final risk he is accepting, neither can he know the true extent of the risks he is avoiding. Furthermore, the practice of an unreasoned raising of the cut-off rate can restrict the flow of profitable opportunities which are necessary for the continued existence and growth of the company.

A further and more acceptable first approach to the quantification of uncertainties, which may lie in business investment, concerns selectivity. By this procedure the project appraiser selects a value from the normal single best guess factor estimates in a proposal evaluation. This particular factor's value is then varied by a specific percentage or quantity: the project's expected rate of return is then recalculated, incorporating the one (arbitrary) variation in the forecast data, in order to find out what effect such a variation would have on the ultimate expected rate of return for the proposal. When this process has been repeated several times, giving a number of percentage variations in the average expected return, then the extent of importance of each factor's forecast in the eventual outcome will be revealed. Here the reader should remember that if the likelihood of the forecasts in Exhibit 88 being achieved is only a 70 per cent chance for each factor, then the likelihood of all of them attaining the forecasted values at *the same time* is only 17 per cent.

Examining the results of a selectivity study will indicate those estimates which are critical to the proposal's outcome. Consequently the areas where further research is necessary into the accuracy of forecasted data, can be emphasized. Extra attention to these areas vital to proposal productivity may well enable the forecasts to be improved. At least the figures should be blessed with sounder bases from which to draw conclusions. The investment's forecasts and its ultimate evaluation will be giving better information to the decision maker, consistent with forecasting cost and available business knowledge. Exhibit 91 demonstrates the value of a selective analysis of the importance of cost and income elements in a proposal's estimated returns.[1] The horizontal line grades percentage changes for the variable factors in a particular investment. Assuming a 5 per cent increase in plant cost, the broken lines on the chart show that a 2 per cent reduction in the rate of return could be expected. Similarly a 5 per cent decrease in building costs should give a 1·7 per cent increase in the expected return from the proposal. Such visual expressions of capital expenditure profitabilities have considerable

[1] See *The Complete Investment Picture* by I. McFall and J. Denholm, *Management Today*, p. 74 (February 1967).

EXHIBIT 91

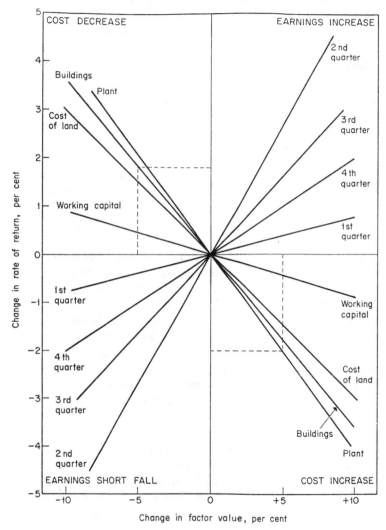

PROJECT RETURN SENSITIVITY TO COST/INCOME VARIATIONS

presentation value for the busy decision makers: their appreciation of the risks involved is easily heightened. It must be emphasized however that the above exhibit does not present a general picture for all investment projects. It is applicable to the circumstances of that project only which is represented in the exhibit.

A further example of project sensitivity to variations in forecast data is given in Exhibits 92 to 94. Here again the forecasted information is shown to have a (limited) range of possible outcomes.

EXHIBIT 92

FORECAST DATA OF INVESTMENT PROPOSAL

Net cash flows per annum	(a) £75
	(b) £100
	(c) £125
	(d) £150
Investment cost	£300
Economic life	From 2 to 10 years
Cost of capital	10 per cent

It is here that present value profiles can be used once more to show the relative worths of the various groups of factor values affecting the investment's forecasted returns. Exhibit 93 demonstrates the sensitivity of the project's returns to variations in (*a*) net cash flows and (*b*) investment life. The point at which the profile line crosses the line of investment initial outlay indicates discounted payback periods for the project, where there are variations in the forecast net cash flows. The graph shows that a doubling of net cash flows from £75 to £150 per annum will reduce the discounted payback by *more* than 50 per cent. The conclusions to be drawn from such a presentation can be impressive where more variables are introduced into the calculations. Next, Exhibit 94 shows the same information being used to produce DCF yields for the several combinations of factors which can influence the projects returns. In this case the possible economic life has been extended to 20 years.

This arbitrary extension of project life gives a clear indication that, after a certain period, length of economic life is of minor importance to the forecasted return. In particular, if the capital expenditure proposal should prove to have a longer profitable life than the 10 years quoted in the original forecast then, with net cash flows of £150 per annum, little improvement in the rate of return can be expected *from such an extension of life*. However with net cash flows of £75 per

EXHIBIT 93

SENSITIVITY ANALYSIS—INFLUENCE ON PROPOSAL'S PRESENT VALUE

COST OF CAPITAL, 10 PER CENT

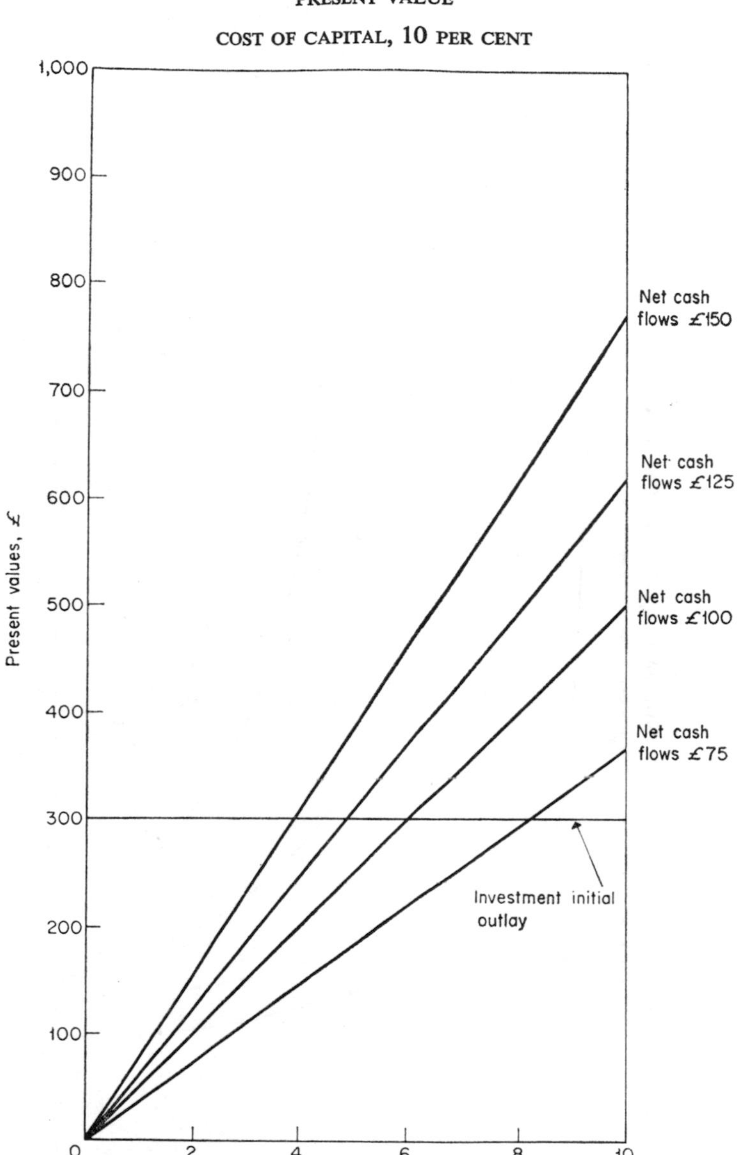

EXHIBIT 94

SENSITIVITY ANALYSIS—INFLUENCE ON PROPOSAL'S YIELD INVESTMENT COST £300—COST OF CAPITAL, 10 PER CENT

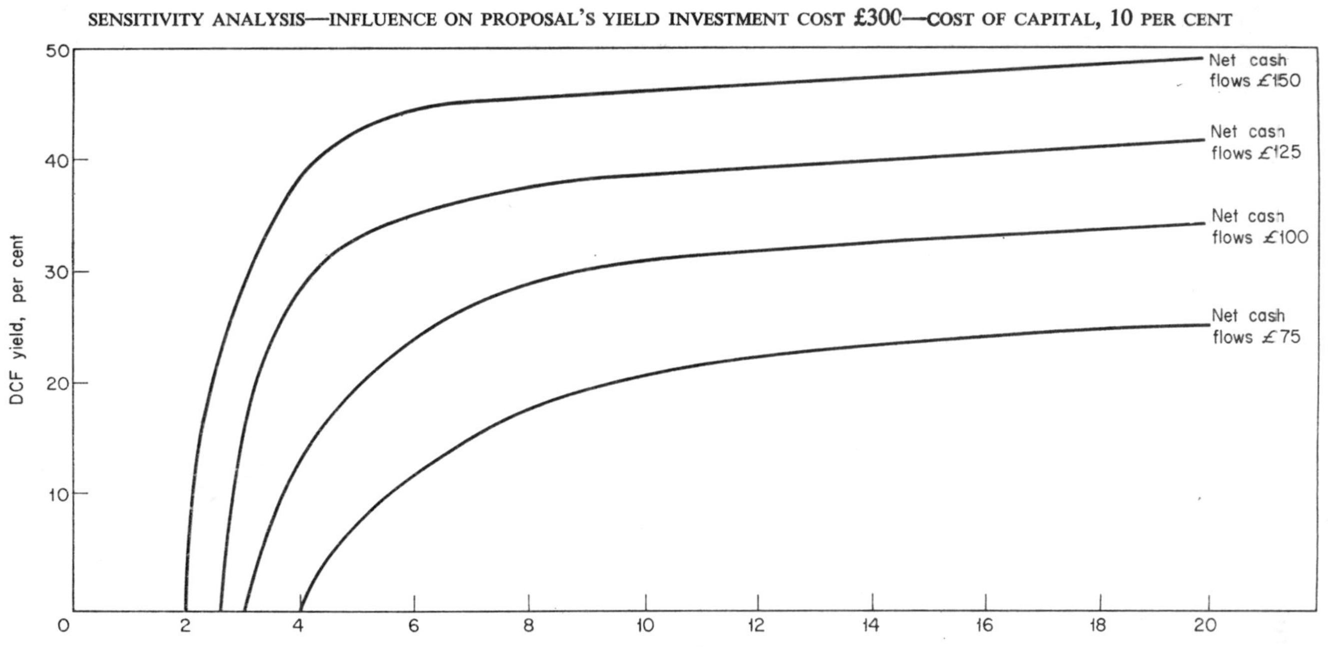

annum, a lengthening of the proposals economic life to 20 years could give a yield increase of approximately 7 per cent *over the forecast 21·5 per cent.*

Risk profiles

The above examples of improvements in forecasting techniques still lack an evaluation of the relative variations' likelihood of arrival. If the decision maker could be told that, for example, a life of 10 years has a 60 per cent probability of occurrence whereas a life of 20 years has only a 20 per cent probability of occurrence, he would possess vital additional information to aid his making a good decision. The presentation of such valuable decisional data needs the involvement of those forecasting and estimating staffs who are concerned in the proposal's evaluation. After the major influencing factors, in any capital expenditure project, have been defined then the managers who produce the estimates should be asked to give the probable ranges of values to be applied to the forecasts with which they have been concerned. At the same time each forecaster should be encouraged to give his estimate of the probability of achievement for each sector of the forecast range of values relating to his own factor group. By these means the intangibles associated with a proposed investment will not be represented by a single figure: the picture will be completed by a probability distribution of the various values attributable to each of the major influencing groups of costs and incomes found in any proposed capital investment.

The next stage in the process of reaching an assessment of the proposed investment would be to find out the rates of return, for the project, which would result from random combinations of the probability values for each of the major influencing factor groups. Common sense will have to lay down some restriction on the 'random' combinations. There would have to be a realistic limit to the share of the market attainable by the investment plus existing resources. The end result will be an assessment of the return to an investment which gives not only the spread of various likely returns, but also gives a *weighting to the likelihood* of the actual return falling at any point within the potential whole range. Exhibit 95 shows the sequence of events in evaluating the risks and uncertainties implicit in planning the installation of long-term capital assets. The final chart of investment risk profile measures, on the vertical axis, the probabilities that

EXHIBIT 95

INVESTMENT RISK PROFILE

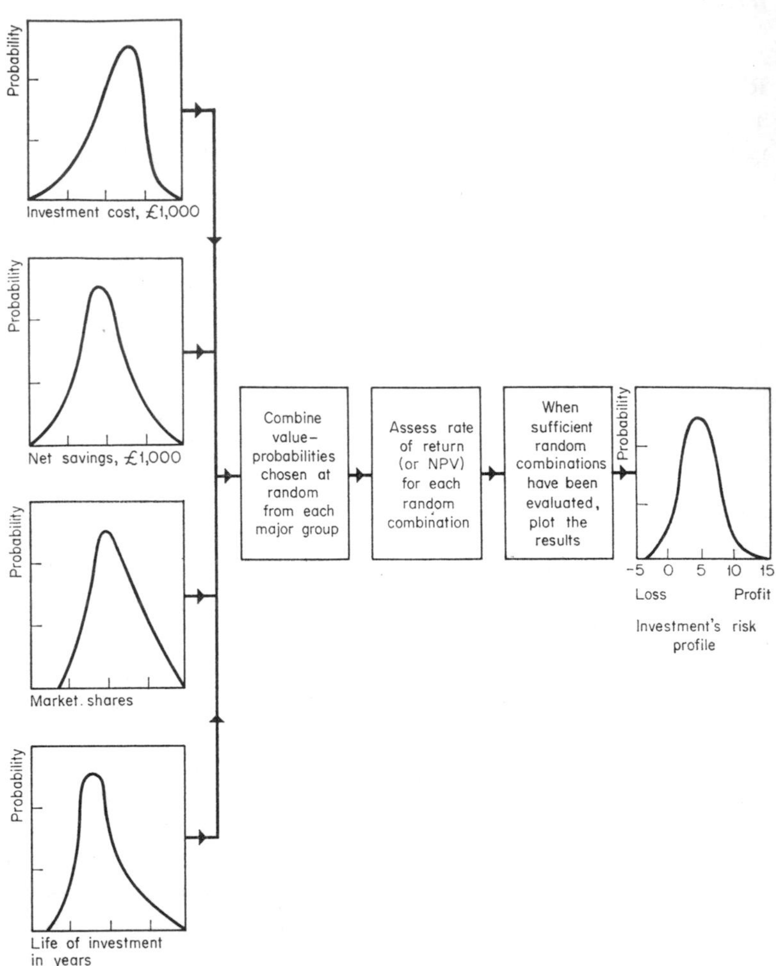

the investment will achieve the returns graduated on the horizontal axis.

The final risk profile, which incorporates the range of all the variable factors for the project, shows not only the average or expected rate of return but also the probability of their being achieved. The

EXHIBIT 96

RISK PROFILES OF ALTERNATIVE INVESTMENTS

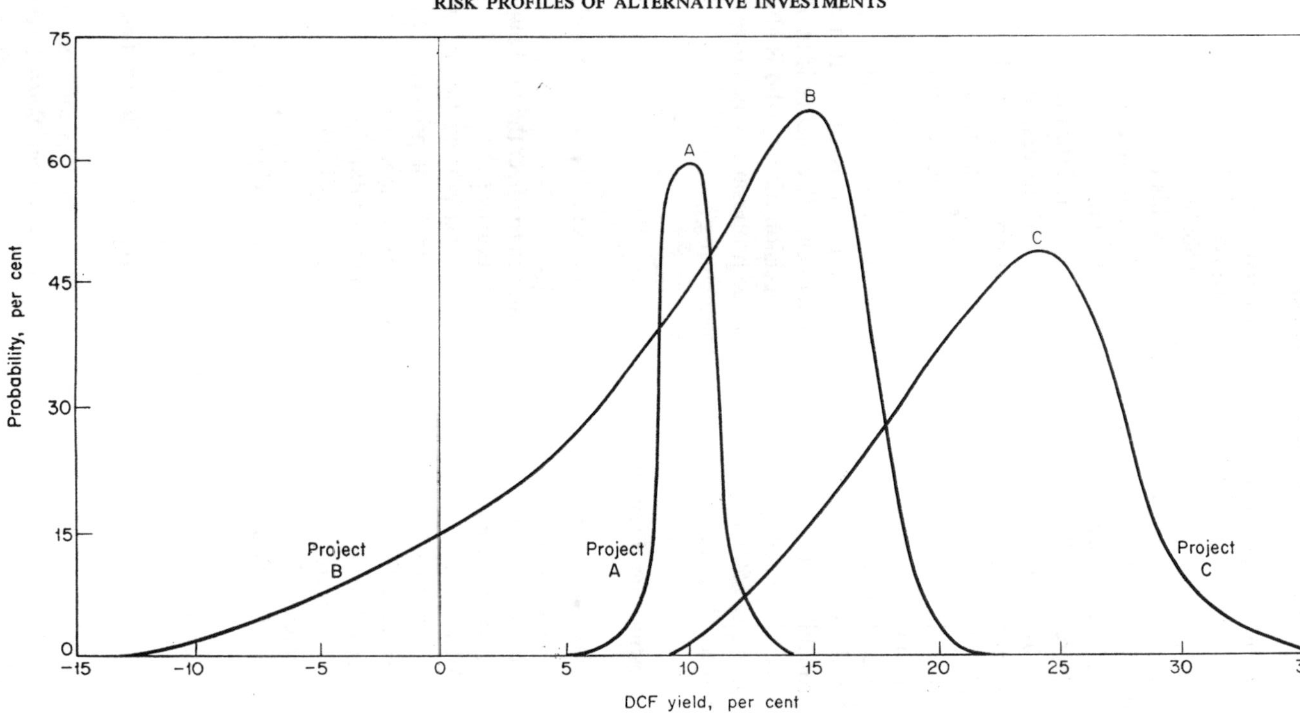

likelihood that other rates of return, expressed by any point on the profile, will be achieved is similarly expressed in probability ratings. Thus the decision maker knows the probability of loss or of large gain and he is the better equipped to place his own subjective value on the worthwhileness of the gamble. The usefulness of such risk profiles is shown to advantage by Exhibit 96.

Here three alternative proposals are presented for the choice of the decision maker. He can have project A with its assured 10 per cent return but with no prospect of high returns, or of loss. Proposal B offers a higher average return of 15 per cent: it also rates a higher probability for the 15 per cent. Unfortunately project B has a 15 per cent probability of loss. Finally proposal C's expected return, 24 per cent, is given the lowest probability rating of the three proposals. On the other hand it offers no prospect of loss and a 10 per cent probability of a high return of 30 per cent. The reader is invited to place himself in the position of the decision maker, who is about to spend say £500,000 on *one* of the three proposals. Which investment project should be chosen for implementing?

Questions for discussion

1. Has the single best guess index of project assessment any place in a sound capital investment planning scheme?
2. Should personal judgement be allowed to affect the final appraisal of an investment's future potential returns?
3. What is the object of calculating a most pessimistic, an average and a most optimistic rate of return for a project? Do such estimates have any value in capital investment evaluation?
4. How would you improve the reliability of data used in forecasts, in order to reduce the element of uncertainty implicit in a project's forecasted rate of return?
5. What do you understand by (*a*) selectivity (*b*) sensitivity?

Recommended reading

HERTZ, D. B., 'Risk analysis in capital investment', *Harvard Business Review*, January/February 1964.

HESPOS, R. F. and STRASSMANN, P. A., 'Stochastic decision trees for the analysis of investment decisions', *Management Science*, August 1965.

SOLOMOM, M. B., JR., 'Uncertainty and its effect on capital investment analysis', *Management Science*, April 1966.

HERTZ, D. B., 'Investment policies that pay off', *Harvard Business Review*, January/February 1968.

HENDERSON, C., 'The treatment of risk in capital investment projects', *European Business*, January 1968.

APPENDIX A

Extract from The Companies Act 1967[1]

Schedule 2—Part 1—General Provisions as to the Balance Sheet and Profit and Loss Account

2. The authorised share capital, issued share capital, liabilities and assets shall be summarised, with such particulars as are necessary to disclose the general nature of the assets and liabilities, and there shall be specified—

(*a*) any part of the issued capital that consists of redeemable preference shares, the earliest and latest dates on which the company has power to redeem those shares, whether those shares must be redeemed in any event or are liable to be redeemed at the option of the company and whether any (and, if so, what) premium is payable on redemption;

(*b*) so far as the information is not given in the profit and loss account, any share capital on which interest has been paid out of capital during the financial year, and the rate at which interest has been so paid;

(*c*) the amount of the share premium account;

(*d*) particulars of any redeemed debentures which the company has power to reissue.

3. There shall be stated under separate headings, so far as they are not written off—

(*a*) the preliminary expenses;

(*b*) any expenses incurred in connection with any issue of share capital or debentures;

[1] This extensive reproduction of the legal requirements regarding the information to be provided in, or annexed to, the published accounts of a public limited company is printed by permission of H.M. Stationery Office. The reader is referred also to The Companies Act 1967 published by the Accountants' Publishing Company Limited, for the Institute of Chartered Accountants of Scotland (published in 1967).

(*c*) any sums paid by way of commission in respect of any shares or debentures;
(*d*) any sums allowed by way of discount in respect of any debentures; and
(*e*) the amount of the discount allowed on any issue of shares at a discount.

4.—(1) The reserves, provisions, liabilities and assets shall be classified under headings appropriate to the company's business:

Provided that—

(*a*) where the amount of any class is not material, it may be included under the same heading as some other class; and
(*b*) where any assets of one class are not separable from assets of another class, those assets may be included under the same heading.

(2) Fixed assets, current assets and assets that are neither fixed nor current shall be separately identified.

(3) The method or methods used to arrive at the amount of the fixed assets under each heading shall be stated.

5.—(1) The method of arriving at the amount of any fixed asset shall, subject to the next following sub-paragraph, be to take the difference between—

(*a*) its cost or, if it stands in the company's books at a valuation, the amount of the valuation; and
(*b*) the aggregate amount provided or written off since the date of acquisition or valuation, as the case may be, for depreciation or diminution in value;

and for the purposes of this paragraph the net amount at which any assets stand in the company's books at the commencement of this Act (after deduction of the amounts previously provided or written off for depreciation or diminution in value) shall, if the figures relating to the period before the commencement of this Act cannot be obtained without unreasonable expense or delay, be treated as if it were the amount of a valuation of those assets made at the commencement of this Act and, where any of those assets are sold, the said net amount less the amount of the sales shall be treated as if it were the amount of a valuation so made of the remaining assets.

(2) The foregoing sub-paragraph shall not apply—

(*a*) to assets for which the figures relating to the period beginning with the commencement of this Act cannot be obtained without unreasonable expense or delay; or

(*b*) to assets the replacement of which is provided for wholly or partly—

(i) by making provision for renewals and charging the cost of replacement against the provision so made; or

(ii) by charging the cost of replacement direct to revenue; or

(*c*) to any quoted investments or to any unquoted investments of which the value as estimated by the directors is shown either as the amount of the investments or by way of note; or

(*d*) to goodwill, patents or trade marks.

(3) For the assets under each heading whose amount is arrived at in accordance with sub-paragraph (1) of this paragraph, there shall be shown—

(*a*) the aggregate of the amounts referred to in paragraph (*a*) of that sub-paragraph; and

(*b*) the aggregate of the amounts referred to in paragraph (*b*) thereof.

(4) As respects the assets under each heading whose amount is not arrived at in accordance with the said sub-paragraph (1) because their replacement is provided for as mentioned in sub-paragraph (2) (*b*) of this paragraph, there shall be stated—

(*a*) the means by which their replacement is provided for; and

(*b*) the aggregate amount of the provision (if any) made for renewals and not used.

5A. In the case of unquoted investments consisting in equity share capital (as defined by subsection (5) of section 154 of this Act) of other bodies corporate (other than any whose values as estimated by the directors are separately shown, either individually or collectively or as to some individually and as to the rest collectively, and are so shown either as the amount thereof, or by way of note), the matters referred to in the following heads shall, if not otherwise shown, be stated by way of note or in a statement or report annexed—

(*a*) the aggregate amount of the company's income for the financial year that is ascribable to the investments;

(*b*) the amount of the company's share before taxation, and the amount of that share after taxation, of the net aggregate amount of the profits of the bodies in which the investments are held, being profits for the several periods to which accounts sent by them during the financial year to the company related, after deducting those bodies' losses for those periods (or vice versa);

(*c*) the amount of the company's share of the net aggregate amount of the undistributed profits accumulated by the bodies in which the investments are held since the time when the investments were acquired, after deducting the losses accumulated by them since that time (or vice versa);

(*d*) the manner in which any losses incurred by the said bodies have been dealt with in the company's accounts.

6. The aggregate amounts respectively of reserves and provisions (other than provisions for depreciation, renewals or diminution in value of assets) shall be stated under separate headings:

Provided that—

(*a*) this paragraph shall not require a separate statement of either of the said amounts which is not material; and

(*b*) the Board of Trade may direct that it shall not require a separate statement of the amount of provisions where they are satisfied that that is not required in the public interest and would prejudice the company, but subject to the condition that any heading stating an amount arrived at after taking into account a provision (other than as aforesaid) shall be so framed or marked as to indicate that fact.

7.—(1) There shall also be shown (unless it is shown in the profit and loss account or a statement or report annexed thereto, or the amount involved is not material)—

(*a*) where the amount of the reserves or of the provisions (other than provisions for depreciation, renewals or diminution in value of assets) shows an increase as compared with the amount at the end of the immediately preceding financial year, the source from which the amount of the increase has been derived; and

(*b*) where—

(i) the amount of the reserves shows a decrease as compared with the amount at the end of the immediately preceding financial year; or

(ii) the amount at the end of the immediately preceding financial year of the provisions (other than provisions for depreciation, renewals or diminution in value of assets) exceeded the aggregate of the sums since applied and amounts still retained for the purposes thereof:

the application of the amounts derived from the difference.

(2) Where the heading showing the reserves or any of the provisions aforesaid is divided into sub-headings, this paragraph shall apply to each of the separate amounts shown in the sub-headings instead of applying to the aggregate amount thereof.

7A. If an amount is set aside for the purpose of its being used to prevent undue fluctuations in charges for taxation, it shall be stated.

8.—(1) There shall be shown under separate headings—

(*a*) the aggregate amounts respectively of the company's quoted investments and unquoted investments;

(*b*) if the amount of the goodwill and of any patents and trade marks or part of that amount is shown as a separate item in or is otherwise ascertainable from the books of the company, or from any contract for the sale or purchase of any property to be acquired by the company, or from any documents in the possession of the company relating to the stamp duty payable in respect of any such contract or the conveyance of any such property, the said amount so shown or ascertained so far as not written off or, as the case may be, the said amount so far as it is so shown or ascertainable and as so shown or ascertained, as the case may be;

(*c*) the aggregate amount of any outstanding loans made under the authority of provisos (*b*) and (*c*) subsection (1) of section fifty-four of this Act;

(*d*) the aggregate amount of bank loans and overdrafts and the aggregate amount of loans made to the company which—

(i) are repayable otherwise than by instalments and fall due for repayment after the expiration of the period of five years beginning with the day next following the expiration of the financial year; or

(ii) are repayable by instalments any of which fall due for payment after the expiration of that period;

not being, in either case, bank loans or overdrafts;

(*e*) the aggregate amount (before deduction of income tax) which is recommended for distribution by way of dividend.

(2) Nothing in head (*b*) of the foregoing sub-paragraph shall be taken as requiring the amount of the goodwill, patents and trade marks to be stated otherwise than as a single item.

(3) The heading showing the amount of the quoted investments shall be subdivided, where necessary to distinguish the investments as respects which there has, and those as respects which there has not, been granted a quotation or permission to deal on a recognised stock exchange.

(4) In relation to each loan falling within head (*d*) of sub-paragraph (1) of this paragraph (other than a bank loan or overdraft), there shall be stated by way of note (if not otherwise stated) the terms on which it is repayable and the rate at which interest is payable thereon:

Provided that if the number of loans is such that, in the opinion of the directors compliance with the foregoing requirement would result in a statement of excessive length, it shall be sufficient to give a general indication of the terms on which the loans are repayable and the rates at which interest is payable thereon.

9. Where any liability of the company is secured otherwise than by operation of law on any assets of the company, the fact that that liability is so secured shall be stated, but it shall not be necessary to specify the assets on which the liability is secured.

10. Where any of the company's debentures are held by a nominee of or trustee for the company, the nominal amount of the debentures and the amount at which they are stated in the books of the company shall be stated.

11.—(1) The matters referred to in the following sub-paragraphs shall be stated by way of note, or in a statement or report annexed, if not otherwise shown.

(2) The number, description and amount of any shares in the company which any person has an option to subscribe for, together with the following particulars of the option, that is to say—

(*a*) the period during which it is exercisable;
(*b*) the price to be paid for shares subscribed for under it.

(3) The amount of any arrears of fixed cumulative dividends on the company's shares and the period for which the dividends or, if there is more than one class, each class of them are in arrear, the amount to be stated before deduction of income tax, except that, in the case of tax free dividends, the amount shall be shown free of tax and the fact that it is so shown shall also be stated.

(4) Particulars of any charge on the assets of the company to secure the liabilities of any other person, including, where practicable, the amount secured.

(5) The general nature of any other contingent liabilities not provided for and, where practicable, the aggregate amount or estimated amount of those liabilities, if it is material.

(6) Where practicable the aggregate amount or estimated amount, if it is material, of contracts for capital expenditure, so far as not provided for and, where practicable, the aggregate amount or estimated amount, if it is material, of capital expenditure authorised by the directors which has not been contracted for.

(6A) In the case of fixed assets under any heading whose amount is required to be arrived at in accordance with paragraph 5 (1) of this Schedule (other than unquoted investments) and is so arrived at by reference to a valuation, the years (so far as they are known to the directors) in which the assets were severally valued and the several values, and, in the case of assets that have been valued during the financial year, the names of the persons who valued them or particulars of their qualifications for doing so and (whichever is stated) the bases of valuation used by them.

(6B) If there are included amongst fixed assets under any heading (other than investments) assets that have been acquired during the financial year, the aggregate amount of the assets acquired as determined for the purpose of making up the balance sheet, and if during that year any fixed assets included under a heading in the balance sheet made up with respect to the immediately preceding financial year (other than investments) have been disposed of or destroyed, the aggregate amount thereof as determined for the purpose of making up that balance sheet.

(6C) Of the amount of fixed assets consisting of land, how much is ascribable to land of freehold tenure and how much to land of leasehold tenure, and, of the latter, how much is ascribable to land held on long lease and how much to land held on short lease.

(7) If in the opinion of the directors any of the current assets have not a value, on realisation in the ordinary course of the company's business, at least equal to the amount at which they are stated, the fact that the directors are of that opinion.

(8) The aggregate market value of the company's quoted investments where it differs from the amount of the investments as stated, and the stock exchange value of any investments of which the market value is shown (whether separately or not) and is taken as being higher than their stock exchange value.

(8A) If a sum set aside for the purpose of its being used to prevent undue fluctuations in charges for taxation has been used during the financial year for another purpose, the amount thereof and the fact that it has been so used.

(8B) If the amount carried forward for stock in trade or work in progress is material for the appreciation by its members of the company's state of affairs or of its profit or loss for the financial year, the manner in which that amount has been computed.

(9) The basis on which foreign currencies have been converted into sterling, where the amount of the assets or liabilities affected is material.

(10) The basis on which the amount, if any, set aside for United Kingdom corporation tax is computed.

(11) Except in the case of the first balance sheet laid before the company after the commencement of this Act, the corresponding amounts at the end of the immediately preceding financial year for all items shown in the balance sheet.

Profit and Loss Account

12.—(1) There shall be shown—

(*a*) the amount charged to revenue by way of provision for depreciation, renewals or diminution in value of fixed assets;

(*b*) the amount of the interest on loans of the following kinds made to the company (whether on the security of debentures or not), namely, bank loans, overdrafts and loans which, not being bank loans or overdrafts:

(i) are repayable otherwise than by instalments and fall due for repayment before the expiration of the period of five years beginning with the day next following the expiration of the financial year; or

(ii) are repayable by instalments the last of which falls due for payment before the expiration of the period;

and the amount of the interest on loans of other kinds so made (whether on the security of debentures or not).

(*c*) the amount of the charge to revenue for United Kingdom corporation tax and, if that amount would have been greater but for relief from double taxation, the amount which it would have been but for such relief, the amount of the charge for United Kingdom income tax and the amount of the charge for taxation imposed outside the United Kingdom of profits, income and (so far as charged to revenue) capital gains;

(*d*) the amounts respectively provided for redemption of share capital and for redemption of loans;

(*e*) the amount, if material, set aside or proposed to be set aside to, or withdrawn from, reserves;

(*f*) subject to sub-paragraph (2) of this paragraph, the amount, if material, set aside to provisions other than provisions for depreciation, renewals or diminution in value of assets or, as the case may be, the amount, if material, withdrawn from such provisions and not applied for the purposes thereof;

(*g*) the amounts respectively of income from quoted investments and income from unquoted investments;

(*ga*) if a substantial part of the company's revenue for the financial year consists in rents from land, the amount thereof (after deduction of ground-rents, rates and other outgoings);

(*gb*) the amount, if material, charged to revenue in respect of sums payable in respect of the hire of plant and machinery;

(*h*) the aggregate amount (before deduction of income tax) of the dividends paid and proposed.

(2) The Board of Trade may direct that a company shall not be obliged to show an amount set aside to provisions in accordance with

sub-paragraph (1) (*f*) of this paragraph, if the Board is satisfied that that is not required in the public interest and would prejudice the company, but subject to the condition that any heading stating an amount arrived at after taking into account the amount set aside as aforesaid shall be so framed or marked as to indicate that fact.

(3) If, in the case of any assets in whose case an amount is charged to revenue by way of provision for depreciation or diminution in value, an amount is also so charged by way of provision for renewal thereof, the last-mentioned amount shall be shown separately.

(4) If the amount charged to revenue by way of provision for depreciation or diminution in value of any fixed assets (other than investments) has been determined otherwise than by reference to the amount of those assets as determined for the purpose of making up the balance sheet, that fact shall be stated.

12A. The amount of any charge arising in consequence of the occurrence of an event in a preceding financial year and of any credit so arising shall, if not included in a heading relating to other matters, be stated under a separate heading.

13. The amount of the remuneration of the auditors shall be shown under a separate heading, and for the purposes of this paragraph, any sums paid by the company in respect of the auditors' expenses shall be deemed to be included in the expression 'remuneration'.

13A.—(1) The matters referred to in sub-paragraphs (2) to (4) below shall be stated by way of note, if not otherwise shown.

(2) The turnover for the financial year, except in so far as it is attributable to the business of banking or discounting or to business of such other class as may be prescribed for the purposes of this sub-paragraph.

(3) If some or all of the turnover is omitted by reason of its being attributable as aforesaid, the fact that it is so omitted.

(4) The method by which turnover stated is arrived at.

(5) A company shall not be subject to the requirements of this paragraph if it is neither a holding company nor a subsidiary of another body corporate and the turnover which, apart from this sub-paragraph, would be required to be stated does not exceed £50,000.

14.—(1) The matters referred to in the following sub-paragraphs shall be stated by way of note, if not otherwise shown.

(2) If depreciation or replacement of fixed assets is provided for by some method other than a depreciation charge or provision for renewals, or is not provided for, the method by which, it is provided for or the fact that it is not provided for, as the case may be.

(3) The basis on which the charge for United Kingdom corporation tax and United Kingdom income tax is computed.

(3A) Any special circumstances which affect liability in respect of taxation of profits, income or capital gains for the financial year or liability in respect of taxation of profits, income or capital gains for succeeding financial years.

(5) Except in the case of the first profit and loss account laid before the company after the commencement of this Act, the corresponding amounts for the immediately preceding financial year for all items shown in the profit and loss account.

(6) Any material respects in which any items shown in the profit and loss account are affected—

(*a*) by transactions of a sort not usually undertaken by the company or otherwise by circumstances of an exceptional or non-recurrent nature; or

(*b*) by any change in the basis of accounting.

APPENDIX B **Recommendations on Accounting Principles**[1]

15. Accounting in relation to changes in the purchasing power of money (issued 30 May 1952)

In amplification of its Recommendation **12** *on* RISING PRICE LEVELS IN RELATION TO ACCOUNTS, *the Council of The Institute of Chartered Accounts in England and Wales makes the following statement to members of the Institute. This statement is designed to present in conjunction with Recommendation* **12** *a brief description of the limitations on the significance of accounts prepared on the generally accepted basis known as historical cost, to examine the main suggestions so far made for new principles designed to overcome those limitations and to make recommendations as to the procedure which should be followed in preparing annual accounts unless and until a generally acceptable alternative to the historical cost basis of accounting is available. The whole subject of accounting in relation to changes in the purchasing power of money is of such importance that the Council proposes, after the International Congress on Accounting in June 1952, to invite other professional bodies to join with it in furthur study of the subject.* Pending the outcome of such further study, it is hoped that this statement will be helpful to members whose advice may be sought by clients, or who have responsibilities as directors or officers of companies.*

* See now the statement appearing after paragraph 31.

Accounting based on historical cost

1 The primary purpose of the annual accounts of a business is to present information to the proprietors, showing how their funds have

[1] This extract from the Recommendations' on Accounting Principles, published by the Institute of Chartered Accountants in England and Wales, is reproduced here by kind permission of the Institute.

been utilised and the profits derived from such use. It has long been accepted in accounting practice that a balance sheet prepared for this purpose is an historical record and not a statement of current worth. Stated briefly its function is to show in monetary terms the capital, reserves and liabilities of a business at the date as at which it is prepared and the manner in which the total moneys representing them have been distributed over the several types of assets. Similarly a profit and loss account is an historical record. It shows as the profit or loss the difference between the revenue for the period covered by the account and the expenditure chargeable in that period, including charges for the amortisation of capital expenditure. Revenue and expenditure are brought into the account at their recorded monetary amounts. This basis of accounting is frequently described as the historical cost basis and in this statement the expression 'monetary profits' is used to denote profits so computed.

2 An important feature of the historical cost basis of preparing annual accounts is that it reduces to a minimum the extent to which the accounts can be affected by the personal opinions of those responsible for them. For example, the cost of a fixed asset is known so that in calculating depreciation provisions based on that cost the only respects in which estimates enter into the matter are in relation to the probable useful life of the asset and its realisable value, if any, at the end of its life. Depreciation provisions computed on this basis are intended, by making charges against revenue over the useful life of an asset, to amortise the capital expenditure incurred in acquiring it. For this purpose, estimates of current value or of replacement cost do not arise. Again, there are limits within which estimates and opinions can properly operate in relation to stock-in-trade, provided the bases of calculation are sound in principle and used consistently.

3 The significance of accounts prepared on the basis of historical cost is, however, subject to limitations, not the least of which is that the monetary unit in which accounts are prepared is not a stable unit of measurement. During a period of rising prices a decrease occurs in the purchasing power of cash and bank balances and assets such as debts and investments carrying fixed rates of interest or dividend, but this decrease is not treated as a reduction of business profits; nor are business profits shown as being increased by the benefit derived from the fall in the burden, expressed in terms of purchasing power, of

loans and other liabilities incurred before the rise in prices but payable in currency of diminished purchasing power. Moreover, the monetary cost at which stock-in-trade is charged against revenue is not sufficient, during a period of rising prices, to meet the cost of replacing the same quantity of stock; and similarly depreciation charges based on the monetary cost of fixed assets will not provide the amount required to meet the cost of replacement of those assets at higher prices if and when they need to be replaced.

4 Monetary profits do not therefore necessarily reflect an increase or decrease in wealth in terms of purchasing power; and in times of material change in prices this limitation upon the significance of monetary profits may be very important. It would be a major development in the building up of a coherent and logical structure of accounting principles if the limitations of accounts based on historical cost could be eliminated or reduced by the adoption of new principles, capable of practical application to all kinds of businesses in a manner which would be independent of personal opinion to a degree comparable with the existing principles based on historical cost.

The main suggestions for new accounting principles

5 The main suggestions which have so far been made for new accounting principles to overcome the limitations of the historical cost basis, may be considered in the following four broad categories:

- The replacement cost method of dealing with fixed assets
- The writing-up of fixed assets
- The current value method of dealing with stock-in-trade and depreciation of fixed assets
- The index method of adjusting accounts to reflect changes in the purchasing power of money.

The replacement cost method of dealing with fixed assets

6 The object of the replacement cost method of dealing with fixed assets is to make charges to profit and loss account to provide the amount needed to meet the cost of replacement. Under this method

therefore provisions for replacement would be charged, instead of depreciation charges designed to amortise the cost of fixed assets over their useful life. The method was followed more extensively in the past than it is today, particularly though not exclusively by public utility undertakings.

7 Considerable uncertainty attaches to the calculations required by the replacement cost method. Unless an asset is to be replaced within a very short period, the replacement cost cannot be estimated with any accuracy and the method therefore leaves wide scope for extremes of personal opinion in determining each year the charge to be made in computing profits. Moreover, improved methods of production and new inventions often render existing plant obsolete with the result that when it is replaced the new equipment is of a different character from the old.

8 In conditions where prices continue to rise, the uncertainty of the method is emphasised because the estimated replacement cost of assets increases year by year. If each year's charge has been calculated on the basis of one year's proportion of the replacement cost estimated at the time of making the calculation, then the aggregate of the amounts so provided will not be sufficient to meet the actual cost of replacement. If in order to meet this difficulty the calculation each year is made on a cumulative basis so as to make up the deficiency in past provisions, the effect would be to place undue burdens upon particular years. On the other hand if the deficiency were not so made good, the amounts shown as profits would not have been arrived at after providing for the replacement of fixed assets. In the latter event, the effect of applying the method would be to show as profits each year amounts which are neither monetary profits nor profits after providing fully for the replacement of fixed assets; the more persistent the rise in prices the less significance the profits computed in this way would have, because each further rise in prices would increase the deficiency in the past provisions.

9 In addition to the foregoing difficulties of calculation and treatment, the method involves other considerations which become apparent when replacement occurs. At that point two courses are open, namely either (*a*) to bring into the balance sheet the cost of the new asset, thus maintaining in the balance sheet the cost of the

fixed assets in current use; or (*b*) to charge the cost of the new asset against the accumulated replacement provisions. If the first course is followed the cost of the asset replaced will be charged against the accumulated replacement provisions; but if prices have been rising these provisions will exceed the amount charged against them and this excess will be treated as a reserve, thus being recognised in the balance sheet as part of the proprietorship interest. This involves the inconsistency that the profits of each year during which the provisions are accumulated will be ascertained after deducting amounts which it is known must in due course be recognised as reserves and could become available for distribution to proprietors. Such a reserve would not be disclosed in the balance sheet if the second course were followed (namely the charging of the cost of the new asset against the accumulated replacement provisions), because the balance sheet would not show the cost of existing assets; instead it would continue to include the cost of the asset which has been replaced and if this procedure were followed on each successive replacement the amount standing in the balance sheet would be the original cost of an asset which may have been replaced many times.

10 Another consideration arises in a period of falling prices when replacement would cost less than historical cost. If each year's charge is calculated on the basis of one year's proportion of the replacement cost estimated at the time of making the calculation, then the aggregate of the amounts so provided will fall short of the amount required to amortise the cost of the existing assets. It cannot be assumed that there will be reserves against which to charge the deficiency and it would therefore seem that the charge must be to the profit and loss account. The effect of such a charge would be to adjust the aggregate depreciation charges to what they would have been under the historical cost method. The replacement cost method is therefore not capable of application in a period of falling prices, unless an additional charge is made in order to provide for the full amortisation of capital expenditure actually incurred.

The writing-up of fixed assets

11 In some countries businesses have been permitted for taxation purposes to write-up fixed assets in accordance with a legally

established index and thereafter to charge depreciation on the written-up amounts.

12 The writing-up of fixed assets has the effect of treating the business as ceasing and starting afresh on a new basis as from the date of writing-up; and this is why it is in practice considered to be appropriate and desirable in certain special circumstances, such as where a subsidiary is acquired and the assets are written-up to reflect the cost to the acquiring company, or where subscriptions for new capital are invited on the basis of a current valuation of the assets. Apart from such special purposes, the writing-up of assets appears to be suitable only for the readjustment of all balance sheets by government action as part of a process of stabilising a currency.

13 If fixed assets are written up, the subsequent charges for depreciation will be the amounts required to amortise the written-up amounts of the assets over their remaining life. The figures shown as profits for years subsequent to the writing-up will therefore be arrived at after charging depreciation on amounts which are neither the historical cost nor the estimated replacement cost of the fixed assets. If the writing-up were not based on a legally established or generally accepted index there would be wide scope for the factor of personal opinion in so computing depreciation charges. The method also involves an inconsistency similar to that arising under the replacement cost method. At the time of writing-up, the excess of the written-up amount over the historical cost of the assets concerned would be treated in the balance sheet as a capital reserve, later, when the written-up amount has been fully amortised by subsequent depreciation charges, the reserve could become available for distribution to the proprietors although it will never have appeared as profit in the profit and loss account.

The current value method of dealing with depreciation and stock-in-trade

14 The object of the current value method of dealing with depreciation and stock-in-trade is to express charges for consumption of assets in current values and not in terms of the monetary cost of the assets consumed.

15 Charges for depreciation of fixed assets would not be regarded as the spreading of historical cost or as provisions for future replacement. They would be regarded as a measurement of asset consumption during the year, calculated by applying the depreciation rates to the estimated current value of the fixed assets instead of to their historical cost. Broadly the effect would be that the charges in any particular year for depreciation of fixed assets would be adjusted to approximately what they would have been if the assets had been purchased at prices ruling in that year instead of when they were in fact purchased. Some advocates of this basis of ascertaining profits suggest that the method by which the current value of fixed assets is estimated should be that best suited to the particular type of business; for example valuation by the company's engineering staff, or current insurance values, or price indices according to the year of purchase. Such a proposal serves to emphasise the dependence of the method upon personal opinion.

16 In a period of rising prices when current values are greater than historical cost, the depreciation charges calculated on current values would exceed depreciation calculated on historical cost and the method requires this excess to be shown in the balance sheet as a capital reserve. This would involve the inconsistency that an amount which is treated as a deduction in computing profits is recognised in the balance sheet as forming part of the interest of the proprietors and could even become available for distribution to them in the event of the reserve being regarded as no longer of a capital nature. In a period of falling prices when current values are less than historical cost, the method would not be capable of application unless an additional charge were made to provide for the full amortisation of capital expenditure actually incurred.

17 As already indicated, the current value method does not purport to be a means of providing for the replacement of fixed assets. If therefore prices continue to rise and it were desired to accumulate the full amount required to replace fixed assets, it would be necessary to set aside additional sums over and above the depreciation charges calculated on current values. These additional sums would be treated in the profit and loss account as transfers to reserve. The total reserve shown in the balance sheet under the current value method would then be the same as that which can be achieved under existing

accounting principles; but whereas under existing principles the creation of that reserve would be shown in the profit and loss account as having been made out of profits, under the current value method part of the amount taken to reserve would be treated, as stated in the preceding paragraph, as a charge in arriving at profits.

18 The current value method also requires charges for consumption of stock-in-trade to have regard to current values rather than to historical cost. Some advocates of the method suggest that the manner of charging consumption in current values should be left open for consideration in the special circumstances of each case but that certain methods of valuing stock-in-trade, namely LIFO (last in, first out), NIFO (next in, first out) base stock and variants of these should be recognised as means of achieving the desired end and that whatever method is adopted should be indicated in the accounts.

19 In a period of rising prices the effect of charging consumption of stock-in-trade on the basis of current values would be that the difference between the cost of an article and the higher amount for which it could be replaced at the time of its sale would not form part of the profit on the transaction. In a period of falling prices when stock-in-trade could be replaced at less than its historical cost, the current value method could not be applied unless an additional charge were made to cover the excess of the historical cost over the current value. Whether prices are rising or falling however the difference between the cost of an article and its current value may often result to a much greater extent from market fluctuations in the prices of particular goods than any general trend in the purchasing power of money. Such market fluctuations are an ordinary business hazard affecting profit or loss and their incidence on a particular business may be dependent to a considerable extent upon judgment in buying and on management generally, whereas under the current value method the effect of these fluctuations would be excluded in computing profits.

The index method of adjusting accounts to reflect changes in the purchasing power of money

20 The object of the index method of adjusting accounts is to eliminate from profits the effect of fluctuations in the purchasing power of money.

21 The method is not strictly a proposal for a change from accounting based on historical cost; it is *more in the nature of a proposal for adjusting* accounts which have been prepared on the basis of historical cost. The ascertainment of profits involves bringing together in one account monetary amounts for transactions which have taken place not only at various times during the period covered by the account but also at various times in other periods, for example, stock-in-trade at the commencement of the period and fixed assets acquired many years earlier. The theory of the index method is that if there has been a change in the purchasing power of money between the time when a transaction was entered into and the date as on which the accounts are prepared, the currency in which the transaction took place was a currency different from that now in use and must be converted into the new currency. For the conversion process an index of purchasing power would be used.

22 The technique of applying the index method need not present insuperable difficulties if a satisfactory index were available, although there could be considerable complications in respect of businesses with complex capital structures. An important practical consideration would be that in order to enable the index method to be applied as a part of normal accounting procedure, it would be essential for the index to be available in an up-to-date form month by month; otherwise it would not be available for use as and when required by a particular business for the rapid production of the annual accounts at the normal accounting date. It would seem from the theory underlying the index method that it must apply not merely to transactions effected in earlier years, such as the purchase of fixed assets or stock-in-trade held at the beginning of the accounting period, but also to transactions during the accounting period if during that period there have been material changes in the purchasing power of money.

23 Unless all items were converted into the 'new currency' and not merely selected items such as depreciation of fixed assets and consumption of stock-in-trade, the account would not, in a period of rising prices, reflect the loss in purchasing power arising from the holding of assets such as investments, debtors and bank balances or the gain arising on liabilities of fixed monetary amount. In businesses where such items are material in relation to fixed assets and stock-in-trade it would be inconsistent to ignore such losses and gains and to

take into account only those arising on particular types of assets. To do so would not enable the effects of the diminution in the purchasing power of money to be measured so that they can be eliminated in ascertaining profits or losses. Similar considerations arise in a period of falling prices.

24 Application of the theory underlying the index method would require an index which represents changes in the purchasing power of money and not indices of changes in the prices of particular articles. If an index of purchasing power were not used, it would be necessary to use different indices for various items in the accounts of any one business; this procedure would be a means of applying the current value method to stock-in-trade and depreciation but it would not measure the effect of changes in the general purchasing power of money which is the object of the index method. The view might be taken that the use of an accurate index of changes in general purchasing power is not important and that any reasonable index could enable the effects of such changes to be measured with sufficient accuracy, provided the same index were used by all businesses. On the other hand, prices do not move uniformly for all articles and commodities, so that the application of a general index to a particular business could well be inappropriate. Moreover the effect on a particular business of changes in the purchasing power of money may be offset by the benefits derived from technical improvements. The whole theory of the index method therefore needs further examination before it could be accepted as a valid method of adjusting accounts prepared on the basis of historical cost.

25 If it were established that the theory of a general purchasing power of money is valid and a satisfactory index could be prepared, there would remain the important question of the purpose for which the index method is to be applied. If it were used merely as a means of measuring the effects on the affairs of a business of changes in the purchasing power of money, for the purpose of giving this information in statements supplementary to accounts prepared on the basis of historical cost, it might give information which would be of interest to the management and proprietors. If however the index method were accepted as a means of introducing a new conception of profit, it would carry implications which extend far beyond accounting matters.

Economic and social issues

26 The adoption of any new conception of profit, whether based on the replacement cost method, the writing-up of fixed assets, the current value method, or the index method, would raise much wider questions than the computation of business profits. A conception based on the index method would raise the whole question of the effect of changes in the purchasing power of money on rights expressed in monetary terms. Important economic and social issues would then need consideration and some of these would also arise if a conception of profit based on any of the other three methods were adopted. The following are some of the questions which would need consideration:

a whether there should be legal recognition of changes in the purchasing power of money so as to adjust legal rights which have been expressed in terms of money; for example investments in government and other stocks and shares, rents under leases, pensions, insurance policies, debentures and other liabilities, rights under service agreements and profit-sharing schemes to incomes which are dependent on or vary with profits, and the relative rights of life tenants and remaindermen

b the determination of prices of goods and services, particularly the question whether a new conception of profit would make it necessary for prices to be raised in order to enable a business to pay a fair return to investors, or indeed to make a profit at all; in other words whether the effect would be to cause a further fall in the purchasing power of money and thereby aggravate the problem

c the relative position for taxation purposes of different kinds of businesses and of persons having money incomes, including employees and pensioners of businesses. In the United Kingdom the basis and scale of taxation seriously restrict the extent to which monetary profits may be retained in businesses to meet the increased capital requirements imposed by diminution in the purchasing power of money. A new conception of business profits designed to alleviate this situation would raise the question of what is the proper taxable income of other classes of taxpayer; in a period of rising prices it would relieve businesses of a large amount of taxation and would therefore raise the further question of how the burden of that relief is to be distributed over other taxpayers *d* the effect on the raising of capital for business undertakings if such capital is to be raised on the basis that before dividends can be paid the purchasing power of the capital employed in the business must be maintained, as distinct from the existing position under which it is a matter of policy for directors to consider to what extent monetary profits are to be regarded as available for distribution and to what extent it is desirable to retain profits to meet the future requirements of the business

e the position in the event of the purchasing power of money being increased by falling prices, particularly if the effect of a new conception of profit were to be that the contributed capital would cease to be intact

f the position of persons who have acquired investments on the basis of annual accounts or prospectus statements prepared in accordance with existing accounting principles, if the adoption of a new conception of profit would result in dividends, including those on preference capital, whether or not cumulative, being reduced or passed.

27 These issues affect not merely every business but also every individual and they involve major considerations of general monetary and social policy which go far beyond the question whether one accounting method of computing business profits is more free from limitations than another.

Conclusions and recommendations

28 The Council cannot emphasise too strongly that the significance of accounts prepared on the basis of historical cost is subject to limitations, not the least of which is that the monetary unit in which the accounts are prepared is not a stable unit of measurement. In consequence the results shown by accounts prepared on the basis of historical cost are not a measure of increase or decrease in wealth in terms of purchasing power; nor do the results necessarily represent the amount which can prudently be regarded as available for distribution, having regard to the financial requirements of the business. Similarly the results shown by such accounts are not necessarily suitable for purposes such as price fixing, wage negotiations and taxation, unless in using them for these purposes due

regard is paid to the amount of profit which has been retained in the business for its maintenance.

29 On the other hand the alternatives to historical cost which have so far been suggested appear to have serious defects and their logical application would raise social and economic issues going far beyond the realm of accountancy. The Council is therefore unable to regard any of the suggestions so far made as being acceptable alternatives to the existing accounting principles based on historical cost.

Recommendations

30 Unless and until a practicable and generally acceptable alternative is available, the Council recommends that the accounting principles set out below should continue to be applied:

a historical cost should continue to be the basis on which annual accounts should be prepared and, in consequence, the basis on which profits shown by such accounts are computed

b any amount set aside out of profits in recognition of the effects which changes in the purchasing power of money have had on the affairs of the business (including any amount to finance the increase in the cost of replacements, whether of fixed or current assets) should be treated as a transfer to reserve and not as a charge in arriving at profits. If such a transfer is shown in the profit and loss account as a deduction in arriving at the balance for the year, that balance should be described appropriately, since it is not the whole of the profits

c in order to emphasise that as a matter of prudence the amount so set aside is, for the time being, regarded by directors as not available for distribution, it should normally be treated as a capital reserve

d for balance sheet purposes fixed assets should not (except in special circumstances, such as those referred to in paragraph 12) be written-up, especially in the absence of monetary stability.

31 The Council also recommends to members who are directors or officers of companies or who are asked by clients for advice, that they should stress the limitations on the significance of profits computed on the basis of historical cost in periods of material

changes in the purchasing power of money; and that they should draw attention to the desirability of:

a setting amounts aside from profits to reserve in recognition of the effects which changes in the purchasing power of money have had upon the affairs of the business, particularly their effect on the amount of profit which, as a matter of policy, can prudently be regarded as available for distribution

b showing in the directors' report or otherwise the effects which changes in the purchasing power of money have had on the affairs of the business, including in particular the financial requirements for its maintenance and the directors' policy for meeting those requirements, either by setting aside to reserve or by raising new capital

c experimenting with methods of measuring the effects of changes in the purchasing power of money on profits and on financial requirements. If the results of such experiments are published as part of the documents accompanying the annual accounts, the basis used for the calculations and the significance of the figures in relation to the business concerned should be stated clearly.

Statement by the Council published in 'The Accountant' of 16th January 1954

32 The headnote to the Council's Recommendation **15**, issued on 30th May 1952, stated that the whole subject of accounting in relation to changes in the purchasing power of money was of such importance that the Council proposed, after the International Congress on Accounting in June 1952, to invite other professional bodies to join with it in further study of the subject. Accordingly, in July 1952 the Council issued invitations to The Institute of Chartered Accountants of Scotland, The Society of Incorporated Accountants and Auditors, The Institute of Chartered Accountants in Ireland and The Association of Certified and Corporate Accountants. All these bodies appointed representatives to meet with representatives of the Council with the object of considering whether there is a practicable and generally acceptable alternative to the existing conception of profit computed on the basis of historical cost. A first meeting was held in

November 1952, when Recommendation **15** was discussed and the representatives of the Scottish Institute, the Society and the Association undertook to obtain for consideration at a further meeting the views of their respective Councils. (The representative of the Irish Institute was unable to be present.)

33 Memoranda submitted on behalf of the Councils of each of the three bodies were considered at a second meeting in December 1953. At the end of this meeting the representatives of the Council stated that they were willing to arrange a further meeting or meetings if the representatives of the other bodies so desired, but as none felt there was any likelihood of general agreement being reached between the various bodies it was decided that the discussions should be regarded as closed.

34 During these two meetings nothing has emerged which makes it necessary for the time being for the Council to amend or add to the comprehensive review of the subject which is contained in Recommendation **15**.

APPENDIX C Discounting Techniques Explained

Introduction

1 The object of these examples is to enable the reader to become accustomed to the use of interest tables for determining the *present* value of a sum of money which is *receivable in the future*. Conversely the growth, through the passage of time, of a present sum of money which is invested at a specified rate of interest, will also be demonstrated.

2 A sum of £500 is invested for six years at a 10 per cent per annum interest rate.

Amount of initial investment	£500
First year's interest (£500 × 0·1)	50
On hand at end of first year	550
Second year's interest (£550 × 0·1)	55
On hand at end of second year	605
Third year's interest (£605 × 0·1)	60·5
On hand at end of third year	665·5
Fourth year's interest (£665·5 × 0·1)	66·5
On hand at end of fourth year	732
Fifth year's interest (£732 × 0·1)	73·2
On hand at end of fifth year	805·2
Sixth year's interest (£805·2 × 0·1)	80·5
On hand at end of sixth year	£885·7

The above sequence of computations presents three facts to the analyst. These are:

a Assuming an interest rate of 10 per cent, £500 today is comparable with the right to receive £885·7 in six years' time.
b Conversely, and making the same assumption concerning interest, the receipt of a sum of £885·7 in six years' time has a present value of £500 today, and
c a sum of £500 invested today to produce £885·7 in six years' time has a yield of 10 per cent.

Discounting and compounding

3 Turning to the present value interest tables on page 242 it will be seen that today's value of a £ receivable in six years' time, at a discount rate of 10 per cent, is £0·5645. Therefore to find the present value of £885·7 which is receivable at the end of six years, using the same discounting rate, it is necessary to work the following simple multiplication sum:

$$\pounds 885{\cdot}7 \times 0{\cdot}5645 = \pounds 500$$

In this calculation, the resultant £500 is given after allowing for the very slight approximations which led to the original calculation of the £885·7. Now in this instance £500 is the present value referred to in para. 2(*b*) above: it is the future sum of £885·7 which has been discounted over six years to the present time. It should be noted that *the capital sums are therefore equal after allowing for a financing cost of 10 per cent per annum.*

4 Compounding is the reverse of discounting. It means the aggregation of the original capital invested, plus interest upon interest and upon that invested sum, throughout the life of the investment. Looking back at the example in para. 2 above, in order to ascertain the amount to which £500 will increase in six years' time at a rate of 10 per cent, the reader may use either compound interest tables, or take the reciprocal of the factor shown in para. 3. The arithmetical calculation is

$$£500 \times \frac{1}{0{\cdot}5645} \text{ (i.e. times the reciprocal)}$$

$$= £500 \times 1{\cdot}7714 \text{ (i.e. times the compound interest factor).}$$

$$= \underline{£885{\cdot}7}$$

5 The interest factors for discounting and compounding, etc., can be obtained by referring to various publications devoted to presenting this information.[1] Interest tables such as these will be used in normal circumstances to save laborious calculations. However, the reader ought to understand how they have been derived. Now the discounting factors are arrived at by starting with the value of £1 today; all that one has to remember is that today's pound (year 0) is next year's pound (year 1) plus 10 per cent, assuming this to be the discounting rate, and the arithmetical display is

$$\text{Year 1} \quad 1 \times \frac{100}{110} = 0{\cdot}90909.$$

$$\text{Year 2} \quad 0{\cdot}90909 \times \frac{100}{110} = 0{\cdot}82644$$

$$\text{Year 3} \quad 0{\cdot}82644 \times \frac{100}{110} = 0{\cdot}75131.$$

For years 4, 5, and 6, the interest factors will be found to be 0·68301, 0·62092 and 0·56447 respectively. In this way we are able to obtain the discounting factors, at a 10 per cent interest rate, for a series of years one to six. To simplify the calculations which will follow in para. 6, the interest factors have been restricted to three decimal places.

Capital and interest recovery—present value

6 Assume an investment which can show cash flows of £100 in each of the next six years, and assume also that the capital to carry out this investment can be borrowed at 10 per cent. The above interest factors will show *the present value* of those *future* cash flows, thus:

[1] LAWSON, G. H., and WINDLE, D. W., *Tables for DCF Annuity, Sinking Fund, Compound Interest and Annual Capital Charge Calculations*, Oliver and Boyd, 1965.

Year 1	100 × 0·909 =	£90·9
Year 2	100 × 0·826 =	82·6
Year 3	100 × 0·751 =	75·1
Year 4	100 × 0·683 =	68·3
Year 5	100 × 0·621 =	62·1
Year 6	100 × 0·565 =	56·5
PRESENT VALUE OF CASH FLOWS		£435·5

From this statement it can be said that if the investment costs £435·5 today and this capital sum can be obtained at 10 per cent per annum interest, then the future cash flows will just break even with investment cost. It should be noted that the future cash flows:

a Repay the original capital cost.
b Pay a capital financing charge of 10 per cent.

Capital and interest recovery—net present value

7 If the capital cost of the above investment were LESS than £435·5 then the difference between that lower cost and the £435·5 (shown in para. 6 as the present value of the future return series) would represent the increase in wealth or the profitability stemming from the project. The difference is referred to as the *net present value* of the investment and again it should be very carefully noted that this increase in wealth would have been obtained:

a After repaying the original capital cost.
b After paying a capital financing charge of 10 per cent.

Uniform cash flows and the annuity

8 The interest factors in para. 6 can be used in different ways. The reader will observe that these present value factors total to a sum of 4·355. This use of present value techniques appertains to an annuity which is concerned with equal payments over equal periods of time. Thus the factor of 4·355 informs us that, in order to obtain an income of £1 per year for the next six years at an interest rate of 10 per cent, it

is necessary to invest £4·355 today. Similarly, and by the same conditions, in order to receive £100 in each of the next *three* years it is necessary to invest £248·6 today (the factors for the first three years total to 2·486). Put in another way, the receipt of £100 in each of the next three years, allowing for a financing charge of 10 per cent, will cost £248·6 today.

DCF yield or investment rate of return

9 The above examples of compounding and discounting enable a flat rate of return to be obtained by showing

(*a*) a present value or
(*b*) a terminal value of a series of cashflows.

The yield or investment rate of return (see page 130) is the rate of interest which discounts the future incomes produced by an investment, to the point where investment cost and the present value of future incomes are equal. In simpler vein, this is the same as saying that the yield rate is the rate of interest which could be paid on a bank overdraft, necessary to finance the investment, without the investor showing a profit or a loss. In this case the annual cash flows are then treated as repayments of principal and interest as the table below shows.

EXHIBIT 97

INVESTMENT COSTING £435·5 RETURNS £100 P.A.
IN EACH OF 6 YEARS (INTEREST RATE 10 PER CENT)

Year	Initial advance o/s at beginning of each year	Interest due for year	Principal + interest due at end of year	Cash flows used to repay: Interest	Cash flows used to repay: Principal	O/s at end of year
	£	£	£	£	£	£
1	435·5	43·6	479·1	43·6	56·4	379·1
2	379·1	37·9	417·0	37·9	62·1	317·0
3	317·0	31·7	348·7	31·7	68·3	248·7
4	248·7	24·9	273·6	24·9	75·1	173·6
5	173·6	17·4	191·0	17·4	82·6	91·0
6	91·0	9·0	100·0	9·0	91·0	Nil
				164·5	435·5	
				£600		

APPENDIX D **Tables A and B**

Table A

PRESENT VALUE OF £1

(WHAT £1 DUE IN THE FUTURE IS WORTH TODAY)

$(1 + r)^{-n}$

Year	1%	2%	3%	4%	5%	6%	7%
1	0·9901	0·9804	0·9709	0·9615	0·9524	0·9434	0·9346
2	0·9803	0·9612	0·9426	0·9246	0·9070	0·8900	0·8734
3	0·9706	0·9423	0·9151	0·8890	0·8638	0·8396	0·8163
4	0·9610	0·9238	0·8885	0·8548	0·8227	0·7921	0·7629
5	0·9515	0·9057	0·8626	0·8219	0·7835	0·7473	0·7130
6	0·9420	0·8880	0·8375	0·7903	0·7462	0·7050	0·6663
7	0·9327	0·8706	0·8131	0·7599	0·7107	0·6651	0·6227
8	0·9235	0·8535	0·7894	0·7307	0·6768	0·6274	0·5820
9	0·9143	0·8368	0·7664	0·7026	0·6446	0·5919	0·5439
10	0·9053	0·8203	0·7441	0·6756	0·6139	0·5584	0·5083
11	0·8963	0·8043	0·7224	0·6496	0·5847	0·5268	0·4751
12	0·8874	0·7885	0·7014	0·6246	0·5568	0·4970	0·4440
13	0·8787	0·7730	0·6810	0·6006	0·5303	0·4688	0·4150
14	0·8700	0·7579	0·6611	0·5775	0·5051	0·4423	0·3878
15	0·8613	0·7430	0·6419	0·5553	0·4810	0·4173	0·3624
16	0·8528	0·7284	0·6232	0·5339	0·4581	0·3936	0·3387
17	0·8444	0·7142	0·6050	0·5134	0·4363	0·3714	0·3166
18	0·8360	0·7002	0·5874	0·4936	0·4155	0·3503	0·2959
19	0·8277	0·6864	0·5703	0·4746	0·3957	0·3305	0·2765
20	0·8195	0·6730	0·5537	0·4564	0·3769	0·3118	0·2584
21	0·8114	0·6598	0·5375	0·4388	0·3589	0·2942	0·2415
22	0·8034	0·6468	0·5219	0·4220	0·3419	0·2775	0·2257
23	0·7954	0·6342	0·5067	0·4057	0·3256	0·2618	0·2109
24	0·7876	0·6217	0·4919	0·3901	0·3101	0·2470	0·1971
25	0·7798	0·6095	0·4776	0·3751	0·2953	0·2330	0·1842
26	0·7721	0·5976	0·4637	0·3607	0·2812	0·2198	0·1722
27	0·7644	0·5859	0·4502	0·3468	0·2678	0·2074	0·1609
28	0·7568	0·5744	0·4371	0·3335	0·2551	0·1956	0·1504
29	0·7493	0·5631	0·4243	0·3207	0·2429	0·1846	0·1406
30	0·7419	0·5521	0·4120	0·3083	0·2314	0·1741	0·1314
40	0·6717	0·4529	0·3066	0·2083	0·1420	0·0972	0·0668
50	0·6080	0·3715	0·2281	0·1407	0·0872	0·0543	0·0339

$(1 + r)^{-n}$

Year	8%	9%	10%	12%	14%	15%	16%
1	0·9259	0·9174	0·9091	0·8929	0·8772	0·8696	0·8621
2	0·8573	0·8417	0·8264	0·7972	0·7695	0·7561	0·7432
3	0·7938	0·7722	0·7513	0·7118	0·6750	0·6575	0·6407
4	0·7350	0·7084	0·6830	0·6355	0·5921	0·5718	0·5523
5	0·6806	0·6499	0·6209	0·5674	0·5194	0·4972	0·4761
6	0·6302	0·5963	0·5645	0·5066	0·4556	0·4323	0·4104
7	0·5835	0·5470	0·5132	0·4523	0·3996	0·3759	0·3538
8	0·5403	0·5019	0·4665	0·4039	0·3506	0·3269	0·3050
9	0·5002	0·4604	0·4241	0·3606	0·3075	0·2843	0·2630
10	0·4632	0·4224	0·3855	0·3220	0·2697	0·2472	0·2267
11	0·4289	0·3875	0·3505	0·2875	0·2366	0·2149	0·1954
12	0·3971	0·3555	0·3186	0·2567	0·2076	0·1869	0·1685
13	0·3677	0·3262	0·2897	0·2292	0·1821	0·1625	0·1452
14	0·3405	0·2992	0·2633	0·2046	0·1597	0·1413	0·1252
15	0·3152	0·2745	0·2394	0·1827	0·1401	0·1229	0·1079
16	0·2919	0·2519	0·2176	0·1631	0·1229	0·1069	0·0930
17	0·2703	0·2311	0·1978	0·1456	0·1078	0·0929	0·0802
18	0·2502	0·2120	0·1799	0·1300	0·0946	0·0808	0·0691
19	0·2317	0·1945	0·1635	0·1161	0·0829	0·0703	0·0596
20	0·2145	0·1784	0·1486	0·1037	0·0728	0·0611	0·0514
21	0·1987	0·1637	0·1351	0·0926	0·0638	0·0531	0·0443
22	0·1839	0·1502	0·1228	0·0826	0·0560	0·0462	0·0382
23	0·1703	0·1378	0·1117	0·0738	0·0491	0·0402	0·0329
24	0·1577	0·1264	0·1015	0·0659	0·0431	0·0349	0·0284
25	0·1460	0·1160	0·0923	0·0588	0·0378	0·0304	0·0245
26	0·1352	0·1064	0·0839	0·0525	0·0331	0·0264	0·0211
27	0·1252	0·0976	0·0763	0·0469	0·0291	0·0230	0·0182
28	0·1159	0·0895	0·0693	0·0419	0·0255	0·0200	0·0157
29	0·1073	0·0822	0·0630	0·0374	0·0224	0·0174	0·0135
30	0·0994	0·0754	0·0573	0·0334	0·0196	0·0151	0·0116
40	0·0460	0·0318	0·0221	0·0107	0·0053	0·0037	0·0026
50	0·0213	0·0134	0·0085	0·0035	0·0014	0·0009	0·0006

$(1 + r)^{-n}$

Year	18%	20%	22%	24%	25%	26%	28%
1	0·8475	0·8333	0·8197	0·8065	0·8000	0·7937	0·7813
2	0·7182	0·6944	0·6719	0·6504	0·6400	0·6299	0·6104
3	0·6086	0·5787	0·5507	0·5245	0·5120	0·4999	0·4768
4	0·5158	0·4823	0·4514	0·4230	0·4096	0·3968	0·3725
5	0·4371	0·4019	0·3700	0·3411	0·3277	0·3149	0·2910
6	0·3704	0·3349	0·3033	0·2751	0·2621	0·2499	0·2274
7	0·3139	0·2791	0·2486	0·2218	0·2097	0·1983	0·1776
8	0·2660	0·2326	0·2038	0·1789	0·1678	0·1574	0·1388
9	0·2255	0·1938	0·1670	0·1443	0·1342	0·1249	0·1084
10	0·1911	0·1615	0·1369	0·1164	0·1074	0·0992	0·0847
11	0·1619	0·1346	0·1122	0·0938	0·0859	0·0787	0·0662
12	0·1372	0·1122	0·0920	0·0757	0·0687	0·0625	0·0517
13	0·1163	0·0935	0·0754	0·0610	0·0550	0·0496	0·0404
14	0·0985	0·0779	0·0618	0·0492	0·0440	0·0393	0·0316
15	0·0835	0·0649	0·0507	0·0397	0·0352	0·0312	0·0247
16	0·0708	0·0541	0·0415	0·0320	0·0281	0·0248	0·0193
17	0·0600	0·0451	0·0340	0·0258	0·0225	0·0197	0·0150
18	0·0508	0·0376	0·0279	0·0208	0·0180	0·0156	0·0118
19	0·0431	0·0313	0·0229	0·0168	0·0144	0·0124	0·0092
20	0·0365	0·0261	0·0187	0·0135	0·0115	0·0098	0·0072
21	0·0309	0·0217	0·0154	0·0109	0·0092	0·0078	0·0056
22	0·0262	0·0181	0·0126	0·0088	0·0074	0·0062	0·0044
23	0·0222	0·0151	0·0103	0·0071	0·0059	0·0049	0·0034
24	0·0188	0·0126	0·0084	0·0057	0·0047	0·0039	0·0027
25	0·0160	0·0105	0·0069	0·0046	0·0038	0·0031	0·0021
26	0·0135	0·0087	0·0057	0·0037	0·0030	0·0025	0·0016
27	0·0115	0·0073	0·0047	0·0030	0·0024	0·0019	0·0013
28	0·0097	0·0061	0·0038	0·0024	0·0019	0·0015	0·0010
29	0·0082	0·0051	0·0031	0·0020	0·0015	0·0012	0·0008
30	0·0070	0·0042	0·0026	0·0016	0·0012	0·0010	0·0006
40	0·0013	0·0007	0·0004	0·0002	0·0001		
50	0·0003	0·0001					

$(1 + r)^{-n}$

Year	30%	35%	40%	45%	50%
1	0·7692	0·7407	0·7143	0·6897	0·6667
2	0·5917	0·5487	0·5102	0·4756	0·4444
3	0·4552	0·4064	0·3644	0·3280	0·2963
4	0·3501	0·3011	0·2603	0·2262	0·1975
5	0·2693	0·2230	0·1859	0·1560	0·1317
6	0·2072	0·1652	0·1328	0·1076	0·0878
7	0·1594	0·1224	0·0949	0·0742	0·0585
8	0·1226	0·0906	0·0678	0·0512	0·0390
9	0·0943	0·0671	0·0484	0·0353	0·0260
10	0·0725	0·0497	0·0346	0·0243	0·0173
11	0·0558	0·0368	0·0247	0·0168	0·0116
12	0·0429	0·0273	0·0176	0·0116	0·0077
13	0·0330	0·0202	0·0126	0·0080	0·0051
14	0·0254	0·0150	0·0090	0·0055	0·0034
15	0·0195	0·0111	0·0064	0·0038	0·0023
16	0·0150	0·0082	0·0046	0·0026	0·0015
17	0·0116	0·0061	0·0033	0·0018	0·0010
18	0·0089	0·0045	0·0023	0·0012	0·0007
19	0·0068	0·0033	0·0017	0·0009	0·0005
20	0·0053	0·0025	0·0012	0·0006	0·0003
21	0·0040	0·0018	0·0009	0·0004	0·0002
22	0·0031	0·0014	0·0006	0·0003	0·0001
23	0·0024	0·0010	0·0004	0·0002	
24	0·0018	0·0007	0·0003	0·0001	
25	0·0014	0·0006	0·0002		
26	0·0011	0·0004	0·0002		
27	0·0008	0·0003	0·0001		
28	0·0006	0·0002			
29	0·0005	0·0002			
30	0·0004	0·0001			
40					
50					

Table B

PRESENT VALUE OF £1 PER YEAR
(WHAT £1 RECEIVABLE ANNUALLY IS WORTH TODAY)

$$\frac{1 - (1 + r)^{-n}}{r}$$

Year	1%	2%	3%	4%	5%
1	0·9901	0·9804	0·9709	0·9615	0·9524
2	1·9704	1·9416	1·9135	1·8861	1·8594
3	2·9410	2·8839	2·8286	2·7751	2·7232
4	3·9020	3·8077	3·7171	3·6299	3·5460
5	4·8534	4·7135	4·5797	4·4518	4·3295
6	5·7955	5·6014	5·4172	5·2421	5·0757
7	6·7282	6·4720	6·2303	6·0021	5·7864
8	7·6517	7·3255	7·0197	6·7327	6·4632
9	8·5660	8·1622	7·7861	7·4353	7·1078
10	9·4713	8·9826	8·5302	8·1109	7·7217
11	10·3676	9·7869	9·2526	8·7605	8·3064
12	11·2551	10·5753	9·9540	9·3851	8·8633
13	12·1337	11·3484	10·6350	9·9856	9·3936
14	13·0037	12·1062	11·2961	10·5631	9·8986
15	13·8651	12·8493	11·9379	11·1184	10·3797
16	14·7179	13·5777	12·5611	11·6523	10·8378
17	15·5623	14·2919	13·1661	12·1657	11·2741
18	16·3983	14·9920	13·7535	12·6593	11·6896
19	17·2260	15·6785	14·3238	13·1339	12·0853
20	18·0456	16·3514	14·8775	13·5903	12·4622
21	18·8570	17·0112	15·4150	14·0292	12·8212
22	19·6604	17·6580	15·9369	14·4511	13·1630
23	20·4558	18·2922	16·4436	14·8568	13·4886
24	21·2434	18·9139	16·9355	15·2470	13·7986
25	22·0232	19·5235	17·4131	15·6221	14·0939
26	22·7952	20·1210	17·8768	15·9838	14·3752
27	23·5596	20·7069	18·3270	16·3296	14·6430
28	24·3164	21·2813	18·7641	16·6631	14·8981
29	25·0658	21·8444	19·1885	16·9837	15·1411
30	25·8077	22·3965	19·6004	17·2920	15·3725
40	32·8347	27·3555	23·1148	19·7928	17·1591
50	39·1961	31·4236	25·7298	21·4822	18·2559

$$\frac{1-(1+r)^{-n}}{r}$$

Year	6%	7%	8%	9%	10%
1	0·9434	0·9346	0·9259	0·9174	0·9091
2	1·8334	1·8080	1·7833	1·7591	1·7355
3	2·6730	2·6243	2·5771	2·5313	2·4869
4	3·4651	3·3872	3·3121	3·2397	3·1699
5	4·2124	4·1002	3·9927	3·8897	3·7908
6	4·9173	4·7665	4·6229	4·4859	4·3553
7	5·5824	5·3893	5·2064	5·0330	4·8684
8	6·2098	5·9713	5·7466	5·5348	5·3349
9	6·8071	6·5152	6·2469	5·9952	5·7590
10	7·3601	7·0236	6·7101	6·4177	6·1446
11	7·8869	7·4987	7·1390	6·8052	6·4951
12	8·3838	7·9427	7·5361	7·1607	6·8137
13	8·8527	8·3577	7·9038	7·4869	7·1034
14	9·2950	8·7455	8·2442	7·7862	7·3667
15	9·7122	9·1079	8·5595	8·0607	7·6061
16	10·1059	9·4466	8·8514	8·3126	7·8237
17	10·4773	9·7632	9·1216	8·5436	8·0216
18	10·8276	10·0591	9·3719	8·7556	8·2014
19	11·1581	10·3356	9·6036	8·9501	8·3649
20	11·4699	10·5940	9·8181	9·1285	8·5136
21	11·7641	10·8355	10·0168	9·2922	8·6487
22	12·0416	11·0612	10·2007	9·4424	8·7715
23	12·3034	11·2722	10·3711	9·5802	8·8832
24	12·5504	11·4693	10·5288	9·7066	8·9847
25	12·7834	11·6536	10·6748	9·8226	9·0770
26	13·0032	11·8258	10·8100	9·9290	9·1609
27	13·2105	11·9867	10·9352	10·0266	9·2372
28	13·4062	12·1371	11·0511	10·1161	9·3066
29	13·5907	12·2777	11·1584	10·1983	9·3696
30	13·7648	12·4090	11·2578	10·2737	9·4269
40	15·0463	13·3317	11·9246	10·7574	9·7791
50	15·7619	13·8007	12·2335	10·9617	9·9148

$$\frac{1-(1+r)^{-n}}{r}$$

Year	12%	14%	15%	16%	18%
1	0·8929	0·8722	0·8696	0·8621	0·8475
2	1·6901	1·6497	1·6257	1·6052	1·5656
3	2·4018	2·3216	2·2832	2·2459	2·1743
4	3·0373	2·9137	2·8550	2·7982	2·6901
5	3·6048	3·4331	3·3522	3·2743	3·1272
6	4·1114	3·8887	3·7845	3·6847	3·4976
7	4·5638	4·2883	4·1604	4·0386	3·8115
8	4·9676	4·6389	4·4873	4·3436	4·0776
9	5·3282	4·9464	4·7716	4·6065	4·3030
10	5·6502	5·2161	5·0188	4·8332	4·4941
11	5·9377	5·4527	5·2337	5·0286	4·6560
12	6·1944	5·6603	5·4206	5·1971	4·7932
13	5·4235	5·8424	5·5832	5·3423	4·9095
14	6·6282	6·0021	5·7245	5·4675	5·0081
15	6·8109	6·1422	5·8474	5·5755	5·0916
16	6·9740	6·2651	5·9542	5·6685	5·1624
17	7·1196	6·3729	6·0472	5·7487	5·2223
18	7·2497	6·4674	6·1280	5·8178	5·2732
19	7·3658	6·5504	6·1982	5·8775	5·3162
20	7·4694	6·6231	6·2593	5·9288	5·3527
21	7·5620	6·6870	6·3125	5·9731	5·3837
22	7·6446	6·7429	6·3587	6·0113	5·4099
23	7·7184	6·7921	6·3988	6·0442	5·4321
24	7·7843	6·8351	6·4338	6·0726	5·4509
25	7·8431	6·8729	6·4642	6·0971	5·4669
26	7·8957	6·9061	6·4906	6·1182	5·4804
27	7·9426	6·9352	6·5135	6·1364	5·4919
28	7·9844	6·9607	6·5335	6·1520	5·5016
29	8·0218	6·9830	6·5509	6·1656	5·5098
30	8·0552	7·0027	6·5660	6·1772	5·5168
40	8·2438	7·1050	6·6418	6·2335	5·5482
50	8·3045	7·1327	6·6605	6·2463	5·5541

$$\frac{1-(1+r)^{-n}}{r}$$

Year	20%	22%	24%	25%	26%	28%
1	0·8333	0·8197	0·8065	0·8000	0·7937	0·7813
2	1·5278	1·4915	1·4568	1·4400	1·4235	1·3916
3	2·1065	2·0422	1·9813	1·9520	1·9234	1·8684
4	2·5887	2·4936	2·4043	2·6346	2·3202	2·2410
5	2·9906	2·8636	2·7454	2·6893	2·6351	2·5320
6	3·3255	3·1669	3·0205	2·9514	2·8850	2·7594
7	3·6046	3·4155	3·2423	3·1611	3·0833	2·9370
8	3·8372	3·6193	3·4212	3·3289	3·2407	3·0758
9	4·0310	3·7863	3·5655	3·4631	3·3657	3·1842
10	4·1925	3·9232	3·6819	3·5705	3·4648	3·2689
11	4·3271	4·0354	3·7757	3·6564	3·5435	3·3351
12	4·4392	4·1274	3·8514	3·7251	3·6059	3·3868
13	4·5327	4·2028	3·9124	3·7801	3·6555	3·4272
14	4·6106	4·2646	3·9616	3·8241	3·6949	3·4587
15	4·6755	4·3152	4·0013	3·8593	3·7261	3·4834
16	4·7296	4·3567	4·0333	3·8874	3·7509	3·5026
17	4·7746	4·3908	4·0591	3·9099	3·7705	3·5177
18	4·8122	4·4187	4·0799	3·9279	3·7861	3·5294
19	4·8435	4·4415	4·0967	3·9424	3·7985	3·5386
20	4·8696	4·4603	4·1103	3·9539	3·8083	3·5458
21	4·8913	4·4756	4·1212	3·9631	3·8161	3·5514
22	4·9094	4·4882	4·1300	3·9705	3·8223	3·5558
23	4·9245	4·4985	4·1371	3·9764	3·8273	3·5592
24	4·9371	4·5070	4·1428	3·9811	3·8312	3·5619
25	4·9476	4·5139	4·1474	3·9849	3·8342	3·5640
26	4·9563	4·5196	4·1512	3·9879	3·8367	3·5656
27	4·9636	4·5243	4·1542	3·9903	3·8387	3·5669
28	4·9697	4·5281	4·1566	3·9923	3·8402	3·5679
29	4·9747	4·5312	4·1585	3·9938	3·8414	3·5687
30	4·9789	4·5338	4·1601	3·9951	3·8424	3·5693
40	4·9966	4·5439	4·1659	3·9995	3·8458	3·5712
50	4·9995	4·5452	4·1666	3·9999	3·8461	3·5714

$$\frac{1-(1+r)^{-n}}{r}$$

Year	30%	35%	40%	45%	50%
1	0·7692	0·7407	0·7143	0·6897	0·6667
2	1·3609	1·2894	1·2245	1·1653	1·1111
3	1·8161	1·6959	1·5889	1·4933	1·4074
4	2·1662	1·9969	1·8492	1·7195	1·6049
5	2·4356	2·2200	2·0352	1·8755	1·7366
6	2·6427	2·3852	2·1680	1·9831	1·8244
7	2·8021	2·5075	2·2628	2·0573	1·8829
8	2·9247	2·5982	2·3306	2·1085	1·9220
9	3·0190	2·6653	2·3790	2·1438	1·9480
10	3·0915	2·7150	2·4136	2·1681	1·9653
11	3·1473	2·7519	2·4383	2·1849	1·9769
12	3·1903	2·7792	2·4559	2·1965	1·9846
13	3·2233	2·7994	2·4685	2·2045	1·9897
14	3·2487	2·8144	2·4775	2·2100	1·9931
15	3·2682	2·8255	2·4839	2·2138	1·9954
16	3·2832	2·8337	2·4885	2·2164	1·9970
17	3·2948	2·8398	2·4918	2·2182	1·9980
18	3·3037	2·8443	2·4941	2·2195	1·9986
19	3·3105	2·8476	2·4958	2·2203	1·9991
20	3·3158	2·8501	2·4970	2·2209	1·9994
21	3·3198	2·8519	2·4979	2·2213	1·9996
22	3·3230	2·8533	2·4985	2·2216	1·9997
23	3·3254	2·8543	2·4989	2·2218	1·9998
24	3·3272	2·8550	2·4992	2·2219	1·9999
25	3·3286	2·8556	2·4994	2·2220	1·9999
26	3·3297	2·8560	2·4996	2·2221	1·9999
27	3·3305	2·8563	2·4997	2·2221	2·0000
28	3·3312	2·8565	2·4998	2·2222	2·0000
29	3·3317	2·8567	2·4999	2·2222	2·0000
30	3·3321	2·8568	2·4999	2·2222	2·0000
40	3·3332	2·8571	2·5000	2·2222	2·0000
50	3·3333	2·8571	2·5000	2·2222	2·0000

Index